ROBERT NIXON AND POLICE TORTURE IN CHICAGO, 1871–1971

ROBERT NIXON AND

POLICE TORTURE

IN CHICAGO, 1871–1971

Elizabeth Dale

NIU Press, DeKalb, IL

Northern Illinois University Press, DeKalb 60115
© 2016 by Northern Illinois University Press
Printed in the United States of America
25 24 23 22 21 20 19 18 17 16   1 2 3 4 5
978-0-87580-739-3 (cloth)
978-1-60909-200-9 (ebook)
Book and cover design by Shaun Allshouse

Library of Congress Cataloging-in-Publication Data
Names: Dale, Elizabeth, author.
Title: Robert Nixon and police torture in Chicago, 1871-1971 /
    Elizabeth Dale.
Description: DeKalb : Northern Illinois University Press, 2016.
Identifiers: LCCN 2016005471| ISBN 9780875807393 (hardback) | ISBN
    9781609092009 (ebook)
Subjects: LCSH: Police brutality—Illinois—Chicago—History. | Police
    misconduct—Illinois—Chicago--History. |
    Torture—Illinois—Chicago—History. | BISAC: HISTORY / United States /
    State & Local / Midwest (IA, IL, IN, KS, MI, MN, MO, ND, NE, OH, SD, WI).
    | TRUE CRIME / General.
Classification: LCC HV8148.C4 .D35 2016 | DDC 363.2/32—dc23
LC record available at http://lccn.loc.gov/2016005471

Contents

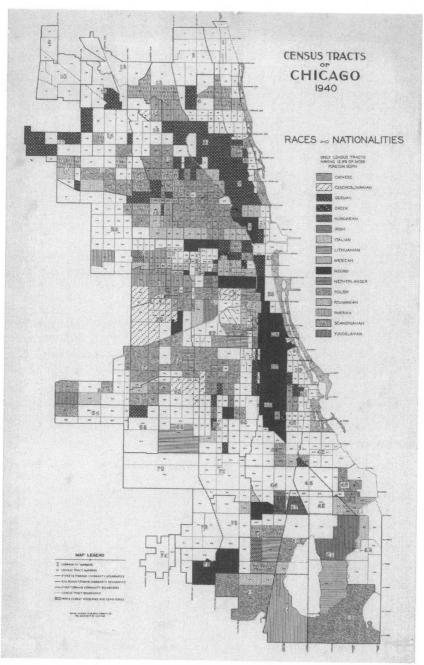

Census Tracts of Chicago, 1940: Races and Nationalities Map. Social Science Research Committee. Reprinted with permission from the Map Collection at the University of Chicago and the Department of Sociology at the University of Chicago.

Robert Nixon in police custody sometime after his arrest for the murder of Florence Johnson. His shirt has already been taken from him for testing. Photograph courtesy of Associated Press.

INTRODUCTION

ON MAY 5, 2015, the Chicago City Council passed an ordinance apologizing to the mostly African American victims of torture conducted by Jon Burge and other police officers at Areas Two and Three police headquarters between 1972 and 1991. The ordinance promised to pay "individuals with a credible claim of torture," a group estimated at between 50 and 88 people, up to $100,000 each in damages, and to provide those victims, their children, and grandchildren job training and free education at the city colleges. It also pledged that Chicago public schools would teach eight and tenth graders about the Burge case in history classes. Passage of the ordinance was a historic moment: speaking in the council chambers that morning, Mayor Rahm Emanuel praised it as "another step but an essential step in righting a wrong." And he thanked those who had worked to pass the ordinance, including many victims of the police torture and their families, for helping the city "come face-to-face with the past and be honest enough and strong enough to say when we are wrong and to try to make right what we've done wrong."[1]

Trying to explain what happened in Chicago between 1972 and 1991, most suggest that when Jon Burge joined the force, he introduced his team to the abusive interrogation techniques he had learned in the military when he served in Vietnam. John Conroy, the author of the newspaper series (which turned into a book-length study) about what happened in Area Two of Chicago, went further, speculating that Burge was "a guy who was failed by his supervisors." If, Conroy went on, someone had called Burge in the first time that he roughed up a suspect and said, "'Burge, you do that one more time and I'll have you guarding the parking lot at 11th and State," it would not have happened again. That theory that Chicago's torture tragedy in the 1970s and 1980s resulted from lack of proper guidance by high-ranking police officers was repeated by federal judge Joan Lefkow when she sentenced Burge for obstruction of justice and perjury in 2011.[2]

Yet perhaps it is not that simple. Certainly, police torture in Chicago did not begin with Jon Burge. The evidence is difficult to come by; as the historian Alfred McCoy noted in another context, police departments "tend to destroy or conceal their records." But after a search of several publicly available records, I have been able to find at least four hundred claims that officers in the Chicago Police Department used torture on witnesses or suspects between 1871 and 1971. At the time they were made, most of those claims were ignored, discounted, or dismissed by the criminal justice system. Now their history has been forgotten and left out of our attempts to explain what happened in Area Two between 1972 and 1991.[3]

This book is intended to help us begin to recapture that lost history. It does so by setting out many of those early claims, using them to reveal the patterns of police torture across that period. As Darius Rejali noted in *Torture and Democracy*, "getting the patterns right, specifying claims about the shape of these patterns, is important to any further research." So too, it is important to tie those claims to names as often as possible, to recognize those whose stories have been lost to our historical memory. It is not enough, however, to simply record the names, the dates, and the claims. To understand how and why police torture happened in Chicago, to consider why it lasted as long as it did, to explore why those claims disappeared from our memory, we need to go beyond lists, to look at how the criminal justice system and the people of Chicago responded to claims of torture when they were made. To do that, this book offers some snapshots of a number of the torture claims made between 1871 and 1971 and looks closely at a single case from 1938. In that case, Robert Nixon, a young black man, was tried for murdering Florence Johnson, the white wife of a Chicago firefighter. A jury found Nixon guilty and that verdict was affirmed on appeal. On June 15, 1939, the people of Illinois put Robert Nixon to death in the electric chair. Robert Nixon went to his death claiming that he had falsely confessed to the Johnson murder after being tortured at police headquarters at 11th and State. The drama surrounding his arrest and trial help us see the context in which torture claims arose. Nixon's problems proving that he was tortured help us understand how the criminal justice system could help perpetuate torture even as it officially rejected the practice.[4]

There are several reasons why I have chosen to focus on Robert Nixon's case. In part, it is because a version of Nixon's trial is already familiar. Two years after Nixon's execution, Richard Wright published *Native Son*, his novel about the failures of racial and economic justice on Chicago's South Side. According to Wright, "many of the newspaper items and some of the scenes in *Native Son* are but fictionalized versions of Robert Nixon's trial." Yet for all that Wright used Nixon's 1938 trial to expose the problems of race and justice in Chicago, in one crucial way Bigger Thomas was not Robert Nixon and *Native Son* could never be the history of Nixon's trial. Although Robert Nixon lived much of the social and economic injustice that *Native Son* exposed and subsequent histories have recorded, Wright's novel ignored the most important lessons Robert Nixon's trial taught about the failures of criminal justice: it said almost nothing about police torture. There is the merest hint of it at the start of Book Three, the very beginning of the section that Wright called "Fate," which opens by describing Bigger Thomas's silence even though the police "carried him from one police station to another, though they threatened him, persuaded him, bullied him, and stormed at him." Yet in the scene when Bigger broke his silence and confessed to State's Attorney Buckley, there was no hint that force had been involved.[5]

Wright's failure to call attention to the police torture claims that were central to Robert Nixon's trial was probably the result of a deliberate decision to emphasize other social ills. Yet it was an artistic judgment that came at a crucial moment, and the timing of Robert Nixon's case is the second reason why I have chosen to examine it closely in this study. In the first decades of the twentieth century, it was an open secret in Chicago that the police used torture techniques, more often known as sweating or the third degree, to get suspects and witnesses to talk. By the mid-1920s, shifts in public opinion and increased scrutiny by courts meant that police could not do so as openly. In 1936, the United States Supreme Court declared that the use of torture to obtain confessions from criminal defendants was an unconstitutional denial of due process. Scholars have, by and large, concluded that those shifts in public and legal opinion meant that by the late 1930s police torture in the United States finally had been brought to an end. Nixon's case suggests, to the contrary, that torture continued in Chicago police stations behind closed doors, in forms that left no marks. In *Torture and Democracy*, Rejali argues that this sort of disappearance is typical in democracies, where governments sweep their less satisfactory or disturbing practices out of sight and out of mind. What the people cannot see, they will not try to stop. Other scholars, notably Stanley Cohen and Jinee Lokaneeta, argue that torture also happens when citizens are unwilling to look too closely at what their governments are doing, particularly because they are afraid and think government wrongdoing is the only way to stop whatever it is they fear.[6]

The history of police torture claims in Chicago between 1871 and 1971 offers evidence that torture did continue even after the law, and public opinion, ostensibly rejected it. Robert Nixon's case offers an explanation of why that may have happened, showing how the court procedures meant to out-law torture instead made it possible for the police to hide what they were doing and for juries and judges to let them do so. Other claims recounted in this book suggest that torture also continued because claims of torture were increasingly left out of accounts in newspapers and other popular treatments of trials. That silence turned the claims of torture that were reported into anomalies, the work of rogue cops, occasional accidents of overzealous policing. That is a problem that transcends Jon Burge.[7]

CHAPTER ONE

POLICE TORTURE IN CHICAGO, 1871–1936

LONG BEFORE JON BURGE joined the Chicago Police Department in March 1970, people complained of being tortured by the city's police. In 1931, the National Commission on Law Observance and Enforcement, popularly known as the Wickersham Commission, charged that the police in Chicago, and in several other major cities in the United States, often used torture, usually known as the third degree, when they interrogated suspects. That report defined the third degree as "the employment of methods which inflict suffering, physical or mental, upon a person in order to obtain information about a crime" and found that police officers in Chicago typically used one or more of three different approaches:

Physical abuse: Law enforcement officers beat suspects or witnesses with rubber hoses, belts, or other items; struck them with their fists or slapped them, kicked or kneed them; hung them by their wrists or neck; or exposed their victims to physical extremes such as rooms that were too cold or too hot (often known as "the sweatbox" or "sweating").

Deprivation: Officers held victims in isolation from friends or family for days (also known as holding someone incommunicado); or deprived them of food, drink, sleep, or necessary medical treatment (or drugs, in the case of addicts).

Psychological pressure: Officers threatened suspects, witnesses, or a family member with violence, prosecution, increased punishment, or being turned over to a mob; or subjected witnesses or suspects to extensive and extended interrogation that was conducted over a period of days or late at night.[1]

Torture in Chicago in the Late Nineteenth Century

The Wickersham Commission's report looked at claims of torture in Chicago in the 1920s, but there were complaints long before that. Charges that law enforcement personnel used torture to try to obtain confessions appear in Illinois court records and news accounts shortly after the Civil War. In 1869, William Stallings of Venice, Illinois sued, asserting that after he was arrested for larceny the arresting officers took him to a nearby wood, placed him under a tree, took out a rope, and told him he would be hanged if he did not confess. Around the same time, John Francis insisted that he confessed to a robbery in Clark County, Illinois only after being taken from his home by a mob of men and hanged from a tree until he was nearly senseless.[2] Presumably to stop the practice, the Illinois General Assembly passed a law in 1874 that declared it a crime to use force or imprisonment to compel confessions.[3]

Beginning in the 1880s, several suspects taken into custody by Pinkerton agents in Chicago claimed the agents tortured them by putting them in a "sweatbox." Sweatboxes, which had been used during the Civil War and by some slave owners before that war, were small, intensely hot, often smelly or airless rooms. Suspects and witnesses were held in the sweatbox until the discomfort made them willing to talk.[4] In 1885, Frank Bernard claimed that after being arrested on a warrant by a Pinkerton agent he was detained for several days at the agency's Chicago office, where he spent most of his time in the sweatbox. John B. Owens was taken to Chicago in 1887 and put in "the Pinkerton 'sweat-box'" until he confessed to robbing a train. In 1893, Walter Martin said he was tricked into going to Chicago to meet a man who seized him and took him to the Pinkerton offices, where he was held for two weeks. At night he was chained to a bed; during the day he was locked in a small closet and threatened with the "sweat-box" if he did not confess to committing arson. While the sweatbox, usually in combination with being held incommunicado for several days and nights, seemed to be the Pinkertons' preferred technique, some men claimed that private detectives in Chicago used other forms of torture: W. J. Gallagher, suspected of election fraud in 1884, complained he had been arrested and kept in the offices of a Chicago detective agency overnight, chained to an investigator. Gallagher said that whenever he fell asleep his companion jerked the chain to wake him up and began to question him, effectively subjecting him to sleep deprivation.[5]

In the last decades of the nineteenth century, news stories suggested that federal and state agencies in Chicago also used the sweatbox or held suspects incommunicado. News accounts in 1878 reported that special federal agent James Stuart, investigating a claim of mail theft in Chicago, put Carl August Namuth in the sweatbox to get him to confess. A year later, Henry Sloan, a witness questioned concerning a suspected confidence game, was put in the sweatbox by federal officials to try to get the story of the crime out of him. In 1895, agents in the United States Secret Service kept C. O. Jones, a local newspaper artist, in the sweatbox for five hours as they investigated stamp counterfeiting in Chicago. Two years before, state fire inspectors investigating arson cases held Otto Jirsa and other suspects incommunicado in a secret room at the Gault House, a local hotel.[6]

Claims that Chicago police officers were using similar forms of torture began after the city reorganized its police department between 1875 and 1885. Reorganization was prompted by a combination of elite and business fears of labor militancy and the expansion of the city with the incorporation of the suburbs in Lake View, Hyde Park, and Englewood. It brought with it a series of reforms designed to remake Chicago's police into professional crime stoppers. The department grew dramatically between 1883 and 1884, from 637 men, a number that included officers and clerical staff, to 924 employees, of whom 576 were patrolmen.[7] In 1884, the police department admitted that Lawrence Beatty, suspected leader in a burglary ring, had escaped from the sweatbox at the Central police station. Two other men who were suspected of being part of his gang were too big to slip out of the hole Beatty made in a window; they remained in the sweatbox as police tried to convince them to confess. During a murder investigation a year later, the police officers at the Desplaines station made little secret of the fact they were holding a number of Italian immigrants incommunicado as they tried to induce them to confess. Suspects in other cases said police officers used threats or other means to scare them into confessing: Frank Chapek, a suspected anarchist, claimed in 1888 that police officers threatened him with dynamite and held a knife to his neck to try to make him confess. Other efforts were more imaginative: the *Milwaukee Journal* reported that Chicago police at the Fifteenth Street station used a skull with eyes that lit up to try to frighten a confession out of one suspect in 1896.[8]

Police torture claims figured in the investigations into Chicago's most notorious cases in the 1880s and 1890s. During the investigation into the Haymarket bombing in 1886, reports in the *Chicago Tribune* made it clear that police officers under the command of Inspector John Bonfield were holding suspects incommunicado and threatening them to make them confess. At least one witness questioned during the investigation, Vaclav Djemek, made more serious charges. He insisted that when he said that he knew nothing about the Haymarket bombing and would not turn state's evidence, he was cursed at and kicked by officers, who threatened he would be hanged. One of the Haymarket defendants, George Engle, said that police officers held him incommunicado and put him in "the sweat-box."[9]

Three years later, during the investigation into the murder of Dr. Patrick Cronin at the hands of the Clan-Na-Gael, an Irish Republican organization,

Chicago police officers held Martin Burke, one of the suspects, incommunicado. When Burke's lawyer filed a petition for a writ of habeas corpus to try to get access to his client, the chief of police, George Hubbard, refused on the grounds that the Chicago police officer who had taken him to Chicago from Canada was serving the interests of the federal government and was thus outside the reach of the state court. The judge who heard the petition agreed, and Burke stayed under police control until the trial. Several years later, when one of Burke's codefendants was retried for the Cronin murder, defense attorney W. R. Wing argued to the jury that Burke, who had died of tuberculosis in prison waiting for the appeal, had been subjected to physical tortures by the police as they tried to get him to confess in 1889. The judge in the second trial did not allow Wing to develop that argument, which meant that any attempt to establish what the Chicago police did to Martin Burke died with him.[10] At the end of the century, during the investigation into the notorious workings of Dr. Holmes, the serial murderer immortalized in *Devil in the White City*, the police put Patrick Quinlan, Holmes's handyman, through "the sweat-box" at the Harrison Street police station on several different days, at least once for five hours. Quinlan's wife and her good friend Mrs. L. Doyle were both sweated by the police from 9:00 in the morning until 1:00 in the afternoon, and another witness, Joseph Owens, was sweated at the Harrison Street station for more than five hours by officers trying to find out what he knew about Dr. Holmes's plans.[11]

By the 1890s, undergoing a "sweating" in Chicago referred either to being put in a special room or being subjected to "sweatbox methods," which often meant an intensive and extensive interrogation conducted by relays of police officers. Whether a place or a practice, sweating was a coercive and physically difficult process.[12] There is considerable evidence that across the 1890s it also became a well-established part of criminal investigations in the city. In 1893, George Craig, suspected of murdering a small child, was sweated at the West Chicago Avenue station. A year later, after two special police officers were killed, police officers at that same station put two suspects, Henry Griswold and William Lake, through the sweatbox for five hours each. In 1894, officers at the Attrill police station used the sweatbox on Joseph Shuppick, while their counterparts at the East Chicago station sweated eight suspects in another murder case. Laek Lindell, a young man accused of attempted murder, was put in the sweatbox at the Woodlawn station in 1896; and Red Sullivan, a suspected robber, "had to undergo the pumping process in the sweatbox" that same year. The next year, the technique flourished. Two murder suspects whom the police refused to name were sweated at the East Chicago station in April; Henry Dunker was sweated at the Hyde

Park station in August; in October, officers put Nick Redmond through the sweatbox at the Maxwell Street station; Joe Keller was sweated at the Central station in November; and Mike Romelius and John Akacz were sweated at another station (perhaps Englewood) in December. Officers at Rawson Street put murder suspects Otto and Charles Brandt through the sweatbox for five straight days in 1898. That same year officers at the Harrison station sweated Thomas Rutledge and John Ransom for two hours. A year later, murder suspects were sweated at the stations at Warren Avenue, Englewood, Hyde Park, and the Stock Yards.[13]

Although many of the people sweated in the late nineteenth century were suspected of murder, newspapers reported that the police sweated those suspected of other crimes as well. A man named Smith, who was simply arrested on suspicion in 1888, was sweated at the Central station. Another, known only as Morgan, was given a sweating at the Harrison Street station in 1893 following his arrest for theft. That same year, police at the Harrison Street station sweated John Oliver, suspected of robbing a safe. "Samuel of Posen," a suspected pickpocket, and Frank Dale, who had been implicated in an embezzlement case, were both sweated by officers at the Central station in 1894, while officers at the Woodlawn station gave William Haney, suspected of burglary, a sweating in 1895. In 1896, several men suspected of being part of a robbery gang were put through the sweatbox at the Maxwell Street station, members of a supposed stickup team were sweated at police headquarters, officers at the Central station sweated men they thought were part of a robbery ring, Thomas Higgins was given a sweating by officers at the Harrison Street station who were investigating a robbery, and Frank Harper and James Robinson, both suspected of attempted theft, got a sweating at the East Chicago station. A year later, William Wright was sweated at the Harrison Street station as part of an investigation into meter fraud, while officers at the Central station investigating a theft sweated Daniel Cronin and Edward Grant. That same year, the *Chicago Tribune* matter-of-factly reported that officers at the Cottage Grove police station held John Keller incommunicado for two weeks before they put him through a sweating. Keller had been implicated in a series of burglaries in the neighborhood.[14]

As that list suggests, most of those sweated by the Chicago police in the late nineteenth century were adult males. In the late nineteenth century, they were typically also white. Chicago's police seemed, however, to be willing to use the sweatbox on anyone. Sometimes they sweated African Americans, like Smith, the man arrested on suspicion in 1888; Haney, arrested as a burglary suspect in 1895; or Edward McIntosh, accused of hiring another man to kill his wife in 1896. Reports indicated that they also used sweatbox methods on minors: in 1895, twelve-year-old Maud Cooper, suspected of burglary at the house where she worked as a servant, was sweated for two hours. That same year, nine boys, the oldest of whom was nineteen and the youngest of whom was twelve, were sweated at the East Chicago station to try to get them to confess to the murder of a fisherman named Klank. In 1898, sixteen-year-old Josie Bragg, suspected of attempted murder, was taken to a station and, in the words of the *Chicago Tribune*, "put in the sweatbox just as grown suspects are." As the cases of Maud Cooper and Josie Bragg made clear, the police were also perfectly willing to sweat women. In 1895, Minnie Dahlke, a witness, was put in the sweatbox twice during the investigation into the murders by Dr. Holmes. A year later, Hannah Martinson, suspected with her husband, Ole, of robbery, was given a sweating by police at the Maxwell Street station, and Agnes Mehan, a witness to another crime, was put through the sweatbox by officers at the Warren Avenue station. In 1897, officers at the Central station used sweatbox methods on Mrs. Jones and two other women; all three were married to suspects in a murder case. Chicago's police also sweated witnesses. Patrick Keeler and Henry Eagan, who were witnesses to a murder, were given a sweating at the Harrison Street station in 1892 and four years later, Chief Badenoch sweated Stubby Hicks, a witness in an investigation into a series of stickups, until Hicks had "not one shred of information left."[15]

Not all attempts at sweating suspects were successful: Lawrence Beatty's escape from the Central station sweatbox in 1884 was one way to beat the system, while other suspects simply managed to hold tough. Adolph Luetgert, a butcher whom police believed had killed his wife and then ground her up like sausage, was sweated in October 1897 to no avail. Inspector Shea at the Maxwell Street station, famous, the *Chicago Tribune* reported, for "his ability to force confessions," used sweatbox methods on Tom Hickey over several days in late November 1897, but was unable to get him to confess to murder.[16]

These practices did not go unchallenged, although most often objections to the sweatbox in the late nineteenth century focused on private detective agencies. The *Tribune* grumbled about the way detective agencies used the sweatbox in 1888, and the state legislature debated bills about the issue in 1887 and 1889. Neither bill was passed. A state court judge denounced private detective agencies and their use of the sweatbox during a hearing in 1889, a grand jury indicted Matt Pinkerton for his mistreatment of Walter Martin in 1895, and another grand jury undertook an investigation of the sweatbox methods of private detective agencies in 1896. After the investigation, the grand jury reported that it found no "strong-room, cell, or dungeon, nor did we find any such room commonly known as a 'sweat-box,'" but its report did condemn agencies that held suspects incommunicado for extended periods of time. The grand jury was skeptical of the agencies' claims that the suspects agreed to be held, concluding that most of those agreements were obtained under threat. The grand jury condemned that practice as kidnapping.[17]

On rare occasions, police tactics were called into question, but usually only if some respectable or well-to-do person was inconvenienced. In 1896, two professional men, one a dentist, were arrested and taken to the Central police station, where detectives put them through the sweatbox. They were finally released, with apologies, when someone believed their claims of innocence. The two threatened to bring charges against the arresting officer, but it is unclear whether they ever did.[18] More often, police use of the sweatbox was ignored, while on occasion it was excused or celebrated. In 1898, the employer of two suspects in a bombing case declared that the best way to get at the truth in the case was to put the two men in the sweatbox; he denounced the police for failing to do so. A lengthy article published in the *Chicago Tribune* in 1896 noted that although the practice was illegal, Chicago police often held suspects incommunicado for "one day, or three days, or three weeks," while officers tried to find evidence tying the suspect to a crime. Police only turned to the sweatbox, the paper explained, when they could not locate evidence. Even then, the article emphasized, while "wild stories have been told about the brutal manner in which prisoners have been bulldozed at the Central Station," Chicago's police never used violence on a suspect "unless a prisoner shows fight." Reassuring as that caveat surely was, the *Tribune's* account ended on a somber note. Recognizing that sweatbox methods could and did coerce innocent people to confess, the paper conceded there were few remedies available for those who did so.[19]

Police Torture at the Turn of the Century

In contrast to the general indifference to sweatbox methods that marked most discussions of police interrogation techniques in the nineteenth century, the twentieth century opened with several sharp attacks on the practice. In 1901, Carl Lindenman brought charges against two detectives at Chicago's East Chicago station. He claimed the officers beat him, threw him down the stairs, and put him in a cell with rats to try to make him confess to robbery. Lindenman, a lawyer, charged that the same officers abused his father when he protested his son's arrest and insisted that officers at the Harrison

Street station mistreated two of his clients, Arthur Mask and Albert Warren, to get them to admit to other crimes. A year later, Walter B. Haynes complained that when he was in the sweatbox at West Lake Street station he was subjected to abusive language and struck by the officers interrogating him as part of their investigation into the murder of two police officers.[20]

That same year, 1902, the apparent mistreatment of Oscar Thompson by officers at the Hyde Park police station "aroused the indignation of the citizens," the condemnation of the noted reformer Jane Addams, and the denunciation of several former and sitting judges. Thompson, a suspect in a murder case, said the officers at Hyde Park deprived him of sleep and subjected him to extensive and abusive interrogations over several days. The result, the *Tribune* reported, had brought Thompson close to a breakdown and seemed to be driving him to madness. The chief of police dismissed the complaints, mocking those who feared the police put suspects in "a small room, unventilated and capable of being heated to a high temperature by steam." Perhaps, he speculated, "public belief furnishes the 'sweat box' with a rack, thumbscrew, and other forms of torturing machinery," but nothing, he assured Chicagoans, could be further from the truth. Suspects interrogated by the Chicago police were questioned in a pleasant room. Chief O'Neill's assurances notwithstanding, protests escalated when it was reported that officers at the Hyde Park station subjected Edward Counselman to an abusive interrogation simply because they hoped he had evidence against Oscar Thompson. The police department's sweatbox methods became a nine days' wonder. Letters were written to the editor deploring the inhumanity of police techniques. Newspapers editorialized against sweating, and the *Chicago Tribune* report explicitly equated the sweatbox with torture.[21]

In the end, for all the publicity that the "sweatbox methods" briefly generated, the complaints and protests in 1902 came to nothing and news accounts indicated that the police continued to employ those methods on suspects. Seventeen-year-old Frank Kolar and eighteen-year-old John Hajny, suspects in a murder case, claimed they confessed only as a result of being subjected to the third degree at the Warren Avenue station, while John Wagner, fifteen, was sweated at the Hyde Park station during a robbery investigation. That same year, D. C. Kelly and Hugh O'Reilly, suspected in the murder of a police officer, were put through the sweatbox at the Stock Yards station. The *Tribune* reported that O'Reilly emerged from his interrogation with his "face bruised and blackened, his eyes swollen," and added that "groans escaped him as he was led to the cellroom below." That same year John Giroux and Walter Geary, suspected of murder, said they were struck in the face, beaten, and threatened with a hanging while they were interrogated by detectives at the Harrison Street station.[22]

The debates over sweating in 1902 were not without moments of irony. Captain Herman Schuettler, commander at the Lake View District station, announced that he did not condone the use of force on suspects during the Oscar Thompson case. That same year, the *Tribune* reported he put Ernest Boese and Hammond Lawrence through a sweating to get them to confess to bribery. Despite his claimed opposition to sweatbox methods, Schuettler's use of those tools in 1902 was not unexpected. He was a protégé of Inspectors Bonfield and Schaak, well known for sweating suspects in the late nineteenth century, and his association with sweatbox methods was long-standing. During the Cronin case, one of the attorneys charged that his client, who had been put through the sweatbox, had been "Schuettlerized," a process by which men went into an interview room with Schuettler, only to come out later to tell "prodigies of stories."[23]

As that suggests, reports frequently associated certain names and stations with sweatbox methods at the turn of the century. In 1900, police at Chicago's Maxwell Street station sweated Frank Goodhugh and Peter McLean, suspected in the murder of a police officer. The sweating was led by Captain Wheeler, who also helped sweat James McMahon, suspected of robbery at the end of the year. Two years later, Wheeler and the officers at the Maxwell Street station sweated Edward Hughes, John Kemmery, Michael Lahey, and Edward Morgenstern during an investigation into a robbery. In September that same year, officers at the Maxwell Street station sweated Edward Geary, who they believed was guilty of attempted burglary. In 1902, Inspector Hunt and the officers at the Hyde Park station used the sweatbox on Peter Borner and John Wagner. In 1904, that noted opponent of sweating, Assistant Chief Schuettler, sweated three men being interrogated about a robbery and a number of other men rounded up in an effort to stop holdups. In 1905, officers at the Chicago Avenue station, investigating the murder of Maud Reese, subjected Frank Klein, William Halpin, and Daniel O'Connell to a sweating, while Schuettler sweated James Kendall, another suspect in that case. Leonard Leopold, suspected of murder in 1906, said he was denied food, sleep, and access to his attorney. He also claimed that the officers at the Harrison Street station prodded him through the bars of his cell, shook their fists in his face, and cuffed him to a chair for three hours, and that Captain Collins kicked him during the interrogation. Based on those claims, a Cook County judge ordered that Leopold be taken out of police custody and put in the Cook County Jail to protect him from police abuse. Leopold's alleged accomplice, Howard E. Nelson, was put through what was called a "severe and continuous examination" for five days at the East Chicago station by Collins, Schuettler, and several other officers. In 1907, Richard Walton, an African American, charged that Inspector Hunt and other officers at the Hyde Park station deprived him of sleep and subjected him to an extended interrogation as they investigated the murder of a local white woman. Charles Evans, also African American, who was suspected of warning Walton, also was put through sweatbox methods by Hunt and the others during that investigation.[24]

The names of some officers, like Schuettler, Wheeler, and Hunt, or of particular stations, like Hyde Park and Maxwell Street, often seemed to be associated with sweatbox methods, but in the first decade of the twentieth century there were reports suspects were sweated in stations throughout the city. In 1900, police at the Harrison Street station who were investigating a meter-tampering case sweated George Pigott and Clarence Wolfe. A year later, newspapers reported that officers at the South Chicago station said that they sweated several men they thought had committed a train robbery, while police at the West Chicago station put Michael Ettleson through a sweating to get a confession in an arson case.[25] In 1903, Joseph Koestner claimed the officers at the Cottage Grove station beat him nearly every hour and kept him awake for forty-eight straight hours until he confessed. The *Chicago Tribune* confirmed that Koestner's "appearance bears out his words."[26] In 1907, Laura Nightingale, a witness being questioned at the Warren Avenue station during an investigation into a murder, was subject to such a "relentless" interrogation, over several days, that she tried to kill herself. After two police officers were killed in 1908, the police department declared war on holdup men and other thugs who carried guns. A huge dragnet followed; patrolmen in every station picked up hundreds of men on suspicion. Central station alone brought in over thirty men. News accounts reported that all thirty were given the third degree.[27]

The hostility to sweatbox methods that marked the beginning of the first decade of the twentieth century briefly resurfaced at decade's end. In 1907, after a jury found two men accused of murder to be not guilty, the *Chicago Tribune* attributed that disturbing outcome to squeamishness. "The only reason" for that verdict, the paper explained in an editorial, "is the claim of the defendants that the confession of one of them was procured by brutality on the part of the police." Unfortunately, the paper noted, while the third degree was often useful, the public "does not take kindly to the idea of confessions extorted by the thumbscrew, the rack, the knout, or their equivalents." While it shared the sense that obtaining confessions by means of torture was inappropriate, the *Tribune* was exasperated by the remedy the jurors proposed:

"Admitting that the police were wrong, the jury seems to have attached an undue weight to those uncomfortable hours." That year the Illinois General Assembly debated a bill designed to prohibit the use of sweatbox methods, making it a crime to use force or threats of force to obtain a confession. The proponent of the bill, Representative B. M. Chiperfield, assured his colleagues that he had heard complaints of all sorts of assaults by the Chicago police, including use of the "water cure," in which interrogators forced water into suspects either by pouring it through their nostrils or down their throat by means of a hose or through funnels. Interest in the bill was high; the *Tribune* published competing guest editorials, one, written after the bill was considered, in defense of sweatbox methods and one, written before the bill was voted on, opposed. In the end, however, while the bill passed the Illinois House it was defeated in the Senate. Two years later, the *Tribune* editorialized against sweatbox methods, noting once again the problem that some juries seemed inclined to acquit people who claimed they had confessed as a result of a "brutal" interrogation.[28]

1910–1920

By the *Tribune*'s own account, the public's views of police torture, like its own, were infinitely malleable. In 1910, an editorial in that paper conceded "that every now and then men arrested on suspicion have been badgered or maltreated by the police in the hope of extracting a confession," though "probably not so often as has been alleged." But the paper insisted that credit for the practice needed to go where credit was due: The problem was not the police; rather, the "indifference of the community" tempted officers to violate the law.[29]

At the start of the new decade, the practice showed no sign of coming to an end, though the terms used to describe it changed as "the third degree" increasingly replaced "a sweating" or "sweatbox methods." In May 1910, the police department investigated charges that Stephen Orth, Stephen Zack, and Joseph Pribila, suspected in the murder of a police officer, were subjected to "two days and nights of mental torture," which ultimately drove Zacak to kill himself. A subsequent police investigation, conducted by Herman Schuettler, completely exonerated the officers at the Stock Yards station, concluding that the prisoners were not coerced. Schuettler emphasized that both Orth and Pribila told him that they were "humanely treated" at the station. Pribila had a bruise over his right eye, which he claimed he got when he fell out of bed, but Schuettler concluded he received it when the rope he tried to use to hang himself broke and he fell to the ground. Schuet-tler did admit that it was possible a police wagon driver stuck Pribila in the face when Pribila lit a cigarette in the wagon, and recommended that that be investigated further. In contrast, Schuettler credited Officer Berounsky's claim that he did not pull Orth from his cell by his hair, or grab him around the neck to show him that he would be hanged if he did not reveal where the murder weapon was hidden.[30]

Other instances of sweating did not prompt investigation. In 1910, the *Tribune* reported that Vito Laglaia was subjected to hours of sweating by Inspector Healy before he confessed to killing an unidentified man. Four years later, George Arndt, suspected of drowning his fiancée in Lake Michigan, was given the third degree at the Sheffield Avenue station. In 1915, the parents of Russell Pethrick claimed that he only confessed to mur-dering Ella Coppersmith and her two-year-old son after being given the third degree at the Grand Crossing station. And the year after that, attorneys for Iva Barnes, who had confessed to murdering her husband, attacked her confession and charged that teams of officers at the Hyde Park station kept their client awake all night and put her through "every torture known to the sweatbox." The next year, twenty-one-year-old Joseph Haller, suspected of attempted rape, said he was given the third degree for four hours. That same year, when Arthur Quinn, son of a prominent political leader, was arrested on suspicion of being part of a jewel theft ring, Quinn was subjected to the third degree by Chief Schuettler and Captain Russell late at night. When his attorneys tried to file a petition for habeas corpus to get him out of police custody, Russell began to move Quinn around the city in an elaborate game of hide and seek: he was taken to the state's attorney's office, then back to a police station, and then to a number of other unnamed places around the city. Finally, he was taken to criminal court, where he was released on bail. In 1919, when Mabel Jackman, a medium, went on trial for plotting to kill her former partner, she maintained the Chicago police used the third degree on her to try to get her to confess.[31]

While many claimed that they were subjected to the familiar mix of extended interrogation, sleep deprivation, and being held incommunicado, others charged there was violence as well. In January 1913, William Kirk, a Chicago real estate agent, filed a report after he saw officers at the 22nd Street station kick and beat Frank Haas, a telegraph officer who had been arrested on the mistaken impression that he was a man wanted for mur-der. Kirk charged that he saw several officers standing over Haas with their jackets off and their shirtsleeves rolled up, beating him as he crouched on his hands and knees. In response, Charles Thompson, 25th Ward alderman, called for a city council hearing into what he called the "torture chamber" methods of the police. Faced with a credible eyewitness, the police did not deny they had beaten Haas. Instead they said they did so because he had resisted arrest.[32]

That same year, Tony Campagna, a suspect in a burglary case, alleged that two officers at the Fillmore Street station used a carpenter's chisel on him to get him to confess. The story in the *Chicago Tribune* recounted that Campagna had a deep gash on his right leg, scratches on his neck and face, and a number of bruises on his neck, back, and chest. The police denied any abuse occurred, insisting that they had to use force to subdue Campagna when he tried to escape through an open window. In 1914, Daniel Hill, arrested on suspicion of burglary, said he was subjected to a severe beating by officers at the Chicago Avenue station and finally confessed to five crimes he did not commit in order to make the beating stop. Hill claimed Sergeant James Carney beat him; ten days before Hill made that charge William Shaw said Carney beat him during an interrogation at the same station. That same year, sixteen-year-old Daniel O'Callahan insisted he was beaten by four officers at the Stock Yards station to get him to confess to stealing an automobile. In support of his claim, he offered the evidence of a black eye "partly closed by a long blue streak directly across it" and a lump on his head. In 1916, a gangster known as "Little Polly" Kramer said he was knocked down several times by police officers during a "brutal third degree." In 1918, Albert Klein, Leo Stern, and Joseph Sullivan, all charged with conspiracy, alleged they were beaten during an interrogation conducted at the state's attorney's office by an assistant state's attorney and a Chicago police officer. That same year, Joseph Sullivan said he confessed to freight car thefts only after he was beaten until he was unconscious. A year later, two young black men, Charles Johnson and Walter Colvin, were arrested for murder during Chicago's race riot. Both charged the police abused them to get them to confess. Johnson (who was eighteen years old) asserted he had been struck in the head and beaten with clubs, hit in the mouth, and called names during his interrogation; Colvin (who was only sixteen) said he confessed after having been struck in the face, choked, and locked up with only bread and water to eat for three days.[33]

When Albert Klein said that he was subjected to the third degree by Edward Fleming, who was secretary to the state's attorney, and John Murphy, a Chicago police officer working with the state's attorney's office, he was not the first to make a claim that implicated lawyers in the third degree. In 1913, Isaac Brofman sued Maclay Hoyne, state's attorney of Cook County, two of his assistants, Chief of Police John McWeeny, and another police officer for subjecting him to the third degree. Brofman claimed he had been falsely arrested for illegally selling gasoline, taken into custody, and held incommunicado for two days until he was released. Brofman also alleged he was insulted and called names by the arresting officers and assistant state's attorney. Less than a week later, yet another man, John Mullen, sued Hoyne, McWeeny, and several police officers, claiming that he had been arrested, taken to the 50th Street station, and held incommunicado four days while the police and state's attorney gave him the third degree to attempt to get him to confess that he was really a suspect named Eddie Watts. In 1919, Louis and Joseph Goldberg, suspected of graft, claimed they were subject to the third degree at the state's attorney's office and then at the East Chicago station.[34]

An article by Burton Rascoe on Chicago's unsolved murders, published in 1916, made it clear that it was an open secret that the police used the third degree, along with "promises of immunity and threats," to try to solve crimes. At times, the department conceded that they did so: in 1915, officers at the Central station admitted that they subjected seventeen-year-old Frank Logue to "a determined third degree" to try to get him to confess to the murder of police officer John Burke. In 1917, after Meda Yerion was found murdered in an alley near 31st Street, the Chicago Police Department announced that it intended to subject her three companions to "sweatbox methods" to get to the bottom of the killing. More often, as the Haas and Campagna cases indicated, the department denied that the third degree existed. Police officers insisted that Russell Pethrick confessed in 1915 after being shown fingerprint evidence (rather than getting the third degree as his parents alleged). That same year, the department celebrated the fact that an investigation into the claims that Detective Sergeant Howe had beaten seventeen-year-old Robbie O'Donnell determined the claims were unfounded. Unfortunately, the report's findings were more ambiguous than the department was willing to admit. There was no question that O'Donnell was seriously ill when the two-hour-long interrogation was finished, and although O'Donnell admitted that Howe did nothing more than push him into the interrogation room, he also insisted that Howe stood over him the entire time in a way that made him think Howe was going to hit him."[35]

Opposing the Third Degree

Because the police were unwilling to investigate claims against their officers, after 1910 a number of outside groups began to look into the practice that the *Tribune* increasingly called torture. The results were mixed. In 1910, a subcommittee of the United States Senate investigated use of the third degree by federal agencies; it issued a report condemning the practice in 1911. Because that report did not consider what was happening in police departments at the state or local level, it had no impact on Chicago's police. Three years later, a report by the American Bar Association concluded, over the strenuous objections of one member of the committee, that police departments around the country did not practice the third degree. Others thought differently. In 1912, an editorial in the *Journal of Criminal Law* condemned the techniques the Chicago police used to obtain confessions from Charles and Lillian Conway, who were both subsequently charged with murder, as "unfair and unlawful." Conway, who had gangrene in one leg, claimed he was denied treatment until he confessed and was forced to sleep on a board for three nights. His wife was also subjected to the third degree. The editorial called for legislation that would bar any confession inadmissible at trial and declare it a misdemeanor "for any police officer to exert any force, mental, physical or psychological against an accused person for the purpose of extorting any admission or confession." Chicago's police responded by declaring that the department did not practice the third degree. The moral clarity of that assertion was, however, somewhat weakened by the comments of James Markham, secretary to the detective bureau. Markham explained that enforcement of a statute like the one the *Journal of Criminal Law* proposed would increase crime and bring about "conditions equivalent to anarchy."[36]

In the second decade of the twentieth century, trial court judges took action to try to stop the practice. In April 1913, Frank Eckert was arrested on suspicion that he had been sending blackmail letters to his neighbor. He was taken to the Lake View station, where he was held incommunicado for two days. While he was in custody, his wife and child were taken to the Central police station, where they were interrogated by Herman Schuettler. Both were told they would be sent to jail unless they told the truth; the child, a little girl not yet ten, gave a statement the police said implicated her father. She subsequently said she told the police what they wanted her to say, and at the preliminary hearing on Eckert's case Judge Scully denounced the entire investigation and threw the case out of court. In 1917, Judge Fitch refused to admit Joseph Haller's confession in his trial for attempted rape. Fitch asserted that the fact Haller was away from his cell for a four-hour period, during which time he allegedly confessed, strongly suggested that he had been subjected to the third degree. The jury convicted Haller anyway, and State's Attorney Maclay Hoyne denounced Fitch, proclaiming:

"The greatest trouble the prosecutor has in this community is with judges who are so tender of the feelings of confessed criminals." Hoyne added that during his term in office he had "yet to find a well authenticated case of a confession following the so-called third degree." Other challenges were marginally more successful. In 1918, Albert Klein's claim that he was given the third degree by staff at State's Attorney Hoyne's office was taken before a grand jury by members of the local bar association. That same year, Judge Brentano threw out the confession by Joseph Sullivan after hearing Sullivan's claim that he confessed to a series of freight car thefts only after being beaten insensible by Officer Michael Whitty at the 22nd Street station.[37]

As the state's attorney's comments made clear, there were plenty of apologists for the third degree in the first decades of the twentieth century. Several were members of the judiciary. In 1918, Leo Doyle, a judge on the municipal court, testified that the beating of a prisoner by a police officer could not be a felony. Doyle, a witness in the inquiry into Albert Klein's claim he was beaten during the third degree at the state's attorney's office, added that it was wrong to begin criminal prosecutions against the police department. In 1919, Henry Guerin, a judge in the criminal courts, directed a jury to acquit Joseph Radakowitz on charges of murder after hearing Radakowitz's claim that he had confessed after he was given whiskey and then threatened with whips and clubs to induce him to confess. Guerin also called for a grand jury investigation into the charges against the police and state's attorney's office. Chicago police chief John Garrity said there was no need for an investigation and assured everyone that his officers did not rely on the third degree because he had forbidden the practice in a memo. Other judges, including the chief justice of the criminal court, supported Garrity and averred they never saw any evidence that defendants who appeared before them had been subjected to the third degree. Although State's Attorney Maclay Hoyne claimed he welcomed the inquiry, he wrote a scathing letter to the editor denouncing Guerin and other "maudlin and weak minded judges" who complained about police abuse and demanded that critics of the police department produce a single "reputable citizen" who had been subjected to the third degree in Chicago. On the chance that the distinction he was drawing was not clear, Hoyne added that "my police may have been rough with murderers, gunmen, highway robbers, drug crazed fiends, and may not have been sensitive about their 'constitutional rights' when the public was endangered, but we have judges who worry over liberty of criminals more than the life and safety of citizens, which is worse."[38]

Police Torture in the 1920s

The twenties began where the teens left off, with a string of judicial efforts to rein in police torture. At a hearing in 1920, the attorney for one of the women arrested in a raid on a disorderly house charged that some of the suspects seized in the raid had been subject to the third degree at the Desplaines Avenue station, and the presiding judge reprimanded the lieutenant in charge of the district. When Daniel Schissler claimed that he confessed after four officers at the detective bureau used the third degree on him, and offered two discolored and bruised ears as evidence of the abuse he suffered, Judge McKinley issued warrants for their arrest. That same year, when Irving Schlig was brought to trial for robbery, the judge threw out the case when he determined that it was based on a confession the police had obtained by beating the sixteen-year-old with a rubber hose. In 1922, Judge Marcus Kavanaugh held a hearing on the third degree. Witnesses testified that they were beaten with blackjacks and rubber hoses, kicked and struck, and burned with cigars. Reporting on Kavanaugh's investigation, the *Chicago Tribune* noted that many of the claims seemed to be made against officers at the detective bureau.[39]

There were other investigations into the claims of the third degree in the early 1920s. In 1923, Edmund Fitch's claim he was subjected to the third degree by detectives in the bureau's "gold fish room" prompted the Chicago City Council to hold a hearing to investigate his claims. Aldermen were shocked when Fitch removed his shirt to reveal welts on his back caused by a rubber hose and showed them bruises on his head and his swollen hand. Three officers Fitch identified were suspended and charges were brought against them. The outrage did not end the practice: four months after the city council hearing a police beating left an unnamed African American suspect suffering from a broken jaw. Judges continued to transfer suspects out of police custody when their lawyers complained their clients had been subjected to the third degree. In December 1922, Judge Hebel ordered that Arthur Foster, suspected of killing Kate Mitchell, be taken to the county jail to protect him from officers at the detective bureau who were allegedly using the third degree on him to try to get him to confess. Three years later, another judge sent George Connell to county jail after being told that Chicago police officers investigating a jewel theft had given him the third degree.[40]

Those investigations were reinforced by a series of decisions by the Illinois Supreme Court. In those opinions, that court often denounced the practice in the strongest terms. In *Illinois v. Colvin*, decided in 1920, the court considered the defendants' claims that they had confessed to murder only after being subjected to extended physical and mental abuse and declared that if the defendants' claims were true, "a gross outrage was committed, which not only deserves the severest condemnation, but which would exclude as evidence any admissions obtained by such means." Two years later, in *Illinois v. Rogers*, the court spoke out even more strongly against the third degree. There, nineteen-year-old Harvey Rogers was tried and found guilty of participating in an armed robbery. In the course of reviewing the verdict on appeal, that court endorsed the trial court's decision to exclude Rogers's confession after he claimed that he had been beaten to make him talk, asserting that "the practice of punishing a suspect by bellows [*sic*] or other violence when he refused to confess is a violation of criminal law itself and renders a policeman subject to criminal prosecution for such conduct." "It is," the court added, "just as much the duty of a State's attorney to prosecute an officer who has thus violated the law as it is to prosecute any other man charged with a crime." The court repeated that point at the very end of the decade, in *Illinois v. Frugoli*, where it reversed the verdict of the lower court and remanded the case for a new trial on the grounds that the verdict had been based on a confession that might have been involuntary. In its opinion, the court emphasized that the use of violence or threats to obtain a confession was illegal, citing the two sections of the Illinois Criminal Code that made it a crime to commit an assault or battery or threaten a person in order to obtain a confession.[41]

Unfortunately, some victims of police torture were unwilling to press charges for fear of reprisal. In 1924, when two suspects in a murder case complained about police torture and were asked to appear before the city council to outline their experiences, they refused and left town. Friends explained they feared the police. There was also backlash by the police. In 1922, when Judge Fitch took issue with the methods the police used to obtain confessions, his comments prompted a near riot by police officers who claimed that the judges were interfering with their work. One officer was quoted in a newspaper as saying, "We are permitted to do less and less every day." He added, "Pretty soon there won't be a police department."[42]

The idea that police officers were handcuffed by a judiciary that put the interests of criminals before the community was not confined to patrolmen. In 1921, the *Chicago Tribune* ran a cartoon, titled "How We Protect Our Murderers." In it, two men sat chatting in a jail cell. One told the other: "I pleads not guilty, renigs on my confesh, and tells th' world it was a phony one dragged out o' me by third degree torture, etc." A year later, the *Chicago*

Tribune explained that there was "a pretty general acceptance of the theory that the police must beat up a suspected man, if he has a criminal record, to get the facts out of him." Other newspapers made similar claims; as the *Herald Examiner* put it, the police felt that if they could not use third degree methods, they would not be able to charge any suspects. In 1923, Chief of Police Fitzmorris denounced the city council's investigation into the third degree as an attempt to break down "the public bulwark against crime." These arguments were echoed in a debate in the Illinois General Assembly over a bill that would have made it possible to punish police officers who tricked or abused people into making confessions. A proponent of the bill, a representative from Chicago, made the familiar argument that a law was necessary since too many cases were thrown out in that city because of police tactics; an opponent argued to the contrary that too much effort was being put into protecting criminals and not enough into protecting society from their behavior. In the end, the notion that the problem was the judiciary, not the police, apparently prevailed and the bill was withdrawn.[43]

That did not bring an end to the struggle between the police and the judiciary. Frustrated in their efforts to arrest gunmen and gangsters in 1924, Chicago chief of police Morgan Collins, and Michael Hughes, chief of detectives, denounced judges who granted writs of habeas corpus or released gunmen on bail after hearing claims of torture. Another "wise old policeman," unnamed, declared that the police would be able to solve more cases if they were allowed to use the third degree. In 1927, Michael Hughes, by this time chief of police, responded to claims that the police beat a hotel clerk to force him to confess to the theft of sixty-six dollars by announcing that as long as he was chief of police, criminals in Chicago would not be handled gently. The trouble with reformers and criminologists, he went on, was that they "want to protect the criminals and kick the police. I'm for protecting the police and kicking the criminals."[44] Hughes added, however, that he agreed that the police should not beat "innocent men."[45]

There were apparently very few innocent men being arrested in Chicago in the 1920s, because suspects and their lawyers continued to charge the Chicago police engaged in torture throughout the decade. In 1921, James Bartlett contended that during his extended detention at the Central police station he was deprived of food until he confessed, and Bernard Grant claimed he was given the third degree until he confessed to the murder of a patrol officer. In 1922, Arthur Foster, suspected in the murder of a widow who refused his suit, complained the officers at the detective bureau kept him awake for days and deprived him of food. Two years later, Beulah Annan prevailed at her trial for murder. Although the verdict apparently reflected the fact that the jurors believed her claim she murdered Harry Kalstedt in self-defense, she also presented testimony that she confessed to murdering him after a jealous quarrel because she was given the third degree at the Hyde Park police station. In another case from 1924, Deputy Superintendent of Police John Alcock, who was working with federal investigators looking into allegations that jurors in a trial had been bribed, gave one of the suspects in the case, William Mulvin, what was called "an old fashioned third degree." In 1925, Bernardt Mylin asserted that he confessed to murdering an express messenger only because he had been given the third degree. Three years later, twenty-two-year-old Michael Clos claimed he confessed to murder only after being subjected to the third degree.[46]

Blanket claims of being subject to "the third degree" make it hard to tell precisely what happened, but there were enough specific claims of physical force to suggest that violence figured prominently. Andrew Chrfrikas, arrested in 1920, said he was beaten by the police until he confessed to murder, and Harvey Rogers made a similar claim a year later. In 1921, Daniel Schissler said he confessed after being subjected to a violent third degree at the Detective Bureau, a claim that seemed to be confirmed by the fact both his ears were bruised. In 1925, Ira Perry, a burglary suspect, said he was hit with fists and beaten with a rubber hose during his interrogation.[47]

A year later, Azar Holick claimed he confessed to murder after being interrogated for more than ten hours and beaten. In 1927, Timothy Yahanan said he confessed after being beaten and kicked, and Patrick Coffey, arrested with Yahanan for theft, claimed at trial that he confessed after being beaten. His complaint was substantiated by the testimony of a fellow inmate at Cook County Jail, who said that when Coffey was brought to his cell he was badly bruised and scarred. In 1929, three African Americans suspected of murder, Leonard Shadlow, LaFon Fisher, and Leon Brown, maintained that they only confessed after officers kicked and slapped them during interrogations. One of the men, Fisher, was beaten so hard he was paralyzed from the waist down.[48]

Sometimes, the use of the third degree by one branch of the criminal justice system prompted denunciations of the practice by another. In 1929, one of the suspects claimed that the special investigator for the grand jury, Sheldon Bruseaux, had used the third degree on several witnesses. One of those witnesses said he was beaten in the office of the special prosecutor during an interrogation. In an odd twist, which presumably reflected political differences as much as respect for the rights of a witness, Police Chief Michael Hughes was reprimanded by the special prosecutor for obstructing justice when he removed five police detectives from the special prosecutor's staff. In response, Hughes agreed to reinstate all but one of the men, based on evidence that the officer had slapped a witness. Asked about the decision, Hughes explained that he would not employ "any man on the force who will lift a hand against any one."[49]

The 1930s: End of an Era?

The 1920s ended much as the decade had begun, with an attack on the police department. In his chapter on the Chicago Police Department in the *Illinois Crime Survey*, published in 1929, August Vollmer condemned the department for its incompetence, corruption, lack of professionalism, and ties to organized crime. He recommended hiring better men, giving them more training, and supplementing the current investigative practices with better record keeping and more science and technology. Puzzlingly, Vollmer did not criticize, or even mention, the department's use of the third degree. Instead, the *Survey*'s discussion of the third degree appeared, briefly, in the chapter on Chicago prosecutors. There, Chicago's police were condemned for lack of training in modern policing. As a result, the report concluded, they were criticized by press and public alike for their inability to catch criminals, "and, smarting under the criticism of failure, they have resorted to the 'third degree' and other improper and dishonest police methods." While the authors of the *Illinois Crime Survey* condemned the practice and the police who relied on it so heavily, their concerns were more pragmatic than principled. They argued that when Chicago's police relied on violence to obtain confessions, they failed to make any effort to get other proof to substantiate their charges. Then, if a judge threw out the confession, there was no other evidence available to the prosecution and the apparently guilty criminal went free.[50]

In 1930, at the first meeting of the Chicago chapter of the Association of Law Enforcement Officers of America, several of the participants echoed the assumptions of the *Illinois Crime Survey*, expressing the belief that various new scientific methods—including the lie detector and truth serum—would eliminate the need for the third degree. That same year, the NAACP took up the problem of the third degree at its national convention. The next year, the Wickersham Commission devoted an entire volume, significantly entitled *The Report on Lawlessness in Law Enforcement*, to the third degree. The commission's report particularly condemned the use of the third degree by police departments in a number of cities, and it offered an extensive and highly critical description of the abusive practices of Chicago's police, assistant state's attorneys, and state's attorney's investigators. The report noted that the third degree "employed by the State attorney's investigators in the solution of outstanding crimes" was "more severe and exceptional" than the type of third degree administered by the police.[51]

Still, the Wickersham Commission also pointed to reasons for optimism that the third degree was coming to an end, even in Chicago. Its report pointed to the fact that the Illinois Supreme Court had issued a number of opinions condemning the third degree over the course of the 1920s, opinions that established procedures by which courts could assess third degree claims and bar confessions when the claims were substantiated. More generally, the report raised the possibility that when and if Prohibition came to an end, there would be no need for the third degree and similar police methods. Others were even more optimistic. When the 1930s began, the *Chicago Tribune* was certain that law enforcement in Chicago was finally ready to give up the third degree and credited the Wickersham Commission's report with helping turn the tide. In an editorial praising the commission's report, the paper explained that the new administration of the Chicago Police Department, particularly Acting Commissioner Alcock, opposed the third degree. And there seemed to be ground for optimism. In the fall of 1931, when Joseph Donovan appeared in court bearing unmistakable bruises and claimed that he had confessed to robbery after being beaten by police at the Shakespeare Avenue station, Alcock ordered an investigation and vowed that any officers found to have beaten Donovan would be taken before the disciplinary board. In 1932, a lengthy article in the *Tribune* assured its readers that a new, humanitarian leadership at the top of the police department had done much to bring third degree practices to an end.[52]

The middle of the decade brought an even greater reason for hope that the third degree would finally end. In 1936, the United States Supreme Court decided *Brown v. Mississippi*, a case involving three African American men who claimed that sheriff's officers in Mississippi had tortured them into confessing to a murder that they did not commit. At trial, the jury convicted the three of murder and sentenced them to death. On appeal, the United States Supreme Court struck down their convictions and declared police torture intended to obtain confessions was a deprivation of due process.[53]

That seemed to change matters considerably. Police torture was no longer unprofessional or problematic because it could lead to a case being thrown out of court. It was illegal because it was unconstitutional. The *Chicago Tribune* and the *Chicago Defender* both seized on the opinion and publicized it widely. The *Tribune* printed a full-page analysis of the opinion two weeks after it was issued. That paper also published two editorials on the opinion, including one that discussed, at length, the claims of torture in the case. The opinion, the paper argued, was a significant protection against police brutality and one of several important decisions protecting the rights of African Americans by the Supreme Court that year. The *Defender* was no less impassioned. It covered preparation for oral argument in the case and published the entire opinion by Chief Justice Hughes when it was handed down. The *Defender* also reprinted the *Tribune*'s editorial on the decision and excerpted editorials from other newspapers around the country praising the result and deploring police efforts to extort confessions.[54]

By and large, scholars have come to the same conclusion, finding that police torture declined significantly in the 1930s after the Wickersham Commission's report and the Supreme Court's decision in *Brown*. Yet there is ample evidence that Chicago was not ready for reform. Acting Chief Alcock's strong words against abuse in the Donovan case were all but forgotten in that same year when he denounced the Wickersham Commission report. Alcock denied that police in Chicago had ever engaged in the practice and pointedly wondered if the commission "heard anything from any person whose word could be believed."[55]

That was indeed the problem, though not, perhaps, in the way Chief Alcock meant. Claims of torture continued to be made in the 1930s, but as we will see in the next chapters, they were rarely made by people whose words the courts, the press, or the public wanted to believe.

CHAPTER TWO

MURDER IN BLACK AND WHITE

TO UNDERSTAND HOW AND why police torture continued after *Brown*, it helps to look closely at one case in which claims of police torture arose. Unpacking that case will help reveal the combination of pressures and decisions that helped perpetuate the problem.

The Murder of Florence Johnson

This particular case began at sunrise on Friday, May 27, 1938.

Margaret Whitton woke with a start at 5:15. The sun was just coming up over Lake Michigan, less than half a mile from her bedroom window. The night before had been mild, so mild that Margaret and her sister had cracked open the apartment's windows to let in the breeze, and that dawn the weather already was warm and fair. It promised a pleasant close to a busy week for Whitton, who lived with her sister, Florence, and her brother-in-law, Elmer Johnson, in an apartment on Chicago's South Side. Elmer's brother Harry and Harry's new wife had just finished a visit, and nice as it had been, the addition of two more adults made the two-bedroom apartment cramped. The rain that had come down almost nonstop since Monday had done nothing to help; by midweek, Margaret's niece and nephew had been cooped up too long. On Wednesday five-year-old Kenneth broke a window playing in their bedroom, and his father had to clear out the broken glass and find something to cover it. Thursday morning, Elmer Johnson left before 8:00 a.m. to begin his twenty-four-hour shift at the Company 3 Fire Station, leaving Margaret and Florence to deal with the guests and children. And in the midst of all that, Margaret had her own work as a registered nurse at Englewood Hospital.[1]

Still, the spring-like weather that Margaret Whitton woke up to early that Friday morning could not conceal the fact that Chicago was already busy and loud. At 5:15, a northbound Illinois Central train was nearing the

47th Street station less than a hundred yards away from her window and its southbound counterpart was chugging around the curve of Lake Michigan just a few blocks to the north. Milk trucks were beginning their rounds on her neighborhood's streets. A few hundred yards to the south at 47th Street, a busy commercial thoroughfare, bartenders were closing up, shopkeepers preparing to open, and the streetcar was running its route. At the corner of 47th and Lake Park, less than half a mile from the Johnson apartment, a road crew resurfacing the intersection already was setting up their barricades.[2]

That particular Friday morning, noise was only one of Chicago's problems. May 27, 1938, was the first anniversary of one of the most deadly incidents in the city's bloody labor history: the Memorial Day Massacre. The year before, striking steelworkers held a Memorial Day picnic and rally on Chicago's far South Side and then marched across a vacant lot toward the Republic Steel plant. A few hundred yards from the front of the plant, the marchers were blocked by a line of several hundred police officers. Twelve months later, people still disagreed about what happened next; but when the dust settled on the field ten of the marchers were dead or dying and more than thirty others had been seriously injured. Most of the injured and all of the dead had been shot in the back or the side. Reaction to the event exposed Chicago's deep divides. The state's attorney of Cook County brought criminal charges against the striking workers, a huge public meeting was held in Chicago's Loop to protest the police violence, and a Senate subcommittee conducted an investigation into management and law enforcement practices during the strike.[3]

In the 1930s, violence in Chicago was complemented by crime. Early editions of the local papers broadcast the day's tally: police on the city's North Side were on the lookout for a team of Yiddish-speaking swindlers who had defrauded several city residents of money and jewelry, while a few miles away a mob of women had attacked a man who had exposed himself in a forest preserve. Across town a considerably more inept thief had been captured after he delayed his getaway long enough to try to make a date with the woman he had just robbed. Not all the crime news was so laughable. Thursday evening twenty police officers surrounded the Hotel Edwards on West Harrison Street and exchanged several rounds of gunfire with a robbery suspect before they captured him.[4]

As the shootout made clear, Prohibition may have been over, but Chicago was still a mobbed-up town. Yet in 1938, the city's police had other concerns. Sex crimes seemed to be on the rise in the 1930s; frequent reports in the local papers about so-called sex morons attacking women made everybody apprehensive. The police department established a sex crimes unit to combat "night prowlers who have been raping and killing women," and the Cook County state's attorney established a sex bureau for the same purpose. Still, the numbers were daunting. In the five years between 1936 and 1940, Chicago police investigated an average of 151 rapes a year, compared to 325 homicides. In neither case were the results particularly satisfying; the police made arrests in only 57 percent of the rape cases and 59 percent of the homicides.[5]

Later Margaret Whitton said that she woke up because she heard a sound inside the apartment; she thought it was a cry or a groan. Worried that meant something was wrong with either her nephew Kenneth or his three-year-old sister Florence, she put on her robe to go check on them. As she stepped through the doorway of her bedroom what had begun as a fairly routine early morning chore became something else. Outside her bedroom Whitton saw a man—with brown-skin—walk past her on his way into the children's room next door.

It must have been a shock, since the only adult male who lived there, Elmer Johnson, was still on duty at the fire station more than a mile away. Furthermore, Whitton and the Johnsons were white and racial tensions were very real in the part of Chicago where Margaret Whitton woke up that morning. Although housing segregation had existed in Chicago before the turn of the twentieth century, in the years around World War I, maintaining segregation became a bloody business. In 1919, a race riot sparked when white youths killed a young black man who had floated into a whites-only bathing area while swimming in Lake Michigan. That riot lasted five days and led to more than thirty-five deaths (the majority black) and several hundred injuries as whites, most of them young and male, attacked African American businesses and raided African American neighborhoods. The end of the riot did not mark the end of racial violence. In 1922, the Chicago Commission on Race Relations reported that in the preceding five years there had been more than fifty bombings of dwellings that blacks tried to move into.[6]

By 1920, most African Americans in Chicago were confined to the city's Black Belt, a narrow strip of land that stretched north and south between 31st and 51st Streets. East and west, the Black Belt ran from the train tracks by Federal Street to the area around Cottage Grove, though above 37th Street it reached further, all the way to the Illinois Central tracks that ran parallel to Lake Michigan. Between 31st and 37th Streets that area stretched from the rail tracks by Federal Street all the way east to the Illinois Central tracks that ran parallel to Lake Michigan. In the 1930s, black families who tried to move out of that area into majority-white areas often continued to face violent opposition. In 1937, when Carl Hansberry purchased a home near Washington Park, a few miles southwest of the Johnson apartment, his family was greeted by rock-throwing whites and legal efforts to enforce the restrictive covenant that barred the sale of the property to blacks. A year later, a few brave black families were moving into apartments only a few blocks to the west of the Johnson apartment building, but Lake Park Avenue, where the Johnsons lived, remained a white enclave.[7]

Whether startled by the unexpected visitor or not, Margaret Whitton coolly stood in her bedroom doorway, waiting and watching as he entered the children's bedroom. Then she followed until she reached the door to the children's room. Standing there, she monitored the mysterious visitor as he crossed the room to an open window, climbed through, and lowered himself to the ground. Then, her interest in his doings apparently at end, Whitton glanced at the two children. Both slept soundly.[8]

That made her wonder once again about the noise that woke her up, so Whitton turned around and walked back past her bedroom door, through the apartment to the small sunroom that was just off the living room. Florence and Elmer used the sunroom as a bedroom, so Margaret went over to check on her sister. The scene that met her eyes was horrific: Florence lay sprawled across the bed, blood gushing from several wounds in her skull. Margaret Whitton's training as a nurse prevailed. She rushed to her sister, bunched up her pillow to prop up her head, and pressed the bed sheet to her wounds to try to stop the bleeding. Unfortunately, it was too little and it was too late. Florence died in Margaret's arms.

At that point, Margaret Whitton screamed.[9]

Investigation

She recovered her composure quickly enough. At 5:40 that morning the desk sergeant at the Hyde Park police station logged a call reporting an attack at the Johnson apartment. The station was less than a mile away; the first officers at the scene, Lieutenant Berounsky and patrol officers McSheffery and Collins, arrived at the apartment around 5:43. Quick as they were, they did not beat the newsmen. Reporters who had heard the report of the crime on police radio were already gathering. Some jostled with the men setting up the barricades at Lake Park and 47th; others crowded around in the hallway as they tried to push their way into the Johnson apartment.

After assigning an officer to keep the reporters under control and out of the apartment, Berounsky led the others to the Johnson home.[10]

The Johnsons lived at 4631 Lake Park, in a building complex on the east side of the tree-lined residential block. The complex, which still stands, consisted of two yellow brick buildings, each three stories high. They faced one another across a modestly terraced courtyard that stretched the width of the block, beginning at an arched gateway that opened onto Lake Park Avenue and ended at a five-foot stone wall that separated the building from the Illinois Central Railroad embankment. Each building in the complex had thirty-six apartments, which were arranged around six separate entryways that opened off the courtyard. The various entries had their own staircases, and at each landing of the stairs there were two apartments. The Johnsons lived in Apartment F, a first floor apartment at the far northeast corner of the courtyard that backed up to the railroad tracks.

Margaret Whitton and a neighbor, Mrs. McCahey, who lived across the hall, met Berounsky and his men at the apartment door. The two women led the officers across the living room to the little sunroom where Florence Johnson still lay on her bed. The first thing Berounsky noticed was the blood; it covered Johnson's face, saturated her hair, and was splattered on the bedclothes and the wall behind her bed. After taking a look, Berounsky called for a doctor. Minutes later, F. K. James, a sixty-five-year-old doctor who lived at 4631 Lake Park with his wife, herself a doctor, knocked on the door. His quick examination of Florence Johnson confirmed the obvious; she was dead. Not long after James left, a second doctor, Thomas Carter, who worked for the coroner's office, arrived to conduct the official examination of the body. After Carter formally confirmed Florence Johnson's death, her body was taken out of the apartment and driven to Boydston's Morgue, a few blocks east at 42nd and Cottage Grove, where Carter performed the preliminary autopsy later that morning.[11]

Once Florence Johnson's death had been established, the first order of business was to determine what killed her. The search for the murder weapon was a surprisingly slapdash affair. Several of the first people on the scene later claimed they failed to see anything that might have been used as a bludgeon: Margaret Whitton admitted she did not see anything when she went to prop up her dying sister that morning, and Dr. James could not recall seeing anything that looked like a weapon during the course of his inspection of the body, though when he testified at trial he said he had a hazy notion there might have been something under Johnson's pillow. Police officer Joseph Kistner, detailed to find the weapon right after he arrived at the apartment around 6:20 that morning, did no better. He admitted he did not see anything that looked suspicious (or even bloody) the first time he searched the sunroom.[12]

Fortunately, others apparently had more finely honed powers of observation: Berounsky saw a bloody brick under Johnson's body when he first looked into the sunroom. Carter recalled seeing a building brick with blood on it tucked beneath Johnson's pillow when he examined her body. Hoping to preserve the crime scene for the investigators, both Berounsky and Carter left the brick where they saw it; but when Raymond Crane, the captain in charge of the Hyde Park station, arrived about 6:30 that morning, he felt no such compunction. When he walked into the sunroom, he immediately went to the bed, reached down, plucked up the brick and wrapped it in the newspaper he was carrying. Then he gave the package to Kistner with orders to take it to the station to inventory.[13]

The issue of the weapon being settled to Crane's satisfaction, the next step was figuring out what had happened. Berounsky took an oral statement from Margaret Whitton not long after he arrived at the apartment. After she told him what she had seen, Whitton took her niece and nephew into her bedroom and Berounsky went to investigate the children's bedroom, a large room at the northeast corner of the building. The room had three windows that faced the Illinois Central track; each window was the common sash-style, with top and lower panels that could be raised or lowered to let in air. On two of the windows, the lower panels had been raised the inch or two from the sill that the burglar guard allowed in order to let in the night breeze, but Berounsky saw that the lower pane of glass in the third window had been entirely broken out. That was the window Kenneth had broken a few days before; unsurprisingly, there were a few bits of glass still in the frame, and there were glass shards and something that looked like linoleum lying on the floor beneath the sill. Berounsky also noted that the lower part of that window had been raised as high as it would go, nearly a foot above the sill, and the window screen had been raised up even higher.

After looking around the room, Berounsky left, leaving a more detailed examination for the members of the investigation bureau who were already at work in the sunroom. Throughout the morning, they took photos, gathered evidence, and dusted for fingerprints. Early news reports eagerly declared that the investigators found several clear fingerprints when they dusted the surfaces in the sunroom and bedroom, and checked the inside and outside of the windowsills in the children's bedroom.[14]

Even in a small apartment, the investigators' work took hours. For a while, Captain Crane directed the investigation, going through the apartment and then outside with some of his men to check around the windows. But the case was too big to leave in his hands; around 8:00 or 8:30 that morning Otto Erlanson arrived at the scene. In contrast to Crane, who spent several years before he became captain at the Hyde Park station in charge of the mayor's police detail, Erlanson was both an administrator and an experienced investigator. He had worked on the St. Valentine's Day Massacre in 1929, and more recently he was a proponent of new policing methods who had helped modernize Chicago's detective bureau by establishing a sex crimes data system. In 1938, he was in charge of the homicide section of the detective bureau. Erlanson sent men out to interview the neighbors. A couple from across the courtyard, Frederick Lutz and his wife, told an officer that they had been awakened before 3:00 a.m., when their dog began barking. They said that when their dog quieted, they briefly heard muffled screams. While Erlanson's men canvased the scene of the crime, Crane left the apartment. After briefly stopping by the morgue to check in on the autopsy, he drove back to his office at the Hyde Park station.[15]

Outside the Johnsons' apartment, the hunt for Florence Johnson's killer was already on. Within minutes of Margaret Whitton's call to the police at 5:40 that morning, an all-points radio call went out to patrol units directing them to be on the lookout for young black men. Over the next twenty-four hours, police arrested at least fifteen to twenty young black men across the city.[16]

When the announcement went out, James Keeley, a detective, was three-quarters of the way through a shift that began at midnight. On May 27, he was working a squad car with Jack Joyce and Joseph Burbach, patrolling a zone that ran north and south between 39th and 71st Streets, and east and west from State Street to Lake Michigan. When they heard the bulletin, Keeley and his partners were in the Fifth District station at Wabash Avenue and 48th Street. They scrambled to their squad car and sped east on 47th Street. As they raced toward the Johnson apartment—Keeley recalled he was driving about fifty miles an hour most of the way—they saw a young African American man walking very quickly along the sidewalk on the south side of 47th Street, heading west.[17]

Keeley slammed on the brakes and got out to investigate. As he walked up to the youth, Keeley noticed he had a cut on one of his fingers and stains of what appeared to be blood on his hands and clothes. When Keeley demanded an explanation about his presence and appearance, the young man responded that his name was Thomas Crosby and said that he had cut his hand during a recent fight on the lakefront. Crosby added that his shirt had been splattered by blood at work when he was skinning chickens. Unconvinced, Keeley bundled Crosby into the squad car and continued to the Johnson apartment. They arrived a few minutes later. After leaving Crosby with officers at a police wagon parked nearby, Keeley hurried into the Johnson apartment to report the arrest. Not long after, he was back outside to collect Crosby, whom he took into the apartment to be viewed by Margaret Whitton. Unfortunately, though her first response was "That's the man!" when she looked again more carefully Whitton decided that Crosby was shorter than the man she had seen in the hallway that morning. That was hardly an identification; but apparently it was good enough for Keeley. He took Crosby back outside, put him into the squad car, and drove him to the Hyde Park station. After locking Crosby in a cell, Keeley went back to the Johnson apartment until about 9:00 a.m. Then, nearly an hour after their shift should have ended, Keeley, Joyce, and Burbach drove Margaret Whitton to the Hyde Park station to be interviewed.[18]

At the station, Keeley took Whitton to the squad room, found her a seat, and went to get Crosby out of his cell in the lockup. This time, when Keeley paraded Crosby in front of Margaret Whitton, she said she was sure that Crosby was the man she had seen in the apartment. Just to be sure, Keeley had another black man who had been arrested that morning, Julius Carothers, brought into the squad room. Whitton reported that the twenty-eight-year-old Carothers was not the man she had seen that morning and repeated that she was sure that she had seen Crosby. That established, Keeley took Crosby to Crane's office on the second floor, where Crane, Erlanson, John Sullivan, the chief of detectives, and Officer McFadden of the detective bureau were meeting about the case. The discussion was interrupted so that they could question Crosby. At some point during that interrogation, Crosby was told to take off the shirt he was wearing under his jacket. That shirt, along with the brick that had been found in the Johnsons' apartment, were given to an officer with orders to take them downtown to a crime lab for testing. At another point, Margaret Whitton was brought into the conference to be asked, once again, if Crosby was the man she had seen in the hallway that morning. This time her answer was more equivocal than it had been on the station's lower floor: she said that he "looked like" the man she had seen in the apartment.[19]

Little as it was, the police decided, once again, that it was enough to keep Crosby in custody. He was taken downstairs to be fingerprinted. There he told an officer that his prints were already on file, under his real name, Robert Nixon, because he had been arrested as a juvenile for robbery in February 1938. Then, at about 11:00 a.m., Keeley, still on duty more than eleven hours after his shift had begun, took Nixon out of the station to a patrol wagon. As the wagon headed north to take Nixon to police headquarters at

1121 South State, Keeley followed behind in his squad car.[20] The entourage arrived at Eleventh and State around noon. Nixon was whisked to the detective bureau, which occupied the building's third and eleventh floors. There, he was questioned in one of the detective bureau offices. Then he was put back into a squad car and driven across the Loop to the Chicago Scientific Crime Detection Lab. Created in the aftermath of the St. Valentine's Day Massacre in 1929, the crime lab was the first forensics lab in the United States. Its scientists and experts trained scientists and officers from other police departments and also did the practical work of testing writing samples, matching bullets to gun barrels, analyzing fingerprints, and running blood tests. The scientists and experts in the lab also worked on trying to develop truth serum and helped pioneer the use of lie detector tests.[21]

Although his shirt and the bloody brick were already somewhere in the crime lab being analyzed, there is no evidence that Nixon gave a blood sample. He had been taken to the lab to be given a lie detector test. The head of the crime lab, Leonarde Keeler, an expert at the polygraph, administered the test to Nixon himself, but the results of the exam were disappointing. Keeler reported that Nixon lied in response to any number of questions, but that the machine stubbornly recorded that Nixon told the truth when he said that he had not been involved in the Johnson murder. Sure that the machine was wrong, the police took Nixon back to the detective bureau and began to employ more homespun means of discerning the truth about the crime. News accounts reported that Nixon was questioned through the rest of the afternoon, across the night, and into the next day by teams of police officers and state's attorneys led by John Sullivan, the head of the detective bureau, and police captain John Prendergast, chief of the uniformed officers. The *Chicago Tribune* added that Prendergast had taken special command of the case.[22]

That afternoon, the coroner's inquest into Florence Johnson's death began. Several firefighters were in attendance, including Charles Crane, chief of the 11th Fire Battalion (and brother of Captain Crane of the Hyde Park station) and James Hughes, captain of the fire house where Elmer Johnson worked. Hughes and Crane announced that the fire department would help the police find Florence Johnson's killer, and Crane added that "It's terrible when a fireman on duty saving life and protecting property comes home to find his wife murdered." Dramatic pronouncements aside, nothing much happened that afternoon. Thomas Carter reported that his autopsy on Florence Johnson established that she had died from skull fractures and lacerations of the brain caused by three deep blows to the front of her head. And with that, the inquest was adjourned pending further police investigation.[23]

Solving the Case

On Saturday morning the investigation continued. Police under Lieu-tenant Erlanson's command compared fingerprints taken at the Johnsons' apartment to those taken from the African American men arrested during the dragnet the day before. Meanwhile, Captain Prendergast sent police offi-cers through the neighborhoods around the Johnson home, and the *Daily News* reported that several more—the article said "scores"—of African American men were arrested as a result. The City of Chicago offered a reward of five hundred dollars to anyone who gave information leading to an arrest and conviction in Florence Johnson's murder.[24]

Late Saturday evening, police efforts began to pay off. At 10:30 p.m., Thomas Harvey, a court reporter who worked for the state's attorney's office, was called to the detective bureau to take down an interrogation. When he arrived, Harvey was taken to a room that held Nixon; Thomas Courtney, the state's attorney of Cook County; John Boyle, an assistant state's attor-ney; Captain Daniel Gilbert, a former Chicago police officer and the chief investigator for the state's attorney; John Sullivan, the chief of detectives, and the deputy chief of detectives, Walter Storms. Harvey settled into the room, and took notes as Nixon was interrogated. At some point in that session, Nixon told his inquisitors that he had spent Thursday evening with Earl Hicks, another young black man. Several police officers were immediately dispatched to Chicago's South Side to locate Hicks. The *Chicago Tribune* explained that the police were particularly interested in talking to Hicks because they feared that "because of his youth, the type of his mind, and probable nervousness, and also because of the long hours during which he had been interrogated," they could not take Nixon's statements at face value.[25]

The police located Hicks around midnight, put him under arrest, and brought him to 11th and State. The interrogation continued; Hicks and Nixon were questioned, separately and together. Finally, during a joint interrogation that took place sometime after 1:00 a.m. on Sunday, Hicks and Nixon both confessed they had a role in the death of Florence Johnson. Each, however, insisted the other had struck the blows that killed her.[26]

Securing confessions from Nixon and Hicks was a major breakthrough, but it was not enough. The police wanted their two suspects to reenact the Johnson murder. So at 4:45 p.m., Sunday, May 29, several members of the detective bureau police arrived at the Johnson apartment with Nixon and Hicks. A crowd that Nixon guessed included thirty people, and one onlooker estimated was nearly one thousand strong, had gathered around the apartment complex, waiting to meet them.[27] Regardless of its size, it was an all-white and not particularly friendly group. The *Chicago Tribune* reported that several women in the crowd called out "Why don't they lynch them." The American Negro Press (ANP) wire service told its readers that it was no accident that the mob was present or enraged because at least one of Chicago's afternoon papers had stirred up public opinion with the false report that Florence Johnson had been raped before she was murdered. The ANP also reported that the police had to call in special backups to protect Nixon and Hicks from the mob.[28]

Against that backdrop, Nixon and Hicks walked the scene of the crime, prompted by the police. As Thomas Harvey struggled to keep up and take notes, the two told an audience that included Boyle, Sullivan, Storms, Crane, Keeley, and others that they had been looking for some money. They went east on 47th Street until they got to the new Illinois Central station at 47th and Lake Park. There, they climbed the stairs to the station and sat for a while, looking at Lake Michigan and talking. After some discussion, they decided they could break into one of the apartments they could see that ran up against the side of the tracks. So they climbed down from the station and began to walk north along the railroad embankment, not stopping until they were parallel to the building at 4631 Lake Park. This spot, they explained, looked promising because one of the windows on the first floor had seemed to be open. Leading the way, they climbed down the embankment, jumped over the five-foot-high retaining wall (followed somewhat more slowly by several police officers and attorneys), and went to the windows on the first floor apartment.

As they re-created their entry into the house, Nixon and Hicks described how they found themselves in the children's bedroom of the Johnson apartment. As they told how they tiptoed past the sleeping children, their stories diverged. Hicks insisted that he stayed at the doorway of the children's room and watched Nixon first go into the kitchen, where he took an apple from a bowl, and then through the apartment. According to Nixon, the two of them walked in and out of the kitchen, then went through the apartment to the living room. They crossed the living room and went into the small sunroom where Florence Johnson slept. There, Nixon said, he started to take the radio and Hicks began to open the desk drawer. But the drawer squeaked, and when it did so Florence Johnson woke up. Quickly one of them—Nixon recalled it was Hicks; Hicks was sure it was Nixon—hit her in the head with a brick picked up outside the apartment. Then, ignoring the windows in the sunroom that would have given them quick access to the courtyard, they dashed through the living room, past the apartment's front door, and back into the children's room, where they clambered back out through the window. Outside, Hicks recalled, Nixon stopped to put his shoes back on and threw away the apple.[29]

Nixon, on the contrary, insisted that the apple fell out of his pocket as he jumped over a fence on the west side of Lake Park as he made his escape. This seemingly inconsequential disagreement led to an impromptu search of the area around the Johnson apartment. Remarkably, one of the men in the crowd remembered that he had kicked away an apple when he was trying to find a good spot to watch the reenactment. He pointed out a half-eaten apple off to the side and Sullivan picked it up, satisfied that it was the apple that Nixon had thrown away two days before. In a surprising lapse of police procedure, rather than give the apple to an officer to be taken to the detective bureau where it could be processed as evidence, Sullivan later testified that he took the half-eaten apple home with him and kept it in his refrigerator.[30]

Most of the rest of the reenactment was anticlimactic. Nixon and Hicks walked the police through their escape routes. Hicks told of scrambling into a hiding place on 47th Street, and waiting there until he could hitch a ride on the back of a milk truck; Nixon described a more complex escape across Lake Park, through a vacant lot, down an alley, and out onto 47th where he was captured by Keeley. Just as the reenactment was wrapping up, it looked as if the crowd would get the drama they yearned for: Elmer Johnson, his brother-in-law John Whitton, and Johnson's two children drove up to the apartment. When Whitton saw Nixon and Hicks he shouted that he'd like to get his hands on them. Eager to avoid a confrontation, the police quickly bundled Nixon and Hicks into a squad car and drove away.[31]

Monday was Memorial Day. Local papers reported that the police were increasingly convinced that Nixon had been involved in several of the rapes and murders of several other white women in Chicago and were hunting for evidence to tie him to those crimes. Meanwhile, the *Chicago Daily News* reported that the Chicago police were in touch with the police in Los Angeles. Officers in Los Angeles said they had identified Nixon as the murderer of Edna Worden and her daughter in 1937 based on a comparison of Nixon's prints and some partial prints found at the scene of the Florence Johnson murder. That squared with a statement Chicago detectives reported had been made by another black youth they had taken up during the dragnet on May 27. Detectives claimed that James Scott told them he had hitchhiked from California to Chicago with Nixon in the fall of 1937, and along the way Nixon had bragged that he had "killed a couple of women" in California.[32]

Tuesday, May 31, was eventful. Florence Johnson's funeral was that morning at St. Ambrose Church, a few blocks from her home and just across 47th

Street from the spot where James Keeley said he first saw Robert Nixon on the morning of May 27, 1938. Early that afternoon, Nixon and Hicks signed their statements confessing to Johnson's murder in a ceremony attended by police, representatives from the state's attorney's office, and several grand jurors. After the signing, Chief of Detectives Sullivan announced that the Chicago Police Department would not cooperate in California's efforts to extradite Nixon to Los Angeles to stand trial for the murder of Edna Worden and her daughter. A few hours later, the police reported that Nixon had confessed to murdering Florence Castle in Chicago in 1936. At 7:30 that evening, Nixon and Hicks were put in a lineup at 11th and State, in front of John Boyle, an assistant state's attorney, Margaret Whitton, a number of members of the general public, and several other prisoners. Whitton identified Nixon, but was unable to identify Hicks. Strangely enough given Whitton's consistent claim that the man she saw walking through the apartment early that morning was black, several of the men in the lineup she viewed that evening were white.[33]

Over the next several days, the police continued to interrogate Nixon about other murders. On Friday, June 3, Chicago police told the press that Nixon had admitted to committing at least five murders and rapes in Chicago between May 1936 and May 1938. That same day, detectives had Nixon reenact three of those crimes, exercises that brought home the startling range and length of his apparent crime spree. One reenactment was at Chicago Hospital, on 49th Street, not far from the Johnsons' apartment. That was where Anna Kuchta, a student nurse, had been murdered in August 1937. Another was downtown at the Hotel Lorraine at the corner of Wabash and Van Buren, where Betty Bryant had been raped and beaten in July 1937. The third reenactment was at the Devonshire Hotel at 17 East Oak Street on the city's near North Side. Florence Castle had been murdered there in 1936.[34]

That same day, the *Chicago Tribune* published a lengthy account of the ways in which the scientists at the crime lab had helped tie Nixon to all the murders. The article explained how pieces of fabric taken from Nixon's shirt, and the brick found in the Johnson apartment, had been taken to the crime lab. Over the next several weeks, Clarence Muehlberger, a forensic toxicologist, subjected both to a series of tests. First, he performed a benzidine test, treating one of the samples he took from the shirt with a mixture of benzidine and other chemicals. The resulting chemical reaction suggested that the stain contained blood. To confirm that, he performed a second test on another sample from the shirt, treating it with acetic acid and then looking at it with a microscope to determine if particular crystals had formed on the stain. The results of that second test confirmed that the stains were blood. In order to learn whether it was human blood, Muehlberger subjected some of the material from Nixon's shirt to a Bordet test. It was a complex process: Muehlberger injected some human blood into a live rabbit. Ten days later he prepared a serum from the rabbit's treated blood and used the serum to test one of the stained pieces from the shirt. The rabbit serum turned cloudy, proving that the blood on Nixon's shirt was human. Muehlberger also examined the hair on the brick with a microscope and established that it had come from a human. In addition, the story in the *Tribune* reminded its readers that fingerprints tied Nixon to the murders of at least five other women who had been killed in Chicago since May 1936, as well as women in Los Angeles.[35]

Confessions

The *Tribune's* enthusiasm for scientific policing notwithstanding, accounts in other papers made it clear that the case against Nixon rested on his multiple confessions.[36] There were three relating to Florence Johnson's murder: the first, by Nixon alone, apparently was made at 11:00 p.m. on Saturday, May 28, but was mysteriously unsigned. The second, made by Hicks and Nixon together at 1:00 a.m. on Sunday, May 29, was signed in front of a number of witnesses on Tuesday, May 31. The third, a transcription of the reenactment by Nixon and Hicks, was made at 4:45 p.m. on Sunday, May 29, and had also been signed in front of the witnesses on May 31.[37]

As one might expect, Nixon and Hicks disagreed about several crucial points in the statements, most obviously on the issue of who struck the blows that killed Florence Johnson. In all three of his statements, Nixon insisted that Hicks had done so; in both his statements, Hicks claimed Nixon had. They also disagreed about a number of minor points: Nixon said that the two of them met on the West Side of Chicago and rode the street car from 47th and Calumet to 47th and Lake Park; Hicks said that they walked the mile and a half between the two spots. Hicks said that he saw Nixon put his shoes on just outside the Johnsons' apartment after they left, while Nixon offered conflicting stories about his shoes, sometimes recalling that he put them back on in a gangway on the north side of the Johnson's building, and other times claiming that he did not put his shoes on until he got across Lake Park.[38]

Some disagreement between the two suspects, particularly on issues that might establish guilt, was to be expected, but their statements were more marked by error than disagreement. Most noticeably, the two misstated the number of blows that were struck. Both Nixon and Hicks agreed that whoever struck Florence Johnson hit her twice, but the autopsy made it clear that she had been struck three times. Nor did either Nixon or Hicks recall any blood in the room after Florence Johnson was struck, which was implausible given what Berounsky saw when he first walked into the sunroom.[39]

Several other claims Nixon and Hicks made in their initial statements had to be corrected to reflect the actual layout of the apartment during the reenactment:

- Brick: Nixon and Hicks quarreled over who had the brick. They also disagreed about where they acquired it. In his statements at the detective bureau, Nixon said that Hicks picked up the brick on the Illinois Central tracks. At the station, Hicks said that Nixon picked it up before they got to the tracks. At the reenactment, Nixon and Hicks initially agreed that the brick was picked up on the tracks near the Johnson apartment building. But when it became obvious that there were no bricks on the track bed, Hicks corrected himself and claimed that Nixon picked up the brick in a vacant lot at the corner of Lake Park and 47th Street, before they got to the Illinois Central station.[40]
- Window: In his initial statement, Nixon claimed that they went into the apartment through a broken window that had no covering on it, other than the window screen. He said the same thing in the joint statement at 1:00 a.m., and then again at the reenactment. When pressed at the reenactment by Sullivan, who asked if there was anything on the window, Nixon said all he remembered was maybe a shade. Hicks then remembered that there was something that was not a shade hanging down on the window. After being prompted by Boyle, who asked if it was not a cloth on the window, Hicks recalled that the window was covered by oilcloth. Oilcloth is not, of course, the same as a piece of linoleum.[41]
- Florence Johnson's bedroom: In his original statement, Nixon recalled that there was a small fireplace in the room that Florence Johnson slept in. During the reenactment, Nixon corrected himself and said what he had thought was a fireplace was a desk.[42]
- Bed: In his original statements at the detective bureau, Nixon said that Florence Johnson was sleeping on a cot. At the reenactment, he realized that she had been sleeping on two beds pushed together.[43]
- Children's room: In his statement at the station, Hicks insisted that he stayed in the doorway of the children's bedroom the entire time, while Nixon killed Florence Johnson. He also said that the two children were

sleeping in a single bed in their bedroom. Nixon, in contrast, said that the two children were in separate beds. Faced with evidence at the reenactment there was a crib and a bed in the children's room, Hicks had to correct his earlier version.[44]

- Escape (I): In his first statement, Nixon insisted that after the two of them left the apartment, he saw Hicks jump over the stone wall behind the apartment and head toward the train tracks. But in their joint statement at 1:00 a.m. Hicks said he went around the building to the north and over to 47th Street.[45]

- Escape (II): In his statement at 1:00 a.m., Hicks said that he left the apartment and went down to 47th Street. He walked west on 47th Street for about six to seven blocks, until he saw a milk truck. He hopped onto the milk truck and rode it eight to nine blocks until he got close to where he lived at 4858 State Street. At the reenactment, Hicks said he left the building and went to about 1233 47th Street, which was only three blocks west of Lake Park and just east of Woodlawn Avenue, where he saw a milk truck. He rode the milk truck four blocks to Cottage Grove, where he got off and walked north to 46th Street. Then he went west on 46th to Vincennes, then back up to 47th Street, and walked down 47th Street to State Street.[46]

As inconsistent as those two versions of Hicks's escape were, either version meant that he was either walking west on 47th Street or riding the back of the milk truck west on that street just when Keeley was driving east on 47th Street. That raised questions about why Keeley did not see and stop him. And those disagreements were not inconsequential; studies have shown that errors of fact are often signs that a confession has been coerced.[47] The high number of errors of fact, corrections, and inconsistencies here raised serious questions about the confessions Nixon and Hicks made.

Criminal Justice in Black and White

In 1940, Richard Wright published *Native Son*, which was loosely based on the Florence Johnson murder, and Robert Nixon was the model for Bigger Thomas. Although *Native Son* has been criticized for its assumption that under racism, alienated young black men inevitably would become brutal criminals, its picture of Chicago as a city deeply divided along racial lines certainly seemed to be reflected in coverage of the Johnson murder.[48] The picture of Nixon that emerged in the local white press was chilling: a young black killer who roamed the city and the country at will, scaling fire escapes and jimmying open windows to enter apartments and hotels where he raped and murdered white women. Chicago's major dailies did their best to make the story even more disturbing: the *Chicago Tribune* reported that when he was threatened by the mob during the reenactment at 4631 Lake Park, Nixon "bared his teeth." An article on the reenactment at the Hotel Lorraine quoted one police officer as saying that Nixon climbed the building "just like an ape." The author of the piece, Charles Leavelle, explained that Nixon lacked the "charm of speech or manner that is characteristic of so many southern darkies." Worse, his very dark skin, hunched shoulders, and "long sinewy arms that dangle almost to his knees," coupled with his "outthrust head and catlike tread" "suggest the animal" or an "earlier link in the species." Leavelle also reminded his readers (incorrectly, as it happened) that Nixon was a rapist, or, as Leavelle put it, a "sex moron," the popular quasi-scientific term for sexual predators.[49]

Other accounts in the city's mainstream, predominantly white press confidently reported that Nixon was the serial rapist and murderer who had been stalking the city's women for more than a year. The papers explained that in addition to Florence Johnson, Nixon had confessed that he killed Anne Kuchta in August 1937, raped Betty Bryant in July 1937, assaulted Virginia Austin in August 1936, and murdered Mary Louise Trammell that same month. And the *Los Angeles Times* reported that Chicago police claimed he had also confessed to several crimes in Los Angeles, including the murder of Rosa Valdez, and attacks on Mrs. H. W. Koll, Elizabeth Ries, Lola Torres, Zoe Dammerell, and Mrs. E. Van Ettan in Los Angeles.[50]

Articles in the African American papers offered a different perspective. Nixon's youth was a particular focus of their accounts, especially in the days before the trial, when papers repeatedly reminded their readers that he was only eighteen. The African American papers also blamed Chicago's mainstream papers for sensationalizing the crime and depriving Nixon of a fair trial through stirring up public hostility by falsely accusing Nixon of raping Florence Johnson. They reported that leaders in Chicago's black community had filed protests with publishers of Chicago's other papers and cast doubt on the fairness of the proceedings.[51]

The black press also found the evidence against Nixon underwhelming. The *Amsterdam News*, published in New York, scathingly noted that "for a time it looked as if Nixon would 'confess' to some slayings that took place before he was born" and pointed out that other men had been tried and convicted for at least some of the murders that Nixon had confessed to or were being laid at his door. It was true for at least a couple of the cases that Nixon had allegedly confessed to: in December 1937, Thomas McCall, a white man, confessed to the assault of Virginia Austin at the Washington Hotel in downtown Chicago in August 1936. A jury found McCall guilty and he was serving five years in the penitentiary for the crime. An African American, Rufo Swain, had been tried, convicted, and executed for the murder of Mary Louise Trammel in August 1936. Swain had also confessed; based on his confession the police tied him to the murders of Florence Thompson Castle and Lillian Guild. At the time, the police had noted (in language that sounded familiar) the strong resemblance between the Castle and Guild deaths and the Trammel murder.[52]

Like Bigger Thomas, both Nixon and Hicks were young, male, and black. In fact, they were very young: at the time of the murder and trial both Nixon and Hicks were under 21. Nixon was at most eighteen years old (his age was disputed); Hicks just seventeen. That meant both were juveniles under Illinois law, and Nixon's arrest in Chicago 1938 for burglary was a juvenile charge.[53]

And like Bigger, Nixon and Hicks were born in the South. Most of the details of Nixon's early life are murky: Nixon said he was the youngest of eight children and had been born in Tallulah, Louisiana, where his mother was the cook for Andrew Servier, the sheriff of Madison Parish. Nixon's statements about his education were inconsistent. At one point, he claimed that he moved to Chicago to stay with his brother in 1933–1934, when he was thirteen; at another, he said that he stayed in Louisiana, and in school, until 1935, when he finished fifth grade. At the age of sixteen, he went west to Los Angeles to live with one of his sisters. He stayed there for about eight months, and then went east to Chicago to stay with his brother. When his brother went east to New York, Nixon headed back west again; first to Reno, Nevada, then to Oakland, California, and finally back to Los Angeles. Then, after briefly returning to Louisiana, he headed back to Chicago, where he arrived in July 1937. From July through September 1937, Nixon said, he worked as a chauffeur for B. H. Robinson, a wholesale businessman who lived on the North Side. When Robinson moved to Denver, Nixon stayed behind in Chicago, living on about four hundred dollars that he claimed he had saved while working as a chauffeur.[54]

While it seems implausible that Nixon saved several hundred dollars from a salary of $17.50 a week, other parts of his story are harder to confirm or dismiss. The two movies he said he worked in both came out in 1938, which means it was possible that Nixon served as an extra while he was in California. Andrew Servier was the sheriff of Madison County, which is where Tallulah was located, and an article in the *Chicago Tribune* seemed to confirm Nixon's claim that he knew Servier, quoting Servier to the effect that "Nixon was raised here and is known as a sneak thief and a house prowler. He has been on the prowl since he was six. Unable to do much with him here because so young. Nothing but death will cure him." But according to the 1930 census, the Servier family had a live-in cook, Willie Shearer, who was white and the 1940 census showed Servier and his wife lived alone without servants. The 1930s manuscript census reports for 1930 turned up no African Americans named Nixon or Nixson (a spelling Nixon himself used on some court documents), in Tallulah or Madison Parish, Louisiana. In fact, the 1930 census did not record anyone, white or black, named Nixon or Nixson, living in Tallulah, Louisiana. The 1930 census did show that there was a young, African American man named Robert Nixon born in Louisiana in 1917, but he lived in New Orleans with his father, mother, and younger sister. Interestingly, the same census had a record for an African American named Thomas Crosby, who had been born in Morehouse Parish, Louisiana in 1920. Morehouse Parish, like Madison Parish, was in the upper northeast part of the state. According to the 1930 census, Crosby's mother was 29, a fairly close match to the details Nixon supplied about his past, although Crosby was the oldest of five children living at home, rather than the youngest. Equally puzzling, a document prepared after Nixon's trial for the Illinois Parole Board indicated that Nixon had been arrested in Vicksburg, Mississippi in April 1935 for prowling and burglary, but showed no arrests in Louisiana or Chicago.[55]

Earl Hicks's life was less mysterious. He said he was seventeen years old in July 1938 and had been born in Greenville, Mississippi, one of eight children (he had four brothers and three sisters). This seemed to be true; the 1930 census shows that an Earle Hicks was the nine-year-old son of Guy and Ollie Hicks in Greenville, where his father was a janitor in the Baptist Church. Hicks claimed he went to school between the ages of seven and fifteen but only finished fourth grade because he spent much of his time working, first in the cotton fields and then for a lumber company in Greenville, until he left for Chicago in 1937 when he was just sixteen. While he held a number of jobs in Chicago—he said he had worked as a porter in a hotel, a bartender's helper, a dishwasher, and a shoeshine—at the time of his arrest he was unemployed and was waiting to hear about a job with the Work Projects Administration. Hicks had never been arrested in Chicago, though he had been arrested once for gambling and once for grand larceny in Mississippi and had served ten months in a Mississippi county jail for the larceny charge in 1936, when he was sixteen. That information was more or less confirmed by a statement by William Taggert, chief of police in Greenville, who told the *Tribune* that Hicks "was always in trouble here, having been arrested numerous times for thievery. In August 1935 we sent him to the State penitentiary for picking pockets. He got out the following July, but didn't come back here. I guess we won't be seeing Earl anymore."[56]

But while they had much in common with Bigger Thomas, neither Nixon nor Hicks was identical to the protagonist of *Native Son*. Bigger lived with his mother and siblings; Hicks and Nixon were not only out of jobs and living apart from their families, they were nearly homeless. Hicks was sharing a room in a boarding house, Nixon was sleeping on a pool house floor. They scrambled between the world of odd jobs and handouts and the space of minor crime and gambling joints. In their study of Chicago, *Black Metropolis*, St. Clair Drake and Horace Cayton describe a world of lower-class African Americans who lived in the tenuous space between kitchenette and penitentiary. At the time of their arrests, Earl Hicks could barely claim a kitchenette, and Robert Nixon had far less.

If Nixon and Hicks seemed to be the embodiment of the masterless young black men that Richard Wright demonstrated worried white Chicago, the Johnson-Whitton families appeared to be equally classic examples of the city's anxious white working class. Florence was the oldest child of John Whitton and his wife, the former Alice Harding, who was French Canadian, and had been born in Chicago in 1904. About three years after Florence was born, the family moved to New York, where her father worked as a chauffeur and her younger sister, Margaret (also known as Marguerite), was born in 1908. Her parents split up when Florence was in her early teens; in 1920 Florence, her mother, and her five younger siblings lived in Chicago, at 35th and Mozart, with her grandfather William Harding and her uncle, George Harding. Although George was a painter by trade, money seemed tight; sixteen-year-old Florence was already working for a telephone company and her younger brother, John (born in 1906), was working as an office boy.[57]

Within the next several years, Florence's life had changed considerably, seemingly for the better. In 1924, she had married Elmer Johnson, who had been born in 1900. Johnson's life before his marriage to Florence has been hard to piece together. His parents emigrated from Germany, but Elmer and his older brother, Harry, were born in Illinois. Harry served in the army during World War I, but Elmer did not, though he would have been old enough to do so. In 1930, Elmer and Florence were living with Harry and his wife, Francis, at 75th and Kingston while Elmer drove a truck for a bakery and Florence worked as a comptometer operator at a notions store. Their first child, Kenneth, was born in 1933, and their daughter, Florence, was born in 1935. In 1937, Elmer joined the Chicago Fire Department and was working out of the new station at 41st and Dearborn. Late that same year, Florence, Elmer, and their two children moved to the apartment at 4631 Lake Park, which was less than a mile away from John Whitton and his family. At some point, Florence's younger sister, Margaret, moved in with them, apparently following the end of her own marriage. Margaret, who was trained as a nurse, worked at Englewood Hospital, a teaching institution at 6001 S. Green.[58]

The distinction between the employed and stable Johnsons and Whitton families, on one hand, and Earl Hicks and Robert Nixon, on the other, could not have been more marked. Yet it was not the distinction between propertied whites and alienated blacks that Wright drew in *Native Son*. The Johnsons were not the Daltons, and much of the white reaction to Florence Johnson's murder rested on the perception that the lives of whites like the Johnsons were precarious. At the start of the twenty-first century, the area north of 47th Street at Lake Park Avenue, where the Johnson family lived, was a gentrifying, predominantly African American neighborhood. In 1938, the Johnsons' neighbors at 4631–4637 Lake Park were exclusively white. Some were middle-class, others were clerical workers or city workers like Elmer Johnson. The 1940 federal census showed the buildings' tenants included musicians, an elevator operator, a retail store manager, several teachers at local public schools, a lawyer, a waitress, a handful of widows (some living with grown children, others sharing apartments with other women), and some office clerks or accountants. Their jobs were middle-class, but the building's residents were not particularly permanent. The 1940 census showed that virtually none of the residents in the complex had lived at that address five years before. That was typical of the residents of the blocks around their apartment. There were a number of apartment hotels, the Woodmere Hotel East and the Eleanor Association (a women's residence) were at 47th and Woodlawn, and the Belvidere Hotel was just to the south of the complex on Lake Park. Other buildings in the neighborhood, though not hotels, served white populations that, if not transient, could not put down deep roots. For some, Florence Johnson's murder seemed to indicate that their community was crumbling because the Black Belt pushed closer.

Habeas Corpus

It was not until Monday, June 7, that the coroner's inquest, which had begun only to be postponed on May 27, 1938, resumed. This time around, the violence that had been threatened at the reenactment on Lake Park was played out. On his way to the witness stand, Elmer Johnson went up to Nixon, who was sitting in a chair shackled to a police officer, and slammed his fist into Nixon's head, bloodying his nose. Remarkably, the shackles that he wore apparently did nothing to restrain Nixon. Accounts in the white press reported that he leapt to his feet and tried to strangle Johnson, but was caught by the officers in attendance just before he could injure him. Chicago's black press presented another perspective on the event, pointedly noting that the police had done nothing when Johnson attacked Nixon (one account claimed that the police officer assigned to guard Nixon seemed to be dozing when Johnson rushed the youth). Not unexpectedly, the attack disrupted the inquest. It took fifteen minutes to restore order, and the *Chicago Tribune* said that the coroner had to excuse Johnson from testifying to quiet things down. After that, the hearing came to a speedy end. The coroner's jury voted to send both Nixon and Hicks to the grand jury on murder charges. The grand jury promptly issued four indictments against Nixon on Tuesday, June 8: one each for the murders of Johnson, Kuchta, and Castle, and a fourth for the rape of Betty Bryant.[59]

Then, after the flurry of activity, there was a strange delay. Although Illinois law required that suspects in custody be brought before a judge promptly after arrest, it took a petition for a writ of habeas corpus before Nixon and Hicks finally were brought to court to be arraigned before Chief Judge Cornelius J. Harrington. Their arraignment was on Monday, June 13. At that point, Nixon had been in custody nineteen days, and Hicks for eighteen.[60]

The habeas petition was prepared by lawyers working for the Chicago branch of the International Labor Defense league. Formed in the 1920s to do work for political prisoners in the United States, the ILD led protests against police brutality in Chicago in the early 1930s after Chicago police killed three Communists involved in a rent protest in Chicago's Black Belt. Nationally, the ILD was actively involved in several major cases of racial justice, including the Scottsboro cases and Angelo Herndon trial, in the first years of the 1930s. In the early 1930s, the ILD combined legal work and mass action, organizing national and international protests in support of the Scottsboro defendants. While that publicity seemed to help galvanize the United States Supreme Court to hear appeals for the Scottsboro defendants, critics charged that the practice of mass action had antagonized white progressives and moderate African American organizations like the NAACP.[61]

That was not the situation in Chicago, where Nixon and Hicks were represented by a coalition of radical and liberal lawyers. At trial, Nixon's lead attorney was thirty-one-year-old Joseph E. Clayton Jr., already an accomplished criminal defense attorney. Clayton lived at the intersection of radical and liberal causes. He had been born in Texas, where his father, Joseph E. Clayton Sr., was a school principal until he quit his job in the 1920s to become an organizer for the Southern Tenant Farmers Union. Joseph Clayton Jr. went to law school at Northwestern and as a young attorney in Chicago worked with Earl Dickersen, a leading African American civil rights attorney who served on the board of the NAACP, was president of the progressive National Lawyers Guild, and argued *Hansberry v. Lee* before the Supreme Court of the United States. At the time of his death from asthma, in 1956, Clayton was one of the top criminal defense lawyers in Chicago and had trained a generation of African American attorneys. His wife, Edith Spurlock Sampson, was a lawyer who worked for the state's attorney's office and became an alternate delegate to the United Nations in 1950. Clayton's co-counsel, Charles Burton, brought a far more radical perspective to Nixon's defense. Burton, who had been born in Mississippi in 1887, had a divinity degree from Yale, and had studied law at John Marshall Law School in Chicago. He was a longtime friend of A. Philip Randolph of the Brotherhood of Sleeping Car Porters, and had been a leader of the Brotherhood's Citizens Committee in Chicago. In 1938, Burton was the executive director of the National Negro Congress, a Communist front organization.[62]

Hicks was represented at trial by Ulysses S. Keys and W. Sylvester White. Keys, who had worked on the initial habeas corpus petition with Roth and the ILD, was roughly the same age as Clayton. Like Burton, he was born in Mississippi, went to college in Chicago at the Lewis Institute (a forerunner to IIT), and then to law school at Chicago's Loyola College of Law. Keys worked with the local NAACP branch, handling cases for them during the 1930s and 1940s. But Keys also worked with the radical, interracial group that supported the packinghouse workers in their efforts to join the CIO. And his wife, Harriet, taught at Chicago's Willard Elementary School, was on the board of directors of the Southpark YWCA, and served as recording secretary for the local chapter of the National Negro Congress. Hicks was assisted by White, who had recently graduated from law school at the University of Chicago. In his first job out of law school White worked for Joseph Clayton, earning five dollars a week. Later he went on to work in the U.S. attorney's office, served as a commissioned officer during World War II, and ended his career as a judge on the Cook County Criminal and Juvenile Courts.[63]

Meanwhile, just as the defense team was predominantly African American, the prosecution team was mostly, but not entirely, a team of white men. The case was prosecuted by the state's attorney for Cook County, Thomas J.

Courtney. Courtney had run for office as a reformer, but contemporary critics and historians agree that his term in office was marked with shady deals, particularly for the mob. Courtney did not actually try the case; instead Wilbert F. Crowley, an assistant state's attorney, handled the trial. Crowley, like Keys, graduated from Loyola College of Law in Chicago. Crowley began his career representing criminal defendants, working for the public defender's office in the early 1930s. Courtney persuaded him to join the state's attorney's office in 1933 and hired him to be the first assistant, the highest-ranking assistant in the office. In that position, Crowley was involved in investigating and prosecuting several major cases; he prosecuted the charges against the striking workers arising from the Memorial Day Massacre in 1937. He remained at the state's attorney's office until 1947, when he was elected to a judgeship. He served as chief judge of the Criminal Court of Cook County in 1956 and 1957, and remained on the bench until his retirement in 1975.

Crowley was aided at trial by another assistant state's attorney, John S. Boyle, a rising star in the state's attorney's office in the 1930s. Boyle had been actively involved in the investigation into Florence Johnson's murder; he questioned first Nixon and then Nixon and Hicks during the confessions on May 28 and 29, and was present at the reenactment. According to his obituary, while he was in the state's attorney's office Boyle won convictions in nearly fifty homicide cases and lost only three jury trials. He served as alderman in the early 1940s, and then ran for mayor in 1943, only to lose. He was elected judge in 1960 and served as chief judge of the Circuit Court of Cook County for many years in the 1960s and 1970s. While the trial team that prosecuted Nixon's case was white, during the investigation into Florence Johnson's murder Boyle worked with an African American lawyer, Edward Wilson. Wilson, who was also an assistant state's attorney, had attended Oberlin and Williams, and then studied law at Howard. In 1938, he had been working at the state's attorney's office in Cook County for more than twenty years, most of them spent in the appellate division, where he handled any number of major criminal appeals for the state's attorney's office. Many of them, perhaps significantly, rested on confessions.[64]

Concerned that the seemingly endless list of crimes Nixon had confessed to suggested that one or both of their clients might be mentally ill, the lawyers that represented the two youths appeared in court with motions to permit Nixon and Hicks to be examined by Walter Adams, an African American psychiatrist who worked at Provident Hospital, and William McKee, an African American psychiatrist at the Institute of Juvenile Research of Cook County. The court promptly granted those motions as well as the prosecution's request to have its own, white experts, Harry R. Hoffman and Harry A. Paskind of the Behavioral Clinic of the Cook County Criminal Court, examine the defendants.[65]

On July 6, the state's experts completed their report, concluding that Nixon's mental condition was as follows:

> Without psychosis; intelligence at the lower limits of normal. Not committable as insane or feeble minded. In our opinion this patient understands the nature of the charge against him and is able to cooperate with counsel.

They offered a similar assessment of Hicks. Nine days later, on July 15, 1938, Judge Rush denied the defense motions to move the trial out of Chicago (the defense had argued that the publicity made it impossible for Nixon and Hicks to get a fair trial) and referred the case to the chief judge for appointment of a trial judge.[66]

As the lawyers made their final preparations for trial, there were troubling issues in the background. Most obviously, there was the problem that Nixon and Hicks had been held incommunicado for more than two weeks. There was a darker problem, as well. Several African American newspapers reported that Nixon and Hicks both claimed that their confessions were false and that the Chicago police had used physical abuse to compel them to confess to the murder.[67]

CHAPTER THREE

WHILE WAITING FOR THE trial to begin, the lawyers for Nixon and Hicks used the radical and African American press to call attention to the case. In an early interview, Charles Burton set the tone. He complained about the "circus" created by the Chicago police and the city's mainstream white papers during the reenactments. He argued that the frenzied mobs, "inflamed by the lurid, lynch hysteria of the press," meant that a change of venue for the trial was the only way to guarantee real justice in the case. The argument did not persuade the court. On July 15 the motion for a change of venue was denied.[1]

Trial Begins

On July 18, the case was assigned to Judge John C. Lewe, who promptly denied the motions for separate trials. Lewe did, however, order a hearing on the question of whether Nixon and Hicks were insane and empaneled a jury to hear the competing evidence from the parties' experts. No transcript of that proceeding exists; but we know that at its end the jurors concluded that neither Hicks nor Nixon was feebleminded or insane. Against the advice of his lawyer, Ulysses Keys, Hicks immediately changed his plea to guilty. An article published by the local African American wire service reported that Hicks pled guilty because he believed he would be set free at the end of Nixon's trial if he agreed to testify for the prosecution, and it quoted unnamed sources (probably Keys) who speculated that the state offered Hicks a deal because it lacked the evidence to convict him.[2]

The trial began on Tuesday, July 26. Over the next two days, the lawyers selected a jury of the twelve men who would try Nixon. All were white, most were working-class, and at least three were naturalized citizens. The jury's composition raises the question of whether it was a result of a deliberate effort by the state to exclude blacks. Yet there was no record of an objection by the defense in Nixon's case, and there is some reason to think that Nixon's lawyers might have been more concerned with class than race when selecting the jurors. In the 1930s, the ILD and the National Negro Congress both tried to create alliances of white and black workers. Regardless, the result was a jury that on paper seemed to have far more in common with Elmer Johnson than it did with Robert Nixon.[3]

With the jury set, John Boyle gave an opening statement for the state. Then Wilbert Crowley called the prosecution's first witness, Elmer Johnson.[4]

Johnson, of course, knew nothing of what happened at his home that Friday morning, since he was at the fire station finishing up his twenty-four-hour shift. The state used his evidence to introduce the jurors to his wife and family: Johnson described how long he and his family had lived at 4631 Lake Park (eight months), when he began work at the fire station at 4005 Dearborn (two years before the murder), the age of his wife at her death (between thirty-four and thirty-five years), and the length of their marriage (nearly thirteen years). Then he described getting a call that Friday morning sometime between 5:30 and 6:00 a.m., telling him to come home immediately because something had happened at home.[5]

That less than consequential but emotional evidence was followed by that of several witnesses who were called to establish that Florence Johnson was dead and had been killed in the City of Chicago. The first was Thomas Carter, who described arriving at 4631 Lake Park early in the morning. He told how he found Florence Johnson covered in blood and determined that she was dead. He also testified about the autopsy he performed later that morning, which established that she had died as a result of receiving three deep blows to the scalp. Carter was followed by F. K. James, the neighborhood doctor. James also described a grisly scene: Florence Johnson was "lying on the bed, and what apparently seemed to be a severe laceration of the right side of the head, her eyes were blackened; there had been a great amount of hemorrhage from the head." Her pillow, he added, was "saturated" with blood, and there was "some blood spotted on the walls above the head of the bed."[6]

Unfortunately for the prosecution, James's testimony seriously confused the timeline for the murder. Asked how long he thought Florence Johnson had been dead by the time he got to the body, James estimated that he first saw her around 5:40 that morning, at which point she had been dead for between an hour and an hour and a half. That put the murder sometime between 4:10 and 4:40, well before Margaret Whitton said she woke up to the sound of her sister's moans. Pressed about the timeline by Crowley,

James hedged his testimony, admitting that he probably did not get to the apartment until about 6:00. But he insisted that when he first saw Florence Johnson it appeared that she had been dead sometime between an hour and an hour and a half, which cast doubt on Margaret Whitton's claim that her sister died in her arms a few minutes before she called the police. Asked if it was possible that Johnson had been killed after 5:15 or 5:20 a.m., James admitted that was possible and also agreed that it was difficult to accurately determine how long a person had been dead.[7]

Margaret Whitton

James was followed by Margaret Whitton, the state's most important witness. At first, her testimony went as expected. She explained that she had been a licensed nurse since 1928 and worked at Englewood Hospital, a few miles from the Johnson apartment. She told the jury that in May 1938 she lived with her sister, her brother-in-law, and their two children at 4631 Lake Park. She recalled that on Thursday, May 26, she went to bed between 10:15 and 10:30, only to be awakened early the next morning by what she told the jurors she believed were the screams of her sister. She got out of bed, put on her robe, and went to the hall. Questioned during cross-examination by Clayton, she insisted that she went to the hall without turning on any lights, because she could see by the light coming through her single bedroom window.[8]

Other parts of her testimony cast doubt on her confident assertion that she could see in the hallway. She told the jurors she saw "a colored fellow" walking past her bedroom door as he headed toward the door to the children's room. Yet her testimony about this remarkable moment was lacking detail: she was not sure how far she was from the man and could not tell whether the man she saw noticed her. On cross-examination she admitted she could not recall what he was wearing, though she remembered that he was dressed in dark clothes and thought that he was wearing a jacket. She added that she could see the collar of his shirt beneath the jacket, but she did not know how far up his jacket was zipped or even whether it was zipped at all. Nor could she say whether the man she saw was wearing a cap or a hat or anything on his head, or whether he had any scars or marks on his face. Her description of the intruder was problematic in other ways: In response to questions, she said that the man she saw was "colored," but when asked to elaborate on what she meant by that, she said that the man she saw was neither "a real dark brown" nor light-skinned. That hardly called to mind

Robert Nixon, who was so dark-skinned he was "nearly black," as Clayton pointed out.[9]

Some details of Whitton's testimony were perplexing. She insisted, repeatedly, that she was not frightened when she woke to moans and was adamant that she was not surprised when she saw a black man in the hall of the apartment. She insisted that once she saw the man go into the children's room, she was not curious enough to see whether he went out that bedroom window, nor did she look out the window to see where he went or do more than peek at the children from the doorway to their bedroom. And she was certain that she did not see the bloody brick under her sister's pillow until after the police had removed her sister's body, which was puzzling given her testimony that she rearranged her sister's pillow to help prop up her head.[10]

Other elements actually contradicted the prosecution's account of the crime. She was certain that she did not hear or see more than one man in the apartment. She insisted that there were no apples in a bowl on top of the refrigerator in the apartment and was sure to the point of quarreling that apples were kept in a bowl on a shelf in a cupboard, where they would have been invisible to someone stumbling through the kitchen at dawn. Her extensive testimony about the window in the children's bedroom was also hard to square with the prosecution's theory of what happened. She was sure that when she looked into the children's bedroom that morning the broken window was still on the burglar latch. That would have meant the window had been raised just four to five inches above the sill, not enough space to let anyone enter or exit. More confusingly, she initially suggested that when she first looked into the children's room that morning the linoleum piece that Elmer Johnson had used to cover the broken window pane was still over the pane, though later she testified that she saw it on the floor. She also told the jury that there was a radiator right beneath the broken window and a dresser right next to it. The presence of either the radiator or the dresser would have seemed to make it very difficult for anyone to climb into the apartment through the window; both should have made entry nearly impossible.[11]

In contrast, Whitton's recollections about the police investigation were straightforward. She was sure she identified Nixon as the man she saw in the hallway when he was first brought into the apartment by Keeley. She described being taken to the Hyde Park station by several police officers sometime after 9:00 that morning, and then going to an office on the station's second floor. She recalled that several police officers were meeting in the room when she arrived and that Nixon was brought in sometime after she sat down. She told the jurors that when he came in she noticed he was wearing a worn and faded blue shirt with some blood stains on his left sleeve and the back of his shirt. She remembered that she was interviewed in that office about what happened that morning and then was driven to the coroner's inquest. And then, she told the jury, a few days later she was taken down to the detective bureau at 11th and State to view a lineup of about seven men, some of whom were white. Although both Nixon and Hicks were in the lineup, Whitton admitted that she was only able to recognize Nixon—whom she had, of course, seen at least three times before in police custody—but was unable to identify Hicks.[12]

Supporting Evidence

The state followed Whitton with a number of police officers whose testimony helped to shore up her less than powerful evidence. Joseph Berounsky described the investigation at the Johnson apartment. Officers, including Otto Erlanson, confirmed that Nixon was brought to the Hyde Park station and questioned in Whitton's presence. Some of these witnesses offered conflicting recollections of the window in the children's room. Berounsky testified that when he saw it, the window "was partially raised," the glass was broken, and the screen was up. Raymond Crane testified that when he first saw the window, the screen was out and he later saw it leaning against the outside wall of the building. Then he corrected himself, recalling that the screen was in the window the first time he saw it, but had been raised as high as it would go.[13]

Others testified that the brick and Nixon's shirt were taken to the crime lab the day of his arrest and then taken back to the crime lab for further investigation a month later. That discussion of Nixon's shirt laid the foundation for testimony by the second important witness for the prosecution, Clarence Muehlberger. But no sooner had he been called to the stand than the defense objected on the grounds that his name did not appear on the list of forty witnesses the prosecution had turned over to the defense before trial. That was no small detail; state law obliged the prosecution to turn over a list of all its witnesses to the defense in order to protect the defendant from surprise. Judge Lewe took the failure seriously, and ordered the jury out of the courtroom to allow the defense attorneys a chance to interview Muehlberger. When they had done so, Clayton repeated his demand that Muehlberger should be barred from testifying. In addition to objecting to the prosecution's failure to follow the law, Clayton noted that Muehlberger's testimony about tests he performed on Nixon's shirt would be impossible to rebut given the length of time it took to do the tests that Muehlberger

performed. After considerable argument, Judge Lewe overruled the objection and called the jury back into the courtroom. Once on the witness stand,
Muehlberger established his extensive academic and scientific credentials,
and then testified about his role as a scientist at the crime lab. He described,
at length, the different tests he performed on samples taken from Nixon's
shirt and the various conclusions that he reached.[14]

It was all very technical, but beneath the haze of scientific terms the
important questions were left unanswered. Muehlberger was quick to tell
the jury that his tests revealed that the blood on Nixon's shirt was human
but never said whether that blood matched Florence Johnson's blood type.
Nor did he tell the jurors whether the blood on the shirt matched the
blood on the brick, or if the blood on the brick matched Johnson's. In fact,
Muehlberger offered no evidence that suggested he ran any tests to type
the blood on Nixon's shirt or on the brick. He testified that all he knew
was that the blood on the shirt was human blood. He also admitted during
cross-examination that he never "made an examination of the blood to
determine the type of blood of Mrs. Johnson," nor did he ever learn Robert
Nixon's blood type.[15]

Presumably it was not that he was unable to do the necessary tests;
Muehlberger was a chemist with a PhD from the University of Wisconsin.
Nor were the tests impossible; in 1938 it was well established that human
blood came in different types, and several processes for testing blood types
had been known to scientists before World War I. Indeed, by the early 1930s
there were at least two processes for typing dried blood. All of that was well
within the scope of the crime lab's state-of-the-art equipment. Given what
was possible, Muehlberger's silence at trial strongly suggested that the results
failed to support the prosecution's case.[16]

When Muehlberger stepped down, the prosecution called the last of its
important witnesses, James Keeley. He described his fortuitous sighting and
arrest of Nixon on 47th Street in some detail, noting in passing that he was
familiar with the neighborhood and knew it was all-white because he lived
nearby. That claim hardly did justice to Keeley's connection to the area; as
he admitted to Clayton during cross-examination, he had lived at 4621 Ellis
with his family, less than a block north of the spot where he said he arrested
Nixon, for about twenty-five years. Just as important, Keeley also admitted
during cross-examination that he knew that several houses in the neighborhood had African American maids, servants, or janitors. As Clayton
pointed out in his closing argument, 6:00 in the morning was about the time
that Keeley might have expected to see an African American janitor getting
off the 47th Street streetcar on his way to work.[17] Although Keeley testified

that Nixon was the only African American he saw on the east side of Cottage Grove, which he identified as the dividing line between the white and black neighborhoods, by 1938 Cottage Grove was a fairly porous boundary. At the end of the 1930s, Chicago's Black Belt stretched all the way from the railroad tracks just west of Federal Street to Cottage Grove on the east. The 1940 census showed that some black families lived between Cottage Grove and Drexel Boulevard at 41st Street, while a few blocks away, between 43rd and 44th Streets, the apartment buildings on both sides of Cottage Grove were majority black. On the east side of Cottage Grove at 46th Street, one building was majority black, the building next door was majority white.[18]

There were some puzzling elements to Keeley's testimony. He contradicted Margaret Whitton's claim that she clearly identified Nixon the first time she saw him in the apartment, recalling that the first time she saw Nixon she identified him as the man she had seen, but then declared that Nixon was shorter than the man in the hallway. That raised the question of why Nixon remained in custody after Whitton first saw him, and other parts of Keeley's testimony suggested additional problems with the initial decision to arrest Nixon. Keeley claimed that when he stopped Nixon, he observed a cut on Nixon's hand and blood on his shirt, but during cross-examination he admitted Nixon was wearing a jacket over his shirt and that there was no sign of blood anywhere on his jacket.[19]

Keeley was followed by police record keepers whose testimony was designed to create the basis for admitting the brick and Nixon's shirt into evidence. Taken together, their testimony was supposed to suggest an investigation that swiftly identified Nixon as a suspect and then painstakingly gathered the clues that helped prove his guilt. Just to make sure, the state called Thomas Harvey, a court reporter, to set the stage to admit the confessions by Nixon and Hicks into evidence.[20]

Harvey testified that he was called to the detective bureau around 10:30 p.m. on Saturday, May 28, to take notes. He first sat through Nixon's confession, and then, around 1:00 a.m. on Sunday, took notes as Nixon and Hicks were interrogated together. Harvey recalled that the state's attorney, Thomas Courtney, his assistant, John Boyle, and Daniel Gilbert, the chief investigator, were all there representing the state's attorney's office while Harvey, John Sullivan, chief of detectives, and Walter Storms, assistant chief of detectives, represented the police. In addition, Harvey testified he was present at the reenactment at 4631 Lake Park on Sunday, May 29, and took notes as Nixon and Hicks described the events of the murder to Boyle, Sullivan, Storms, and several other officers. Finally, he recalled, he took notes during the lineup on May 31, when Margaret Whitton identified Nixon. He described the process of taking down the statements in shorthand, dictating them so they could be typed up, comparing the typed transcripts to his handwritten notes to make sure they were accurate, and finally giving the joint confession to Nixon and Hicks to sign. After Harvey was shown a series of documents that he identified as the statements he took down on the occasions he described, he was followed on the stand by Walter Storms, who briefly confirmed Harvey's account, though somewhat oddly he recalled that Edward Wilson, an assistant state's attorney, was also present during Nixon's first confession on May 28, a fact that Harvey neither recalled in his testimony nor recorded on the confession form. Then, when Storms's testimony was done, the state offered the confessions into evidence.[21]

Confession Hearing

A second later, Clayton was on his feet objecting because the statements were "made as the result of beatings, and duress and under certain promises."[22]

This should not have been a surprise. A month earlier, on June 25, the *Chicago Defender* reported Hicks and Nixon claimed they confessed because they had been tortured by the Chicago police. Other African American papers around the country carried similar stories the week before. In addition, Nixon swore that he had falsely confessed while he was in custody because he was "severely beaten and abused" in a petition in support of a motion to vacate an earlier order denying his request for a separate trial. Nonetheless, Clayton's objection seemed to catch Chicago's press off guard. The morning that the confessions were going to be offered into evidence, the *Chicago Tribune* made light of the possibility that Nixon's attorneys might object to the confessions, reporting that the lawyers were expected to argue against their admission on "the ground that he was pampered into making it with numerous helpings of coconut pie and copious swigs of strawberry pop." The paper explained that Nixon's lawyers planned to claim "this constitutes undue influence just as physical mistreatment would." The atmosphere in the courtroom after Clayton's claim was considerably less lighthearted. After hearing a heated argument about the burden of proof, and some further testimony from the court reporter, the judge ordered the jury out of the courtroom. The hearing began with testimony from Walter Storms and Thomas Harvey, who testified that Nixon was not beaten or offered any inducements before he confessed. Then the defense to put Nixon on the stand to testify about his claims.[23]

Nixon's testimony about his arrest and abuse by the police filled nearly eighty pages of the trial transcript.[24] He described mistreatment that began shortly after he arrived at the bureau, Nixon was taken to what he thought was Deputy Chief Storms's office on the third floor. Although he said he saw both Storms and Sullivan in the building, Nixon said neither was present in Storms's office. Instead, there were seven other officers in the room, one of whom told Nixon he was meeting the "seven devils." They questioned Nixon aggressively for about an hour, asking him not just about the Johnson murder but about whether he had killed other people; when Nixon insisted that he had not killed anyone several of the officers struck him. Then he was taken to the lockup.[25]

Friday night, after he returned from the crime lab, Nixon was taken to Sullivan's office where Storms, Sullivan, and some other officers interrogated him. When Nixon continued to deny that he had killed Johnson, he was taken to the third floor lockup until some officers came to get him. They blindfolded him and took him up in the elevator to another floor (Nixon thought that the officers told the elevator operator to take them to the fifth floor). There, the officers walked him around for some time while he was still blindfolded, then spun him around in circles several times. After that, several officers (Nixon guessed there were about six) had him stand on something while they cuffed his arms to the wall. Once his arms were secured, they kicked whatever he had been standing on out from under him, leaving him hanging by his arms. As he hung there, they turned a very bright, very hot light on him, and started to hit him while they interrogated him about Florence Johnson's murder. Nixon guessed during cross-examination that this lasted about twenty minutes, and then something was put under his feet so that he could rest his arms for a bit. A few minutes whatever he was standing on was removed again, and the officers began to question and beat him some more. This only stopped when Nixon agreed to confess to killing Florence Johnson. When he said that he would tell Sullivan he had murdered Johnson, one of the officers (Nixon thought that it was Walter Paradowski) took Nixon back down to Sullivan's office. There, someone took off his handcuffs and they told him to take off his blindfold. When he had done so, the interrogation started again. Sullivan, Boyle, Storms, and Keeley (Nixon called him Keeler) were present.[26]

This time Nixon told them, falsely, that he had murdered Johnson. Asked who was present during this interrogation, Nixon recalled that Sullivan, Storms, Boyle, and Keeley were the only people there at first. As the interrogation went on, they were joined by several other officers and at some point the court reporter, Harvey, came in and took down his confession. After he finished confessing, Nixon was taken to the lockup for the rest of the night.[27]

Late Saturday morning—Nixon guessed it was sometime around 11:00 or noon—he was taken to Sullivan's office. There, Sullivan, Boyle, and two or three other officers Nixon did not know questioned him about the Florence Castle murder. Around noon, Nixon was moved to Storms's office where he remained, being questioned, for several hours. He continued to deny that he had committed the Castle murder, even after one of the officers hit him six or seven times on the legs with a blackjack and struck him on the side with a fist. At some point, he was taken back to the lockup, where he stayed until about midnight. Then he was taken back to Sullivan's office, where Sullivan, Storms, and Boyle questioned him about whether he had committed any murders when he was living in California. Sometime later, Nixon thought it was around 1:00 a.m., he was taken by elevator to what he believed was the eleventh floor. There, he was surrounded by a number of officers, including one officer he identified in court as Joseph Thurston, and told he had to confess.[28]

He remembered that he was not entirely sure what they wanted him to confess to, because they were all talking at once, but he thought they wanted him to confess to some burglaries on the West Coast. When he refused, someone put a bandage over his mouth and one of the officers pushed him so that he was hanging so far out of an open window that he could look down and see the L tracks that ran down the road behind the police station. The officer holding his legs threatened to drop him if he did not confess to "doing jobs" on the West Coast. When Nixon refused to agree to do so, he was told that he would be dropped at the count of three and some people in the room began counting. At that moment, another officer ran into the room and said that the chief wanted to see Nixon. Although Nixon recalled that the officer holding him "said to tell the chief that it was too late. He had tried to escape and fell out the window," Nixon was pulled back in the window.[29]

Convinced that next time they would let him drop, Nixon told the officers he would tell Sullivan what they wanted. He was taken back down to Sullivan's office where Harvey, Sullivan, Boyle, Storms, and Arthur Fitzgerald were waiting. They began to question Nixon again. At some point during this interrogation, two young men Nixon knew, Harvey Green and Eugene Artieri, were briefly brought into the office. At another point, Earl Hicks was brought in and was interrogated as well. When his statement was done, Nixon was then take back to the lockup.[30]

Nixon testified that he was beaten again around 12:30 p.m. on Sunday, May 29, after he tried to refuse to do the reenactment. This time, an officer beat him on the legs and knees with a blackjack, and punched him on the side; Nixon recalled they told him that if he did not go to the reenactment and say what they had told him to, they would kill him. When he agreed to do so he was put in a police car and taken to 95th and Stony Island, on Chicago's far South Side. They stayed there, parked in the car, for the next three to four hours, and then the police driver turned the car around and they went back north to 4631 Lake Park for the reenactment. After that, Nixon said, he was not beaten again until June 7, when he was taken into Sullivan's office in the morning and told that when he went to the inquest later that day he would need to make a statement. When he refused, he was kicked and struck until he finally agreed to testify at the inquest.[31]

Throughout his testimony at the hearing, Nixon insisted that his confessions were false, and that he only made them to keep from being beaten. There were, however, a number of inconsistencies and contradictions in his testimony that the prosecution made much of during Nixon's cross-examination. Boyle mocked Nixon's inability to identify which officers had beaten him and his confusion about when the various events he recounted had occurred. At one point, he got Nixon to assert he was certain that he was hanging out of the window on the eleventh floor, a claim that would pose significant problems for the defense, later.[32]

All told, the state put on more than forty witnesses to rebut his claims. Thirty-seven of the witnesses were police officers; most were assigned to guard the third floor lockup at 1121 South State at some point between May 27 and June 7. Even so, not all the men assigned to the lockup in that period testified; according to Deputy Chief Storms, seven of the men who had been on lockup duty were on furlough and could not be brought in to testify. But to a man, those who testified agreed that they had never abused Nixon nor seen any other officer do so. In addition, all the men assigned to the lockup denied that they ever saw Nixon taken out of the lockup in a blindfold. Another one of the state's witnesses, Richard Erwin, the building engineer at 1121 South State, took the stand to describe the windows on the east side of the eleventh floor. According to Erwin, the windows on that floor were not standard lift windows, but were three-part windows that could only be opened a few inches. But he had to admit that all the windows on the other floors were standard lift windows, which could be opened wide enough for a man to fit through.[33]

It was an overwhelming effort. But a careful reading of the testimony by the state's witnesses reveals a number of cracks in the wall of evidence.

There were four key dates in Nixon's tale of police torture: May 27 (when he claimed he was beaten and abused on three different occasions); May 28 (when he claimed he was interrogated for more than twelve hours and almost thrown out of a window); May 29 (the day of the first reenactment, when he claimed he was struck until he agreed to do the reenactment and then was held incommunicado on the far South Side until shortly before the reenactment); and June 7 (when he was struck before the coroner's inquest). Most of the state's witnesses did not see Nixon during any of those periods, and so their evidence was not particularly relevant to disproving his claims. Looking only at the testimony from officers who were present on those days, there were significant contradictions and gaps in their testimony:

Friday, May 27: Although the *Chicago Tribune* reported that Nixon was questioned Friday evening after he returned from the Crime Lab, almost none of the witnesses called by the state remembered seeing Nixon in the afternoon or evening of May 27. At one point, Sullivan said that Nixon was questioned in his office around 6:00 that evening, but at another he said that he interrogated Nixon in his office at 6:00 p.m. on Saturday. In either case, Sullivan could not recall who else was in his office during that examination (although he did remember that everyone present seemed to behave "pretty well"). The testimony of the lockup keepers on duty Friday was little help: Michael Hussey, the lockup keeper on duty Friday, May 27, between 8:00 a.m. and 4:00 p.m., said he was positive Nixon was not taken out of the lockup while he was on duty. Forrest Benz, who worked the gunroom next to the lockup that Friday from 8:00 to 4:00, could not recall whether Nixon left the lockup while he was on duty. Of course, Nixon was not in the lockup for at least part of the time that Hussey and Benz were on duty that Friday, since that was the afternoon Nixon was given the lie detector test. John Janusek, who was assigned to the lockup from 4:00 p.m. to midnight on several of the days that Nixon was at 11th and State, recalled generally that Nixon was taken in and out of the lockup, but could not recall specifically if Nixon left the lockup on May 27. Tim Hayes, who also worked the lockup from 4:00 p.m. to midnight on May 27 and several other days, agreed that Nixon was in and out of the lockup while he was on duty, but could not recall specifically if Nixon was taken from the lockup that evening. Charles McMullen, Hayes's partner, also remembered seeing Nixon taken in and out of the lockup, but could not remember precisely when that happened. While they could not recall whether Nixon left the lockup that Friday, all four of the lockup keepers were sure that no one struck, beat, kicked, or abused Nixon in their presence and swore that they had not done any of those things themselves. When asked whether Nixon was hung by his arms on the evening of May 27, Deputy Chief Walter Storms said he had no idea because he was not at the station that night. When asked if he told anyone to string Nixon up by his arms, or beat or strike Nixon, Chief of Detectives John Sullivan said he had not. But he also said he was not at the detective bureau Friday night.[34]

Saturday, May 28: The two men, Thomas Morrison and Stephen Dunne, who worked the lockup from midnight to 8:00 a.m. on Saturday, were pretty sure that Nixon never left his cell while they were on duty, though Morrison admitted that Nixon might have done so. The two men who worked the shift from 8:00 a.m. to 4:00 p.m. offered contrasting recollections. Hussey was sure Nixon was not taken out of the lockup during his shift on Saturday. His partner, George Harding, did recall Nixon being removed from the lockup "numerous" times, but he was not sure whether that happened on Saturday or Sunday. The two men who worked the last shift of the day, James Dougherty and John Janusek, both recalled that Nixon was taken out of the lockup when they were on duty between 4:00 p.m. and midnight. Both said that Nixon was taken out of the lockup around 6:00 p.m. that night, and Dougherty was sure that Nixon was not brought back before midnight. John Sullivan swore that Nixon was in his office for about an hour around noon on Saturday, but none of the officers who testified admitted to taking Nixon there at that time. Three officers, Martin McGuire, George Kush, and Walter Paradowski, testified that around 6:30 that night they took Nixon out of the lockup and brought him to Storms's office. Walter Storms said that Paradowski, Kush, and McGuire brought Nixon to his office at 6:00 p.m. and that Nixon remained there until he took Nixon to Sullivan's office around 10:00 or 11:00 p.m. Arthur Fitzgerald, Storms's driver, recalled that he saw Nixon brought into Storms's office around 6:15 p.m. by three detectives and that Nixon stayed there for four to five hours until he was taken to Sullivan's office. But John Sullivan was sure that Nixon was interrogated in his office around 6:00 or 6:30 p.m. that night. Of course, Sullivan might have been confused; at other times he said that Nixon was in his office at 6:00 p.m. Friday night and that he did not see Nixon Saturday evening until 10:00 p.m.[35]

Paradowski, McGuire, and Kush all denied that they kicked, beat, struck, or otherwise abused Nixon, held him out of a window, or hung him by his arms, but they did not agree about other details. McGuire denied that he ever saw Nixon blindfolded, but Kush answered the question "Did you blindfold Nixon? with a "Yes sir." In addition, McGuire, Kush, and Paradowski had different recollections of how much they saw Nixon Saturday evening. McGuire swore that he saw Nixon when he took him to Storms's office sometime after 6:00 and thought that he next saw Nixon around 9:00 p.m., just before McGuire went home. Paradowski also recalled that he took Nixon to Storms's office with McGuire and Kush around 6:00 p.m., but testified that he did not see Nixon later in the evening. Kush's evidence contradicted them both. In contrast to McGuire's testimony, Kush testified that he and Paradowski took Nixon to Storms's office around 6:00 p.m., and that he, Paradowski, Storms, and Nixon were the only people in the room at the time. In contrast to Paradowski's testimony, Kush recalled seeing Nixon in Storms's office around 9:00 that night, when Sullivan, Storms, McGuire, and Paradowski were present. McGuire, Kush, and Paradowski each denied that they told Nixon they were going to introduce him to the seven devils when they took him to Storms's office on May 28, but that, of course, was not what Nixon said had happened. He claimed the interrogation by the seven devils took place in the afternoon of May 27. None of the other witnesses admitted being at the station until later that evening. Thomas Courtney, the state's attorney from Cook County, and Daniel Gilbert, his chief investigator, both agreed that they did not see Nixon until they arrived at the station around 10:00 p.m. on Saturday. Courtney recalled that James Keeley was in Sullivan's office that Saturday, during the interrogation, but did not say when he arrived. Edward Wilson, an assistant state's attorney, said he did not arrive at the station until sometime after 11:00 p.m. that night.[36]

Wilson's testimony was peculiar in several ways: He was sure that he was called to the station around 11:00 p.m. by an assistant state's attorney named Crawford, but Courtney and Gilbert were insistent that Gilbert called Wilson. Wilson testified that he interrogated Nixon about the Johnson murder, that Nixon described breaking into the Johnson house in some detail, and that Storms also recalled hearing Wilson question Nixon about the murder. But Gilbert and Courtney recalled, instead, that Wilson only questioned Nixon about his treatment and that Courtney was the one who interrogated Nixon about the Johnson case. Most puzzling, the official copies of the statements Harvey prepared did not record that Wilson was present during any of the interrogations.[37]

Sunday, May 29: Michael Hussey and George Harding were once again on duty at the lockup between 8:00 a.m. and 4:00 p.m. Hussey was sure that Nixon was not taken out of the lockup during his shift, which contradicted Storms's testimony that he saw Nixon around 1:15 that afternoon when Nixon was brought to his office and gave Storms a map he had drawn of the

Johnson house. Although everyone denied Nixon's claim that he was taken to 95th and Stony Island for several hours before going to the reenactment, several witnesses agreed that by 2:00, Nixon, Fitzgerald, Hicks, Paradowski, Kush, McGuire, and Storms were heading south on their way to the reenactment. In contrast to his partner, Harding did recall Nixon being removed from the lockup several times but was not sure when.[38]

There were other problems with the prosecution's evidence. Somewhat surprisingly, given Keeley's insistence that he had arrested Nixon because he had a fresh cut on his hand Friday morning, Courtney swore that when he saw Nixon Saturday evening Nixon had no lacerations on his hands. Both Wilson and Courtney agreed that Nixon appeared to be so calm and cool and spoke so freely when they questioned him, that neither felt there was any reason to ask Nixon to take off his jacket or roll up his pants legs so they could examine his body for bruises. For the same reason, Courtney did not think it necessary to have a doctor examine Nixon to see if he was unharmed. There was also a lot of misdirection in the answers provided by the prosecution's witnesses. When questioned during cross-examination about whether he asked Nixon if he had been beaten, Courtney answered: "I asked him whether it was a free statement he was making" and noted that Nixon spoke freely to him. It was only after more specific questioning that Courtney admitted he never asked Nixon if he had been beaten. Raymond Crane was equally precise in his answers. When asked if he hit Nixon on May 27 around 7:30 or 8:00 a.m., he said he was at the morgue then, not the station.[39]

There were also several missing witnesses. The prosecution identified seven officers who were assigned to lockups at the detective bureau in May and June who were on furlough during the trial and were thus unavailable to testify: Morris Freedman, William Glennon, Patrick Barrett, James Patterson, William Higgins, Bernard Bukowski, and Sergeant Parkowski. But several other officers and individuals who were involved in the questioning of Nixon on May 27, May 28, and May 29 never took the stand to refute Nixon's claims of torture: John Boyle, the assistant state's attorney who was present when Nixon was questioned on May 27 and May 28, and was at the reenactment on May 29, not only did not testify, he was one of the attorneys at Nixon's trial and questioned several of the prosecution witnesses during the hearing on Nixon's claim of torture. James Keeley, the police officer who was present while Nixon was interrogated at the Hyde Park station on May 27 and then went back to the detective bureau when Nixon was taken there around 11:00 a.m., was never called to testify during the hearing even though Nixon and Courtney agreed that he was present for some of the interrogations on May 27 and May 28. Neither of the officers who worked with Keeley, John Joyce and Joseph Burbach, were called to testify at all. John Prendergast, the First District commander who the *Chicago Tribune* said had taken charge of the case on May 27, was not called as a witness. Otto Erlanson testified during the trial but not at the hearing and was never questioned about Nixon's claims of torture. In the end, the disputed question of when Nixon was taken out of the lockup and by whom could never be resolved, because all the state's witnesses agreed that there were no records kept of when prisoners were taken out of the lockup or of the officers who took the prisoners out.[40]

Nixon was recalled by Clayton and contradicted many of the prosecution's witnesses. He confirmed that on Friday, May 27, Walter Paradowski and his partner George Kush took him to Deputy Chief Storms's office and swore that during that meeting Paradowski hit him with a fist and then "sapped" him on the legs. He explained that he thought he was taken to the eleventh floor the day that he was dangled out of the window because that was what the officers who had him told the elevator operator. He added that he was sure that the window he was put out of was a window that raised. Nixon recalled that Kush and McGuire were present for at least part of that incident, and that McGuire was the officer who stopped the others from letting him go. He testified that neither Wilson nor Courtney ever asked him if he had been beaten. In fact, he said, he barely spoke to Courtney. Nixon clarified that he was never beaten in the third floor lockup, only on the eleventh and fifth floors (he confusingly insisted he was there when he was beaten in the deputy chief's office, which was on the third floor), and explained that he was not blindfolded on May 28, when he was taken to what he thought was the eleventh floor. He also claimed that he still had some scars on his legs from the beating, and exhibited them to the court. While the state agreed that there seemed to be some marks slightly above his shins, the prosecution did not agree that the marks looked recent.

When Nixon finished testifying, there was an argument, which was not recorded in the transcript, about whether the confessions should be admitted. In the end, Judge Lewe concluded that Nixon's claims that he confessed after being tortured were not credible, and Lewe denied the motion to exclude the statements. So the jury was called back into the courtroom and Crowley read three "statements" into the record and to the jurors. The first was an unsigned statement by Robert Nixon that was dated May 28 at 10:00 p.m. The second, the joint statement by Nixon and Hicks, which was dated May 29 at 1:00 a.m., was signed by both Hicks and Nixon, and witnessed. The final "statement" was actually the transcription of the comments and answers made by Nixon and Hicks at the reenactment on May 29.[41]

A number of important contradictions were lost sight of in the dispute about the admissibility of the confessions. Nixon's description of his arrest directly contradicted Keeley's account and called into question the entire justification for arresting Nixon in the first place. Keeley's testimony made the racial aspect of the case explicit. Cottage Grove, he said, was the line that divided blacks and whites, and Nixon, he claimed, was on the wrong side of that line, which made his presence suspicious. Nixon, in contrast, testified during the hearing that he was arrested around 6:00 in the morning on May 27 as he was coming out of a chili parlor on 47th Street, near St. Lawrence. That put him several blocks west of Cottage Grove, in the heart of the Black Belt.

If Nixon's testimony raised doubts about Keeley's account of the arrest, other minor bits of testimony by state witnesses cast doubt on the confessions by contradicting what Nixon or Hicks "recalled" in their statements. Most notably, Carter's testimony that Florence Johnson had three deep blows to her skull was inconsistent with the claims by both Nixon and Hicks that Johnson had been struck only twice with the brick. As significant, several aspects of Margaret Whitton's testimony contradicted the confessions: Her insistence that the apples in the kitchen were in a cabinet could not be squared with Nixon and Hicks's claim that the apples were in plain view on top of the fridge. Her statement that she did not scream when she saw a black man walking by her bedroom was contrary to Hicks's assertion in the joint confession that he heard her scream. And her recollection that she did not follow Nixon into the children's bedroom to the window was at odds with Hicks's recollection that he saw her at the window when he was outside the apartment. Likewise, Whitton's claim that the broken window had been covered with a piece of linoleum was inconsistent with Nixon's statement that there was nothing covering the window and Hicks's recollection that the window was only covered by something flexible like an oilcloth. And the claims by Berounsky and the doctors about the amount of blood in Florence Johnson's room were hard to square with Nixon's and Hicks's statements that they did not see much blood in the room (and with the fact that Nixon's jacket was not drenched in blood when Keeley saw him).

Wrapping Up the Prosecution

Once the confessions had been read to the jurors, the prosecution brought its evidence to a close. Walter Storms was called back to the witness box to testify about the interrogation of Nixon and Hicks. His evidence essentially repeated what he had said outside during the hearing on Nixon's torture claim. He was followed by three members of the May 1938 grand jury, Charles Arnold, Timothy Dineen, and William Caunt, all of whom had been called in to act as witnesses when Nixon and Hicks signed their statements on May 31. Arnold recalled that before Nixon signed, Chief Sullivan asked him how he had been treated and whether he had been adequately fed, and how he had been treated by the police while he was in custody. Nixon, Arnold recalled, assured both of them that he was fine. Arnold also testified that he saw no marks on Nixon during the signing, but he also admitted that he did not ask Nixon if he had been beaten and did not ask to look at Nixon's hands for marks. Arnold was pretty sure, however, that he saw Nixon's hands when Nixon signed and that they were unmarked. That was also Timothy Dineen's recollection, though he admitted that no one asked Nixon or Hicks to remove their shirts or jackets so that they could look for bruises. Dineen also recalled that Nixon and Hicks were asked about their treatment at the hands of the police, and somewhat improbably recalled that Nixon assured him that the police had extended them every courtesy. He also remembered that Nixon insisted he made the statements of his own free will. William Caunts offered similar testimony, though he added that the grand jurors saw Nixon on several occasions, May 31 at the signing of the statement in the Johnson case, and then again for several hours each on June 1, June 2, and June 3. His recollection was that Nixon was at ease every time he saw him, and repeatedly assured everyone that he had been treated well. But Caunts also admitted that he never asked Nixon to remove his jacket to see whether he had marks or bruises on his body.[42]

The three grand jurors were followed by Thomas Courtney and Edward Wilson, who repeated their testimony from the hearing, though Courtney "corrected" some of his evidence. While he testified during the hearing that Nixon had no visible scars or marks, this second time around Courtney recalled that Nixon had a slight scratch on one of his hands during the interrogation. Once again he admitted that he never asked Nixon to remove his jacket so he could check his body for bruises or scars, because he "saw no reason for it." As a result, he agreed, he was only able to see Nixon's hands, his face, his neck, and a bit of his chest where his jacket was unzipped. He added that Nixon told him that the police had given him "the very best treatment." When he took the stand after Courtney, Wilson also repeated most of what he said during the hearing.[43]

Wilson was followed by John Hanna, who described the discovery of the apple during the reenactment. Hanna explained that the crowd, which he estimated was somewhere between five hundred and one thousand people, scanned the ground after Hicks explained that Nixon had thrown away the apple after leaving the apartment. He told the jury that he had initially kicked the apple away when he was trying to get a good position to watch the reenactment. That seemed inconsistent with the claim that the apple was right where Hicks said Nixon threw it when he ran from the scene. According to Hanna when he heard Hicks claim that Nixon tossed away his apple, he turned to the police officer next to him, who happened to be John Sullivan, and pointed out that there was an apple lying on the ground where he had kicked it. The two of them were right behind the apartment at the time, on a concrete walk that ran next to the railroad retaining wall to the east of the building. John Sullivan picked up the apple and saved it to use as an exhibit.[44]

Sullivan was the state's final witness. He reminded the jurors about the extensive interrogation of Nixon, stretching from May 27 through June 4. That was odd, of course, because no one who testified admitted to interrogating Nixon on May 27. Sullivan also testified, at length, about Hicks's statements (which accused Nixon) on May 28. While that part of his testimony did not add any additional evidence to what the jurors had already heard by way of the statements, it did reinforce that evidence. Sullivan added a few new details to the story of the investigation: he mentioned that a man named Memphis, who claimed to keep the pool hall where Nixon said he worked, was brought to the Hyde Park station on May 27 and denied that he knew Nixon. He mentioned a map that Nixon drew of the apartment before the reenactment, and identified the map as People's Exhibit 16, and he described how he took the apple that Hanna had found and put it in his refrigerator, where it remained until the start of the trial. Then he displayed the apple for the jurors to see.[45]

Defense Case

When the state closed its case, the defense put on its evidence. None of its witnesses was particularly helpful. Susie May Lee testified that she had worked at a grocery store at 225 East 51st Street for several years. She recalled that the Saturday before Florence Johnson was killed, Nixon worked at the grocery store plucking chickens in his shirtsleeves. She added that was the only day he worked there. Edgar Sullivan, also known as Cat-Eye, from the pool hall, took the stand and denied that he knew Nixon or recognized him as someone who came to his club. Dr. Walter Adams, from Provident Hospital, the African American Hospital in Chicago, testified that he was a doctor who specialized in nervous and mental diseases. He told the jurors that he had examined Nixon at the jail on two occasions, first on July 8 and then on July 19, and that based on those examinations, Nixon had an IQ of about 76 and a mental age of roughly 11½. During cross-examination, he and Crowley skirmished about the average mental age of members of the US Army during World War I: Crowley asserted, repeatedly, that it was 11 years, Adams recollected that it was "about fifteen, fourteen or fifteen." As it happened, neither was correct. The army study, which has been roundly criticized since for ignoring the cultural biases in the test and the impact those biases had on immigrants, poor native-born whites, and blacks, found that the average mental age of the soldiers it studied was 13 years. But in the end that did not matter; Crowley got Adams to agree that Nixon was not insane, and that was that.[46]

Then Nixon took the stand once again, this time in the presence of the jury, to testify about his life, his arrest on May 27, and his treatment by the police in the days that followed. Part of his account was an alibi: On May 26, around 6:00 p.m., Nixon said he found himself at the corner of Prairie Avenue and 47th Street, a commercial intersection. He hung out there with some boys, he recalled, until about 7:00 p.m., when he went north to the Republic Theater at 47th and Prairie to catch a show. When the show ended around 10 p.m., he went back down to 51st Street and remained there several hours. Finally, around 1:00 a.m., he went to a gambling club at 47th and Calumet, and stayed there until 6:00 in the morning talking to people. At 6:00, he and another young man from the club, whom he knew only as George, left the club and headed east on 47th Street to a chili parlor that was a few doors down from the corner of St. Lawrence. They grabbed a quick bowl of chili and then went their separate ways: George headed home and Nixon started across 47th Street. As he did so, a police car passed by, siren screaming, and then stopped. One of the policemen inside the car got out, came over to Nixon, and put him under arrest.[47]

Nixon managed to clarify some of his claims about the torture during his testimony. He identified five of the officers who testified, Paradowski, Kush, McGuire, Kistner, and Thurston, as participants in some of his torture. Nixon also explained that the reason none of the lockup keepers could recall seeing him blindfolded was that the blindfold had been put on by an officer right outside the door to the gunroom, not in the lockup. He explained that he had been shown photographs of the Johnson apartment during his interrogation on May 28, which helped explain why he seemed to know how it was organized. He also claimed that he did not draw the floor plan of the Johnson apartment until after the reenactment. In addition, he offered an elaboration of one of his torture claims, noting that when he was hung from the wall, he was not only beaten but was naked, since the officers had made him take off his clothes.[48]

Other parts of his testimony were so confused that they did serious damage to his case. Nixon continued to be unable to pin down dates and times, and frequently guessed about when something happened. This led him to make several claims that were inconsistent with his earlier testimony and with known facts. He testified that he was taken to the crime lab on Saturday, May 28, rather than Friday, May 27, and that he was taken to the fifth floor of police headquarters and hung from his wrists that Saturday evening after his return from the lab. He could not remember when he signed the joint statement, although he could remember who was present. He appeared to contradict himself about whether he was beaten, or only threatened with a beating, in the morning before the reenactment. He also gave inconsistent testimony about when he had worked as a chauffeur. Originally he claimed that it was for several months in 1937 after his return from California. Then he asserted that he worked as a chauffeur from 1933 to 1937, which would have meant he started the job at age thirteen or fourteen. Nixon also made several implausible claims about his finances: he initially claimed that he had several hundred dollars saved from working as a chauffeur, and then said that he had made several hundred dollars working at Twentieth Century Fox while he was in California.[49]

Crowley capitalized on those inconsistencies during his cross-examination. He made much of Nixon's new claim that he was hung from the wall sometime around 7:30–8:00 p.m. on Saturday, May 28, rather than Friday, May 27, as he had asserted during the hearing on his torture claims. He repeatedly pointed out that Nixon did not know the times of his various interrogations and beatings. He made sure that the jurors noticed that Nixon was certain he had been interrogated by Walter Storms on Friday evening, a day that Storms denied seeing Nixon at all. He ridiculed the fact that Nixon did not know the names of people he lived with in Chicago and Nixon's claim to have savings, and Crowley spent a considerable amount of time making sure the jurors realized that Nixon had no permanent home or job in the weeks leading up to his arrest.[50]

It was a devastating cross-examination, though Clayton did his best during redirect to remind the jurors that Nixon did not have a watch or access to a clock while he was in custody. When he got a chance during redirect, Nixon managed to explain several of the apparent discrepancies, pointing out, for example, that he started work as a chauffeur in 1933 and then went back to that job when he returned to Chicago after his travels in the West. But there was not much that either he or Clayton could do, particularly when faced with Crowley's emphasis on the fact that Nixon slept in a pool hall, or with friends, in the weeks before the Johnson murder. Moving from room to room, building to building, and job to job, trying to scratch out a living in gambling joints or running for policy shops, was an experience common to both the small-time hustler and the working poor in Chicago's Black Belt during the Depression. Nixon was a typical resident of what St. Clair Drake and Horace Cayton called "the world of the lower class" in Chicago's African American community in the late 1930s. Typical or not, the state used that evidence to reinforce the idea that Nixon was anything but a poor but honest person falsely caught up in the law's toils.[51]

Nixon was the last witness for the defense. When he stepped down the state called a handful of rebuttal witnesses. A sergeant from the Hyde Park police station testified that Friday morning, after Nixon told him that he lived at the house of a Mrs. Johnson, he went and found her and brought her to the station. She told him that she knew Nixon by that name, and that while he never lived at her home he used to get mail there. Then Crane took the stand to testify that he did not strike Nixon at 8:00 a.m. at the Hyde Park station, because he was not at the station then. Paradowski was called to testify that he did not see Nixon on May 27 and that he arrested Hicks around 8:30 p.m. on Saturday, May 28, a claim that was inconsistent with the time frame of the investigation set out at the time by papers like the *Chicago Tribune*, which reported Hicks was arrested around midnight. He also denied striking or otherwise abusing Nixon on May 27, stringing him up by his arms and beating him around 7:30 p.m. on May 28, taking Nixon to the eleventh floor just after midnight on May 28 and hanging him out of a window, and taking Nixon to 95th and Stony Island for about three hours on Sunday, May 29. In addition, Paradowski denied striking or abusing Nixon on June 7, the day of the inquest, "either in Deputy Storms's office or in Chief Sullivan's office, in the presence of Deputy Storms," or seeing anyone else do so. On cross-examination, Paradowski added that he did not go to the inquest on June 7 and did not see Nixon the morning of the inquest.[52]

Kush followed Paradowski to the stand and also denied that he saw Nixon on May 27. He added that he did not see any other officer strike Nixon between 6:15 and 8:00 p.m. on May 28. He denied that he ever saw Nixon on the fifth floor of the detective bureau and testified that he did not rush to the eleventh floor of the bureau around 1:00 a.m. and announce that Sullivan wanted to see Nixon and that the officers holding Nixon out the window had to save him. He likewise claimed he never told Nixon he had saved his life, never went to the fifth floor of the detective bureau on May 28, and did not see Nixon on the eleventh floor at 11th and State on that date. He did admit, however, that there was a photographic room on the fifth floor with special lights.[53]

Arthur Fitzgerald, Storms's chauffeur, followed Kush to deny that he saw or struck Nixon on May 27. He also testified that he drove Nixon, Storms, Hicks, and several other officers to the South Side on Sunday, May 29, to go to the reenactment, but denied that he drove the car to Stony Island and parked there. He also generally denied seeing any officer strike, beat, or kick Nixon. Storms followed Fitzgerald and testified that he did not see Nixon in the afternoon of May 27 and did not see McGuire strike Nixon twice that afternoon. He denied that he instructed Paradowski, McGuire, or Kush to take Nixon to any floor above the third floor to hang him up by his arms or apply hot lights to him. Storms also denied that Nixon was taken to another floor around 7:00 p.m. that Saturday and beaten by Paradowski, McGuire, and Kush at his request. In fact, Storms claimed that from about 6:00 p.m. on Saturday, May 28, to about 2:15 a.m. on Sunday, May 29, Nixon was never out of his presence for more than a few minutes and was never off the third floor.[54]

Emmet Evans, the identification inspector in charge of the bureau of identification, which had its offices on the fifth floor at 11th and State, testified that police officers were never allowed on that floor without permission. He added that he was trained as a fingerprint specialist and that in his expert opinion it was impossible to take fingerprints from a paving brick because the surface was too rough. Shown the brick that was apparently used to kill Florence Johnson, he expressed the view that it would be impossible to take a print off of its surface. Asked whether the lights in the photography room on the fifth floor were hot enough to burn anyone, he said no and somewhat implausibly denied that there were any special photographic lights in the room.[55]

After Evans, the stream of state rebuttal witnesses continued. McGuire took the stand to deny that he saw Nixon on May 27 or that he ever hit Nixon with a blackjack. In addition, he denied taking Nixon to the fifth floor on May 28 to hang him up by his wrists. During cross-examination, he denied ever taking Nixon to either the fifth or the eleventh floors. John Kistner took the stand to deny that he was at Storms's office on May 27. He added that he never hit, kicked, or beat Nixon on the third floor of the detective bureau. Joseph Thurston testified that the first time he saw Nixon was at the reenactment on May 29. One of the lockup keepers, Arthur Fitzsimmons, testified that he saw Nixon drawing and writing in his cell around 2:20 in the morning on May 29. Harvey testified that when he saw Nixon brought into

Sullivan's office on May 28, he was not wearing a blindfold. He also denied seeing Nixon on Friday, May 27. On cross-examination, Harvey conceded that he left Sullivan's office for a while to run an errand that night and that it was possible Nixon was brought into the room while he was gone and was wearing a blindfold then. On redirect, he said that from 1:00 a.m. to about 2:45 a.m. on Sunday, May 29, Nixon was continuously in his presence, making the joint statement with Hicks that became people's exhibit no. 13. That, of course, contradicted Fitzsimmons's claim that Nixon was in his cell at 2:20 making sketches. On redirect, Harvey explained that Nixon's other statement, people's exhibit no. 12, was made around 11:00 p.m. on Saturday, May 28.[56]

The state closed its rebuttal evidence by calling Sullivan back to the stand. He testified that he was not at the Hyde Park station around 8:00 a.m. on Friday, May 27, and did not see Crane strike Nixon then. He testified that he was at the detective bureau on Friday evening, but did not see Harvey or Boyle. He added that on Saturday, May 28, around 10 p.m., he was in his office with Storms, Harvey, and Boyle when Nixon was brought in, which seemed to contradict Storms's testimony that he brought Nixon to Sullivan's office. Sullivan denied that Nixon was wearing a blindfold when he came into the room. Sullivan also described parts of the building at 11th and State and confirmed that it was impossible to hang anyone out of a window on the eleventh floor. He denied that there was any X-ray or "violet ray" in the detective bureau that could be used to burn anyone and added that no police officer could get onto the fifth floor of the building at night unless he was there on official business. He testified that he never threatened Nixon and that Nixon was never taken off the third floor of the detective bureau between 8:00 p.m. Saturday, May 28, and the early morning hours on Sunday, May 29. In fact, he said, Nixon never left his office between the time he made the statement that became people's exhibit no. 12 and the joint statement with Hicks. Like all the other witnesses, Sullivan testified he never saw Nixon struck by a police officer. Initially, Sullivan claimed he never saw any person, officer or not, strike Nixon, but during cross-examination Clayton got him to admit that he saw someone, Elmer Johnson, strike Nixon during the inquest.[57]

Closing Arguments and a Verdict

At the end of the testimony in the case, Clayton made a motion, which was overruled, that the court strike from the record all the portions of the testimony in the confessions that had been made by Earl Hicks, on the ground that there was no opportunity for the defense to cross-examine Hicks. The court offered Clayton the opportunity to call Hicks to the stand as his own witness, but Clayton, fearing that the jury would think that meant the defense endorsed his testimony, declined. He tried to persuade Judge Lewe to order the state to call Hicks, but Lewe refused to do so.[58]

The state gave the first and the last arguments; Crowley gave the first, Boyle the last. Both of the state's arguments picked up on the themes suggested in the earliest coverage of the murder, casting the trial as a battle of "us" versus "them," citizens and taxpayers against those who were neither. Elmer Johnson and the jurors were most obviously among the former, but the category included the police witnesses as well; at one point Crowley described the building engineer, who testified that the windows on the eleventh floor would not open enough to hold a man outside, as a citizen. Citizens, Crowley explained, were people like Johnson, who worked hard as a firefighter. They had jobs and families; they were people like the police officers who testified at the trial, men "who think something of their reputation." They were men, many of them, who were "too old in life, . . . have lived too long to want to go to their graves sadly with the terrible burden of ever having spoken an untruth against the accused." Citizens were men, like Johnson, like the jurors, who left their families at home when they did their jobs. And they had a right, just as Johnson had a right, to believe that while they were away their families, especially their wives, their sisters, and their daughters were safe in their homes. Nixon, Crowley argued, was not one of "us," he was the antithesis of a citizen. He was not from Chicago. He was not from anywhere. He was born in Louisiana, but had wandered from Chicago, to Los Angeles, to Denver, and to Mexico, and then back to Chicago. He had no wife, no children, no job. He was not out at 5:30 in the morning going to or returning from work. He was out because he preyed upon people whom he chose at random, as he chose Florence Johnson at random. And in his randomness and violence, he posed a threat to Chicago and to the jurors and their families.[59]

Ultimately, Crowley argued, Nixon was unlike the police, the jurors, and state's attorneys, who all wanted to make sure that justice was done and that he received a fair trial. Nixon did not want a fair trial. In a fair trial he would be convicted. So he told lies, making up a "story that we in this business so long recognize as a possibility of a man fighting for his life." He falsely claimed that he confessed because he had been beaten by the police. The state's attorney told the jurors that many criminals claimed to be the victims of police abuse. They concocted those stories in Cook County Jail, with help from the other inmates and their clever attorneys. But, Crowley added, the facts of Nixon's accusations did not add up. Police officers, who had no reason to lie, contradicted Nixon. The janitor at 11th and State contradicted Nixon. High-ranking police officials, state's attorneys, and grand jurors contradicted Nixon. And Nixon contradicted himself. He could not get the times right, he could not get the days right. If he did not know when he was tortured, how could the jurors believe his claims? The police and the state knew that Nixon would lie, because all criminals lie, so they took special efforts to protect the police. They made sure that the confessions were made in the presence of state's attorneys, including a black state's attorney. They made sure that members of the grand jury spoke to Nixon. All those people asked Nixon if he was all right, if he was treated well. He always told them he was. None of them saw any bruises or signs of harm. Surely if he had been harmed, he would have told someone. Surely if he had been harmed, one of those people would have seen it. Left unsaid was the other, very obvious way in which Nixon was unlike the police witnesses, or Elmer Johnson, or the jurors.[60]

In contrast to the unified message offered by the state, the defense offered two, unrelated, and competing theories of the case. The first, set out in the closing argument by Charles Burton, did not address the issue of Nixon's guilt or innocence. It began as a challenge to the jurors to keep true to their oaths to uphold the law and to ignore the fact that Nixon was young and black. Very black, Burton added, in contrast to the "not really dark" man that Margaret Whitton said she saw the morning her sister was killed. Nixon needed them to give him a fair trial, Burton argued, because Nixon stood accused of killing a white woman. That cast the case in terms of the rule of law, and Burton spoke to the jurors about the need to give Nixon a fair trial, attacking the prosecution for failing to let the jurors hear Hicks's evidence. But Burton quickly moved beyond law, to the realm of mutuality and obligation. Offering an alternative to the distinction Crowley drew between "us" and "them," a distinction that Crowley used to argue that the jurors and Nixon had nothing in common, Burton told the jurors that they had a particular duty to Nixon because of the racist milieu in which he had been born and raised. In Louisiana, he had been raised to fear whites and taught that he was inferior to them. Neither his family nor his schools in Louisiana had given him much guidance or prepared him for life. Nor was he responsible for his condition in Chicago. Who was? Burton told the jurors that everyone was: Cook County; Chicago; the state's attorney's office; the jurors themselves. Why? Because Nixon spent the night of May 26 in a gambling den. A den that everyone pretended did not exist, even though they knew it was there. Minors, like Nixon, should have been protected from corrupting places like that. By failing to shut it down, the government and the people of Cook County had failed him and made him what he was. While Burton's closing argument emphasized race, it was not just an attack on racial injustice. He argued the trial was an important one for Cook County because it gave the jurors the opportunity to show the nation that the county was progressive and that the people of Cook County opposed the death penalty. Nixon, Burton pointed out, was not yet twenty-one. He was a minor in the eyes of the law and the evidence of the defense expert demonstrated that he was mentally younger than his physical age. Cook County should not return to the dark ages by putting a child like him to death.[61]

Burton's argument, though a stirring indictment of the racial and economic injustice that Nixon and others like him faced, came perilously close to conceding that Nixon had killed Florence Johnson. In his closing argument, Clayton strenuously argued that the evidence failed to prove Nixon's guilt. His lengthy argument, which took up nearly one hundred pages of the trial transcript, had three parts. First, he attacked the evidence presented by the state. Then he challenged the confessions themselves. And finally he dealt with Nixon's claim of torture. His argument made short work of the state's basic evidence, pointing out that the first three witnesses (Elmer Johnson and the two doctors) could do nothing to tie Nixon to the crime. He spent considerable time on the inconsistencies and implausibilities in Margaret Whitton's testimony. He argued that her claim that she was not frightened when she saw an unknown black man in her apartment was hard to credit, as was her inability to recall whether the man she saw so well was wearing a hat. Clayton spent more time challenging her identification of Nixon, reminding the jurors (as had Burton) that when she described the man she saw she suggested that he was somewhere between brown and light-skinned, a description that could not apply to the very dark-skinned Robert Nixon. He reminded the jurors that the first two times that Whitton saw Nixon she was unwilling to say with certainty that he was the man she had seen in the hallway; it was not until May 31, after she had seen him several times and had been spoken to by several police officers, that her identification became certain.[62]

Clayton also raised questions about the lack of scientific evidence in the case. Muehlberger, he noted, was given both Nixon's shirt and the blood-splattered brick to test. But all he was apparently able to do was claim that the blood on Nixon's shirt was human. He did not testify that the stains on the shirt were Florence Johnson's blood type. He did not testify that the blood on the brick matched her blood type. He did not testify that the blood on the shirt matched the blood on the brick. Since it was obvious, Clayton argued, that the blood on the brick came from Florence Johnson and was therefore human blood, there was no reason for the state to give him the brick unless it wanted him to test it to see if it matched her blood type and the blood type on the shirt. The fact that he did not testify that the blood on the shirt or the brick did match Florence Johnson's type spoke volumes. So did the complete silence on the part of the state about fingerprints. Although the first officers on the scene kept people out of the rooms in the apartment so that they could be tested for fingerprints, and although Nixon said (in one of his confessions) that he cut his finger climbing in the broken window, the state put on no evidence that it found prints that matched Nixon's on the window, the windowsill, the radio he was going to steal, the desk in the sunroom, or anywhere else in the apartment.[63]

Having pointed out the weakness of the evidence that tied Nixon to the crime, Clayton turned his attention to the confessions. Those statements, he noted, contradicted one another and the claims put forward by the state. The problems were so significant that they suggested something had to be amiss with the way they were obtained. The logical explanation was the one offered by Nixon: the confessions were obtained under duress from two young men who were not involved in Johnson's murder. Clayton pointed out the inconsistencies between the statements made by Hicks and Nixon. He ridiculed the state's argument that Nixon's claim of torture should be ignored because he got dates, times, and places wrong, pointing out that Nixon had no watch and was blindfolded when he was taken to different parts of the police station. He reminded the jurors that each of the men who said they saw no signs of harm on Nixon's body admitted that they had not asked Nixon to take off his shirt or even lift up his pants legs to see if he had any bruises beneath his clothes. Clayton wondered why the prosecution, which justified calling the grand jurors to witness Nixon and Hicks when they signed their confessions on the grounds that it needed to protect itself from false claims of coerced confession and torture, did not have Nixon observed by neutral and objective observers. If, he suggested, the police were so concerned, why not have him examined by a doctor? And he noted that all of the officers who claimed that they had not harmed Nixon were very careful to answer precise questions about whether they hurt Nixon at particular times. A specific denial that officers had harmed Nixon at a very precise time, he reminded the jurors, did not foreclose the possibility that they might have harmed Nixon at other times. Finally, Clayton pointed out, several of the people apparently involved in Nixon's interrogation or charged with watching him while he was in custody were not called to testify by the state.[64]

Clayton was followed by Boyle. At the start, Boyle returned to the distinctions Crowley drew in his argument. About Nixon, Boyle said: We "did not bring him up here. He was born and raised in Louisiana. We never got this fellow until '35. That is when we got him. Some other States had him. He was here a short time in '35, he goes to Los Angeles, he goes to Arizona, he goes to Mexico, he is back in Chicago again. What kind of a man do we have on trial here?" He did not need to say it, the answer was clear—Nixon was an outsider, not a citizen of Chicago like Elmer Johnson or the jurors. In addition, Boyle argued, Nixon was a liar. All defendants in criminal cases were liars. "No matter what you do," Boyle told the jurors, "no matter how you tried to protect the obtaining of the statement . . . they go back in the County Jail, and they are there a couple of months and they consult with lawyers." And then, defendants all come out saying the same thing: "Sure, I confess, but the police beat me up. After they consult with a lot of fellows awaiting trial in the County Jail, and they talk to their lawyers, then they come in with a statement that they were beaten up." Echoing the arguments made by the police and state's attorneys in Chicago in the 1920s: If the jurors credited Nixon's claims about abuse, Boyle told the jury, "we might as well take the key to the county jail and turn them all out."[65]

While the jurors should not believe Nixon, Boyle told the jurors that Hicks's statement was obviously true because it was so detailed: he described the vacant lot at 47th and Lake Park, and it was there. He remembered that Nixon got an apple and then threw it away when he was outside the apartment, and in fact an apple had been found at the scene. The jurors could trust Hicks about those precise points, and that meant they could trust him about his other claims.[66]

Ultimately, however, Boyle's argument, like Crowley's argument, was about fear. Fear that Nixon and others like him would "climb through a window and dash your wife's brains out, or your sister's, or your daughter's." Fear that Nixon could have killed anyone that morning: the two small Johnson children if they had awakened, or even the jurors. If Hicks and Nixon had found the window to the Johnson apartment latched, Boyle argued, they would have gone to the next building, or even to the jurors' neighborhood. And in the end, Boyle tied that fear back to Crowley's distinction between "us" and "them:" "And remember this," he told the jurors, "when you go back to consider of your verdict: here is a man on trial who means nothing to the community except as a destroyer."[67]

When Boyle finished, Judge Lewe instructed the jury. One of the instructions he read to them advised the jury that

> as a matter of law if they find from the evidence that the accused was by threat, violence, or fear induced to make a confession, that said confession is not to be considered as evidence by the jury, and if they find that after the making of such confession the accused later made a Statement incriminating himself then you as jurors must disregard such later Statement of the accused unless you are satisfied that the former fear entertained by the accused was wholly removed before the said latter Statements were made by the accused.[68]

The instruction invited the jurors to decide for themselves whether they thought Nixon had been tortured. There is no evidence that they gave the question a moment's thought. The jury took only an hour and ten minutes to find Robert Nixon guilty and sentence him to death. And in those seventy minutes, they had so much time that they were able to grab a quick dinner between their unanimous vote to convict and their vote, also unanimous, to impose the death penalty. Their efficiency impressed the *Chicago Tribune*, which declared it one of the speediest death penalty verdicts on record in Cook County.[69]

CHAPTER FOUR

CLAYTON AND BURTON MADE a motion for a new trial immediately after the jury returned its verdict. On August 12, Judge Lewe promptly denied the motion, formally sentenced Robert Nixon to death, and set the date for Nixon's execution: October 21. Lewe also granted Clayton's motion to let Nixon appeal as a poor person. That made the appeal possible, because it meant that the county would pay to transcribe the transcript and the record on the case.[1]

In 1938, death penalty cases were appealed directly to the Illinois Supreme Court. Even so, the process was not quick. Nixon's attorneys had to prepare and file the Record on Appeal and Bill of Exceptions, a lengthy process in a case with a transcript that was nearly 1,500 pages long. The Bill of Exceptions was not signed, sealed, and filed until November 30, 1938, and the Illinois Supreme Court did not grant Nixon's writ of error until December 15, 1938. All the while, Clayton and another lawyer he enlisted to help him—Richard Westbrook—had to appear before judges or the Illinois Parole Board on five separate occasions to postpone Nixon's execution long enough to let them complete the record. Each time, the state's attorney's office opposed the requests for extensions; four times, the extension was granted. At a hearing before the parole board on December 8, Clayton was told there would be no more stays of execution, which forced him to appeal to Lieutenant Governor John Stelle to get Nixon a final, temporary reprieve while the Illinois Supreme Court decided whether to take the case. That nerve-racking and time-consuming process did not end until the Illinois Supreme Court granted the writ of error; its order setting a briefing schedule for the case automatically stayed Nixon's execution until his appeal was decided.[2]

Appealing to Public Opinion

During those long months of legal maneuvering in the fall of 1938, the racial divisions that marked Nixon's case sharpened, and the "us" versus "them" division set out in the state's attorney's closing arguments became more obviously white versus black. Nixon's case, and the problem of police torture, became a concern limited to a part of the African American community.

After the verdict, a number of Chicago's African American citizens mobilized to write letters concerning the case. On October 18, a group calling itself the "Committee for Justice" sent a telegram to the pardon and parole board asking that Nixon's execution date be stayed until he was able to file an appeal. The telegram was signed by several prominent African American ministers from Chicago and J. S. West, the editor of the *Chicago Defender*. A few weeks later, the Reverend W. L. Sledge sent a petition to the governor of Illinois, Henry Horner. The petition, signed by forty-seven individuals, most of them ministers and leaders in Chicago's African American community, asked Horner to stay Nixon's execution to allow for more investigation into his case. The petition emphasized Nixon's age, arguing that he would be "the first youth eighteen years of age" to be executed by the state. It compared his treatment to that of other, white defendants who had been sentenced to life in prison rather than given the death penalty. And it reminded Horner that the claim that Nixon was a serial killer rested on confessions he claimed had been "forced from him by brutality." Sledge, a Bishop in the AME Church and the director of the Interdenominational Churches of Chicago, was indefatigable in his efforts, sending several personal telegrams to the supreme court on Nixon's behalf. In December, as the threat of an execution grew more real, three other African American associations in Chicago—the Baptist Ministers' Conference of Chicago, the International Literary Society, and the Ethiopian World Federation—sent letters supporting Nixon to Governor Horner. In contrast, there were no white voices raised in Nixon's support; even the ILD was silent about his case after his conviction.[3]

Mainstream papers like the *Chicago Tribune* reported on the delays in bringing Nixon to justice and turned once again to describing Nixon as a "rapist-slayer," but by and large Chicago's white community seemed indifferent to his fate. The only letter written in opposition to Nixon's appeal was sent on December 5, 1938. Written by an anonymous person who identified herself as a citizen and a rape victim, the letter was apparently intended to protest Clayton's final request for a temporary reprieve. Offering an interesting variation on the "us" versus "them" arguments made by the state during the trial, the letter's author complained about "those negro and white criminals" who got away with murder. But the real problem, the author went on, was "the negroes [who] are migrating to your state by the thousand each month." They were "a menace on the south side."[4]

Meanwhile, the state was also busy. On the off chance the Illinois Supreme Court ruled for Nixon, the state's attorney's office prepared to try Nixon for the murder of Florence Castle, using one of the other indictments it had gotten for Nixon back in July. The state also made good use of those indictments during the hearings on the requests for a stay of execution; when arguing against the stay Boyle frequently referred to the indictments or the crimes that gave rise to them. He did so for several reasons. Most obviously, he raised those other crimes to reinforce the state's theory that Nixon was a dangerous one-man crime wave. Boyle also played up the racist images of Nixon. At the hearing before the parole board on December 8, he told the board that during one of the reenactments he saw Nixon swing himself up onto the fire escape with one arm, "just like an animal." Finally, Boyle used the other crimes and indictments to make a more crucial point: it did not matter whether or not Nixon was able to appeal from his conviction for Florence Johnson's murder. If he did appeal and won, the state would just turn around and try him for the murder of Florence Castle or the rape of Betty Bryant. And if Nixon won those cases, there were always the murders that Nixon was wanted for in Los Angeles.[5]

The state was relentless in fighting the defense efforts to stay the execution long enough for an appeal, but Clayton was equally determined. Every time that Boyle described one of the other crimes, Clayton reminded the listeners that there had been no trial that found Nixon guilty of those crimes. Whenever Boyle mentioned Nixon's confessions, Clayton took the opportunity to note that Nixon claimed he had been tortured into falsely confessing. And when Boyle spoke of the evidence in the form of fingerprints and other clues that the state claimed also tied Nixon to those other crimes, Clayton observed that in several of those cases witnesses described white or very light-skinned black men leaving the scene shortly after the crime. No one, Clayton added, would ever describe the very dark-skinned ("as black as your shoe") Robert Nixon in those terms.[6]

Constitutional Precedents

For all that, there were reasons for his proponents to be cautiously optimistic about Nixon's appeal. After largely ignoring the problems of criminal law in state courts for decades, in the 1920s and 1930s the United States Supreme Court had decided a series of cases that began to provide a constitutional definition of a fair trial. In *Moore v. Dempsey*, crowds of armed whites surrounded the courthouse in Phillips County, Arkansas as nearly a hundred African Americans were brought before the court on a range of charges arising from a riot. On appeal, the United States Supreme Court held that a trial violated the due process clause of the Fourteenth Amendment because a trial so dominated by the threat of violence and mob rule could never be fair. Nine years later, in *Powell v. Alabama*, one of the cases arising out of the Scottsboro trials in Alabama, the United States Supreme Court held that due process required the right to a lawyer in a criminal trial, and that the right was denied if a lawyer did not have time to adequately prepare for trial.[7]

In *Moore*, the defendants claimed that the police had beaten them to force them to confess, but the United States Supreme Court did not address that claim. Thirteen years later, in *Brown v. Mississippi*, the court finally returned to that issue. In *Brown*, the court held that due process meant the "rack and torture chamber may not be substituted for the witness stand." In *Brown* the three defendants, Brown, Ellington, and Shields, were black tenant farmers who were indicted for the murder of Raymond Stewart, a white farmer, in Mississippi in 1934. Stewart had been found, brutally beaten, on March 30, 1934, and died later that day. Brown and the other suspects were apprehended shortly thereafter and indicted on April 4. They were brought to trial on April 6. When their confessions were offered into evidence at the trial, their appointed attorney objected and called for a hearing on the confessions outside the presence of the jury. That motion was granted, and the sheriff testified that each defendant freely and voluntarily confessed to the crime in his presence. During cross-examination, the sheriff admitted that he had heard that the defendants had been whipped before they were brought to see him and that he noticed one of the defendants was limping and had problems sitting during his interrogation. After the trial judge ruled the confessions were voluntary, the confessions were allowed into evidence and the state rested. At that point, Brown and the other defendants took the stand and testified that they gave the confessions after they had been "whipped and otherwise mistreated." Each also offered an alibi for the time of the murder. The state then produced some testimony in rebuttal to the effect that fingerprints for one of the defendants had been found at the scene of the murder. When the case went to the jury, it quickly convicted all three defendants. On appeal, the Missouri Supreme Court affirmed the verdict, rejecting the defendants' argument that the use of the confessions at the trial had violated their right against self-incrimination as protected by the Missouri Constitution and the due process clause of the Fourteenth Amendment. With respect to the first claim, the court held that the law was well settled that privilege against self-incrimination could be waived if it was "not specifically claimed." Since it had not specifically been evoked at trial, the court held the defendants had waived the privilege. Nor, in the view of the Mississippi Supreme Court, did the Fourteenth Amendment's due process clause offer a reason to reverse the verdict. Quoting from the United States Supreme Court's opinion in *Twining v. New Jersey,* the court concluded that as a matter of federal constitutional law due process did not require "immunity from self-incrimination."[8]

On appeal, the United States Supreme Court eviscerated that reasoning and the deliberate indifference to the facts of the case upon which it rested. In an opinion joined by every other member of the court, Chief Justice Charles Evans Hughes set out the precise details of the "whipping" the three defendants received before they confessed. One defendant, Ellington, was taken into custody the evening after Stewart died, by a deputy sheriff who took him to the victim's house, where "a number of white men were gathered." When Ellington denied that he had committed the crime, the mob "with the participation of the deputy" hung him from a tree by a rope, took him down, hung him a second time, and then took him down again. When he continued to insist that he was not involved in the murder, they tied him to a tree and whipped him. When he still claimed that he was innocent, he was released only to be seized several days later and taken to a jail in another county. On his way to that jail, Ellington was whipped again by a deputy sheriff, who told him that he would be whipped until he agreed to confess. When Ellington finally did agree to do so, he was taken to the jail and a confession was dictated to him. The two other defendants, Brown and Shields, were arrested and taken to that same jail. At the jail, they were visited by a mob of white men that included at least two deputy sheriffs and the jailer. The mob forced both men to strip, and then whipped them with leather straps with buckles on them. Brown and Shields, who were told that they would be whipped until they confessed, produced confessions during the whipping. The next day, all three men repeated their confessions to the sheriff.[9]

Having established the damning facts, the Supreme Court made quick work of the Mississippi Supreme Court's effort to treat the case as nothing more than a failed effort to assert the privilege against self-incrimination. While it was true, Justice Hughes allowed, that states had the power to establish the "processes of justice by which the accused may be called as a witness and required to testify," there were limits: "Compulsion by torture to extort a confession is a different matter." He continued, "the freedom of the State in establishing its policy is the freedom of constitutional government and is limited by the requirement of due process of law. Because a State may dispense with a jury trial, it does not follow that it may substitute trial by ordeal. The rack and torture chamber may not be substituted for the witness stand. The State may not permit an accused to be hurried to conviction under mob domination—where the whole proceeding is but a mask—without supplying corrective process." As he put it, a "trial is equally a mere pretense where the State authorities have contrived a conviction resting solely upon confessions obtained by violence." And he concluded it "would be difficult to conceive of methods more revolting to the sense of justice than those taken to procure the confessions of these petitioners, and the use of the confessions thus obtained as a basis for conviction and sentence was a clear denial of due process." The Supreme Court reversed the Mississippi Supreme Court and declared the conviction and sentence "utterly void."[10]

Illinois Law

As important as *Brown* was, it did not seem to add much to Illinois law. As the Wickersham Commission noted in its report, during the 1920s the Illinois Supreme Court addressed the third degree in a series of cases. The outcomes in those cases were mixed: In *Illinois v. Frugoli,* decided at the end of that decade, the court reversed the conviction on the ground that the confession was obtained through torture. In contrast, in a decision from the start of the 1920s, *Illinois v. Colvin,* the case involving the two black youths arrested for murder during the race riot of 1919, the court affirmed the verdicts against the defendants, choosing to defer to the jury's determination that the defendants' claims of beatings and abuse at the hands of the police were not to be believed.[11]

In its coerced confession cases, the Illinois Supreme Court's solution to the problem of police torture was a legal procedure: If a defendant claimed to have confessed in response to violence or threats, the court had to hold a hearing outside the presence of the jury on that claim and the state had the burden of proving that there had been no third degree. If the state met that burden and the trial judge decided that the defendant's claim was not credible, the confession could be read to the jury. If the state failed to do so, the confession had to be excluded. In theory, the question of whether a confession was admissible was an issue of law, which could only be decided by the judge, though the Illinois Supreme Court recognized that jurors could hear testimony about the circumstances under which confessions were made in order to determine whether to give the confession credit. Yet in Illinois that rule was not so clear; for decades in the nineteenth and twentieth centuries, the law in Illinois provided that in all criminal trials juries "shall . . . be the judges of the law and the fact." Interpreting that rule, the Illinois Supreme Court had ruled that jurors had a "duty to reflect whether, from their habits of thought, their study and experience, they are better qualified to judge the law than the court." The law changed in 1931, when the Illinois Supreme Court declared that jurors had to accept the legal instructions they received from the judge, and were only qualified to be judges of the facts. As the jury instructions in Nixon's trial made clear, even after that ruling, more often than not Illinois courts allowed the jury to decide whether or not torture had occurred.[12]

In actual practice, trial judges typically did what Judge Lewe did in Nixon's trial. They held a hearing outside the presence of the jury, and then, if they determined that the confession should be admitted into evidence, they let the defendant put on evidence to try to convince the jury that the confession had been coerced by threats or violence. One consequence of this was revealed by the Nixon trial: It focused so much attention on the admissibility of the confessions that there was less emphasis on pointing out the inconsistencies and errors in those confessions. Another was that on appeal the Illinois Supreme Court almost never second-guessed a decision of the judge and jury, because the court treated the issue as a question of fact, not law, and reasoned that those in the courtroom during the testimony and countertestimony about what happened during the interrogation were in the best position to assess the credibility of the different claims.[13]

There were several reasons to question that assumption. The most obvious was one identified in the Wickersham Commission report: "The Chicago public," the commission noted, "is much more concerned with the reduction of crime than with official lawlessness. Much crime in Chicago is committed by brutal ruffians; the public are less inclined to blame the police for beating up such men than for letting them get away scot-free." To the extent that that was true (and the *Chicago Tribune* had been sure it was the case), it meant it was quite possible that jurors in Chicago believed defendants who claimed to have suffered the third degree, but did not care. In effect, that meant jurors were ignoring the well-settled law that a confession obtained through threats or force was illegal, but the Illinois Supreme Court's deference to juries meant that problem could never be addressed.[14]

Another problem with the Illinois Supreme Court's approach was that it required the judge and jury to focus on the specific claims of torture made in a single case. Considered in isolation, a defendant's claims of torture often seemed preposterous. In one of the earliest third degree cases, *Illinois v. Vinci*, that's precisely what happened at the Illinois Supreme Court. The court decided *Vinci* in 1920, and reversed the verdict, rejecting the judge and jurors' conclusion that Vinci's confession was not coerced. But the court did so on the very narrow ground that Vinci had been subject to relentless, extended interrogation over three days and four nights. That was enough, the court held, to make his confession involuntary. Vinci had made other claims: that he was knocked and kicked, that he was threatened by an assistant state's attorney who proposed to throw him out of a window and police officers who offered to shoot him, and that officers made him drunk before they interrogated him. Yet the Illinois Supreme Court ignored those claims, characterizing them as "false and exaggerated" and "ridiculous," noting that Vinci made no complaints of ill treatment to anyone who visited him, and observing that a picture of him taken the Monday after his arrest "showed no signs of physical violence around [his] head or face."[15]

It is, of course, quite possible that Vinci did not complain about his maltreatment to family and friends because it did not happen. It is just as possible he did not do so because he was afraid of further abuse. That was certainly a factor for others who claimed they were tortured by the police. Mott and Wilson were so worried about the possibility that they would be retaliated against in 1924 that they left town rather than appear at a city council hearing investigating the third degree, and in contrast to Vinci they were no longer in police custody. Nor does the fact that pictures of a fully clothed Vinci showed no bruises constitute evidence he was unharmed: Edmund Fitch's demonstration a year earlier of the bruises and welts caused by blows with a rubber hose on his back suggest that the police were perfectly willing, and able, to strike suspects in places where the harm would be concealed by clothing. And certainly the specific details of Vinci's "ridiculous" claims resembled those made by other suspects over the years.[16]

Considering the claim of torture in isolation created yet another problem, because it let jurors and judges dismiss the claims as anomalies. Viewing testimony of a confession induced by torture in isolation allowed the claim to be cast as an exception, the act of "rogue cops," or the inevitable result of overzealous policing. All that made what appeared to be a single claim of torture easy to ignore. If judges and jurors who heard claims of police torture also considered evidence that others had made similar claims against the police, they might have been more willing to conclude that police in Chicago kicked and beat suspects, and they might have been less willing to ignore claims that police officers threatened to drop suspects out of windows, or hung them by their wrists.

Courts considered evidence of patterns of behavior in other cases. When the trial judge in one of the Scottsboro cases held a hearing on whether

African Americans were deliberately excluded from juries, the evidence included testimony from several individuals intended to establish a pattern of exclusion. The Illinois Supreme Court itself had referred to the general knowledge that police abused suspects at least once, in deciding to reverse a conviction based on a confession that had been coerced by torture. In 1928, Edward Grady, suspected in a robbery case, said that the chief of detectives strung him up from a bar by his ankles at Chicago's Gresham station. Ruling on the appeal, the Illinois Supreme Court wrote:

"The defendant's statement that he was shackled and strung up by the heels and was beaten by the chief of detectives of the city of Chicago and the desk sergeant at the police station to force a confession from him was competent evidence and current history indicates that it was not manifestly incredible."[17]

Unfortunately, the court rarely took that larger view. Instead, it typically considered, and allowed lower courts to consider, claims of torture in isolation.[18]

The process that the Illinois Supreme Court established did nothing to solve the problem of competing evidence. As happened in the Nixon case, the state routinely put on any number of witnesses, police officers, and state's attorneys, who testified that nothing untoward occurred. At that point, judges and jurors were faced with a single question: Whom should they believe? As the Nixon trial made clear, the prosecution did everything it could to help them make that decision. In his closing argument in Robert Nixon's case, John Boyle told the jurors to ask themselves who would lie and then answered his own question by assuring the jurors that, of course, the police and state's attorneys had no reason to lie, since all they wanted was for the truth to be revealed, while Robert Nixon and other defendants, who faced the threat of imprisonment or death, had every reason to lie. But there were reasons to lie on both sides: Faced with a weak circumstantial case, the police and prosecution had every reason to get a confession by hook or by crook. And when the consequence of having a confession that was obtained by violence was suppressed, there was every reason to lie about the process. Especially because, as *Brown v. Mississippi* and *Illinois v. Frugoli* made clear, police officers who engaged in the third degree ran the risk of having the confession declared inadmissible and perhaps being charged with a crime.[19]

During the 1930s, as the Illinois Supreme Court wrestled with a number of cases involving claims of police torture, it made its determination to defer to the judge and jurors clearer. *Illinois v. Albers* arose out of a violent strike in southern Illinois. Defendants were on trial for the murder of the young daughter of a deputy sheriff. The defendants presented evidence that they were tortured into making confessions; the state put on a number of witnesses who contradicted all the defendants' claims. On appeal, the Illinois Supreme Court set out the problem: "The trial court could not take any middle ground on the admission or rejection of the confessions, for there was none. It either had to believe the witnesses for the defendants or the witnesses for the prosecution." Faced with that conflict, the solution was to defer to the judge and jury: "The evidence is contradictory on the question of violence, and this court will not reverse the decision of the lower court in admitting confessions unless its action is clearly against the manifest weight of the evidence." That result was not, unfortunately, consistent with the rule that the burden of proving that the confessions were voluntary was on the state. Where one party to a case has the burden of proof, a tie has to be resolved in favor of the party that did not have the burden of proof, which is precisely the opposite of what the Illinois Supreme Court did.[20]

Sometimes, the claims of the police witnesses were so incredible that the decision was easy. In *Illinois v. Basile*, decided in 1934, Basile claimed that he only confessed after he was struck and beaten by officers and threatened with being thrown out of a window if he did not confess. There was also evidence that he, and the other suspects in a murder case, had been kept incommunicado for several days, subjected to extended interrogations, and denied food for prolonged periods of time while they were being interrogated. The state called several police officers to the stand to deny Basile's claims, but they gave, in the words of the Illinois Supreme Court, "very conflicting statements as to how the confessions were obtained and in relating the incidents contradicted themselves and each other." Notwithstanding that, the trial judge admitted the confessions into evidence and the jurors, apparently, credited them and convicted Basile. The Illinois Supreme Court reversed the decision because the officers' contradictory statements raised questions about their claims that the confessions were voluntary.[21]

The result in *Basile* was unusual. More often, when the Illinois Supreme Court examined the evidence relating to a confession closely, it seemed to do so in order to find a reason to admit it. Sometimes, the court looked to see if there was other evidence that either independently established the defendant's guilt or seemed to independently corroborate the confession. In 1934, the Illinois Supreme Court heard an appeal by Walter Evenow, who had been found guilty of the murder of William Rumbler, an off-duty police officer. Evenow claimed that his confession should not have been admitted because it was the result of the third degree. The Illinois Supreme Court agreed that his testimony suggested he had been subjected to cruel and barbaric treatment, but noted that several police officers testified that Evenow had not received the treatment he claimed and had confessed voluntarily. While the court expressed some concern about the conflicting testimony, it concluded that it did not need to exclude the confession because Evenow confessed to his guilt on a second occasion, when there was no coercion. In fact, what the court characterized as Evenow's second confession was hardly that. Sometime after his initial confession, Evenow's codefendant made a statement at the detective bureau. After that confession had been transcribed by the court reporter, it was read to the codefendant, John Senew, in Evenow's presence. After the reading, Senew was asked if the confession was true and said it was. Then Evenow was asked it the statement Senew made was true, and responded: "Senew knew what he was talking about and if he wanted to tell it, it was all right." Since Senew's statement implicated Evenow, the court concluded that Evenow's ambiguous statement was the equivalent of a second confession.[22]

At other times, the Illinois Supreme Court looked to the quantity of the prosecution's evidence. This was often an issue that could result in a ruling for the defendant. In 1931, in *Illinois v. Cope*, the court reversed Cope's conviction for larceny because some of the officers he claimed were present when he was tortured did not testify.[23] The court had reached a similar result a year before Nixon's trial. Jason Arendarczyk, who had been found guilty of incest, claimed that his confession had been prompted by a mix of threats and physical violence. The state called only one witness to refute that claim, an assistant state's attorney who was one of the witnesses when Arendarczyk signed his confession. Citing a number of its earlier decisions, the Illinois Supreme Court ruled that where "there is evidence tending to show the use of violence, threats, torture or promises, all the persons having any authority or control over the person making the confession and charged by the evidence with the use of such means, must be called, if practicable and examined as witnesses before the confession may be admitted." While that appeared to establish a clear rule of evidence, *Arendarczyk* allowed the state a loophole, requiring the state to produce witnesses only if it was "practicable." Applying that standard in later cases, the court often refused to order a new trial simply because a particular officer did not testify at a confession hearing.[24]

Briefs on Appeal

Nixon's appeal took place in that legal context. On December 15, 1938, when the Illinois Supreme Court finally agreed to hear Nixon's appeal, the court set the case for a hearing in February 1939. Once again, things did not go quite as quickly as planned. The opening brief for Nixon was filed on January 27, the state filed its reply on February 16, and Nixon's response was filed on February 25. The briefs on appeal addressed a number of different points. In their initial brief, Clayton and Charles Evins, who joined him on the appeal, chiefly focused on Nixon's claim that his confession had been obtained through torture.[25]

They presented three arguments relating to Nixon's torture claim. The first was a straightforward argument about procedure: Clayton and Evins charged that Judge Lewe ignored well-established precedent during the hearing when he required Nixon to testify in detail about his claim that he was tortured before asking the state to offer evidence that he was not. That, they argued, ignored a long line of cases decided by the Illinois Supreme Court establishing that the state had the burden of proving a confession was voluntary and that "the State must make its showing first." In support of their argument Clayton and Evins cited six separate Illinois Supreme Court cases decided between 1929 and 1938, beginning with *Illinois v. Holick* (1929) and ending with *Illinois v. Roach* (1937).[26]

In a second argument in their brief, Clayton and Evins engaged the question of why a confession obtained through torture should be inadmissible. They relied on the United States Supreme Court's recent decision in *Brown v. Mississippi* (1936), which was a comprehensive refutation of the police department's frequent argument that getting a confession from a guilty person, even when obtained through torture, was not a problem. Since a variation on that argument, cast in legal terms, had been offered by an earlier Illinois Supreme Court opinion, *Illinois v. Fox*, it was necessary to remind the court that this could no longer be the rule after *Brown*. While Clayton and Evins did not cite *Fox*, that was precisely the point they made: confessions obtained by torture could not ever be the basis of a conviction, regardless of whether the confession was true or the person making the confession was clearly guilty, because the use of torture made the admission of such a confession a violation of due process. Then, in a third section, Clayton and Evins reviewed the line of cases setting out the Illinois Supreme Court's opinions relating to the admission of involuntary confessions. They began by repeating the point that the case law established: The burden was on the state to demonstrate that a confession was voluntarily made. They made a second point as well: The rule since *Illinois v. Rogers* was that when a defendant claimed to have confessed under duress, the confession should be excluded unless "all the police department men engaged or present" during the interrogation should be called as witnesses. This point had been reaffirmed as recently as 1937 in *Illinois v. Arendarczyk*. Clayton and Evins relied on *Rogers* and *Arendarczyk* for two specific points. First, they argued that because the prosecution did not produce all the officers who had Nixon in custody or were involved in interrogating him, the state failed to meet its burden of proof. In addition, they noted that the prosecution had not called Earl Hicks, who had been present during at least one interrogation, and argued that also violated that line of cases.[27]

In addition, Clayton and Evins noted that the Illinois Supreme Court had held, in *Illinois v. Sweetin*, that where a first confession was improperly obtained, any subsequent confession was presumed to be involuntary, "unless it appears that from lapses of time or otherwise the influence which induced the original confession had been removed and the confession was no longer dominated by such influence." This meant the court should bar both Nixon's first confession on May 28, and his second, joint statement with Hicks on May 29.[28]

Clayton and Evins also made a number of procedural objections in their brief. They argued that the lower court should have granted their request for a change of venue to get Nixon (and his lawyers) away from the prejudice in the Cook County Criminal Courts. They objected again to the fact that Judge Lewe did not sustain the defense effort to bar Muehlberger's testimony, even though his name was left off the witness list and his testimony could not effectively be refuted given the time it would have taken to replicate his experiments. They complained of the fact that Judge Lewe did not order the prosecution to produce Earl Hicks to testify at trial on the ground that Nixon had a right to "meet the witnesses against him face to face" under Article 2 of the Illinois Constitution. They objected to some of Crowley's comments during closing argument: the fact he repeatedly called Nixon a "killer" and the "brick murderer," and the fact that Crowley claimed, during his argument, that Hicks had told the truth while Nixon had lied. They complained about the former characterizations because they were designed to play into the jurors' fears, rather than encourage deliberation, and the later because Hicks's absence during trial meant it was impossible for the defense to test the honesty of his claims through cross-examination.[29]

Finally, they argued that the evidence offered against Nixon was so poor that it raised a reasonable doubt about his guilt. This argument had several parts: Clayton and Evins asserted that Margaret Whitton's identification of Nixon at the lineup on May 31, the only time she unambiguously identified him as the man she saw in the apartment on May 27, was too tainted by the many other times she had seen Nixon in police custody to be reliable. In addition, they noted the absence of evidence that should have been produced. Although the crime scene had been safeguarded to let fingerprint technicians do their work, no prints that tied Nixon (or Hicks) to the apartment at 4631 Lake Park had been produced. While the police had—rather improbably, Clayton and Evins suggested—produced an apple that they claimed had been found where Nixon threw it as he left the house, there had been no paraffin test done to see if the bite marks in the apple matched Nixon's jaws. The police had never explained why there was blood on Nixon's shirt but none on the jacket that Margaret Whitton said he was wearing over it, or why there had been no tests of the type of blood on his shirt. All this, Clayton and Evins argued, added up to a body of evidence that was inadequate to establish Nixon's guilt, which meant the jury's verdict against him should not be allowed to stand.[30]

In its response rebrief, written by Edward Wilson and several other assistant state's attorneys, the prosecution argued that the law in Illinois was that the order of proof did not matter so long as a hearing on the claim of torture was held. In support of that, the state cited two cases from the 1920s, *Illinois v. Costello* (1926) and *Illinois v. Fox* (1925). Its argument was remarkably sloppy. Although the Illinois Supreme Court in *Costello* did write, on page 104, that "There is no rigid rule as to the order of proof," the state omitted that language entirely from its brief. Instead, it quoted the court, incorrectly, as holding that "if objection is made to a confession on the grounds that it was involuntary the Court must hear, out of the presence of the jury, such evidence as either side may present as to the circumstances of the confession and the decision of the Court that the confession was voluntary and admissible will not be reversed unless manifestly against the weight of the evidence or unless there has been an abuse of discretion."[31]

The inaccurate quotation aside, the greater problem with the state's reliance on *Costello* was that, as Clayton and Evins pointed out in their reply brief, no one had objected to the admission of Costello's confession at trial. That meant that the Supreme Court's discussion of the rules to follow if there were a hearing on a disputed confession was *dicta*, the legal term for an analysis that did not have the weight of law.[32]

The state's reliance on *Fox* was no less problematic. The state cited *Fox* for the proposition that "the order of proof is largely within the discretion of the trial judge." That language, at least, did actually appear in the opinion in *Fox*, but it was not clear that the rule remained good law. In *Fox*, the Illinois Supreme Court apparently concluded that the testimony of a single police officer, who took the stand and denied that a codefendant had been subject to any violence, threats, or coercion in order to make him confess, was enough to establish a prima facie case. One Supreme Court justice, Judge Duncan, dissented and argued at length that the single officer's testimony could not establish a prima facie case because, by his own admission, he was not present throughout the codefendant's interrogation. Duncan's argument was picked up by the Illinois Supreme Court in *Illinois v. Holick*, which it decided four years after *Fox*. In *Holick* the court held the testimony of a single officer was never enough to meet the state's burden of proving that a confession was not coerced.[33]

The ruling in *Holick* seemed to indicate that the rule in *Fox* was no longer good law, but there were at least two other problems with the state's reliance on *Fox*. In *Fox*, the majority began its discussion of the admissibility of the codefendant's confession with a lengthy examination of the law against coerced confessions, concluding that the law's only concern was with admitting *false* confessions. That meant, the majority carefully added, that "the wrong done, however reprehensible, in inducing the accused to make a confession could never, rightly considered, require the rejection of a confession if the court could know as a fact that the confession was true." The implication was that a beating during an interrogation was okay if it was administered to a guilty suspect and resulted in a truthful confession. That was inconsistent with the Illinois Supreme Court's view, set out forcefully in *Rogers* and *Frugoli*, that when a confession was induced by violence the confession could not be admitted because a crime had been committed in order to get the confession.[34]

The final problem with *Fox* was that the majority in that case relied on *Sims v. Florida* to support its conclusions about the proper order of proof. *Sims* was, obviously, not a decision decided by a court in Illinois; it was written by the Supreme Court of Florida, which meant that it did not have the force of law in Illinois. Nor was *Sims* particularly recent; it had been decided in 1910. More to the point, the court in *Sims* did not set out any precise process for a hearing on a confession. Rather, it asserted generally that when "it appears *prima facie* that a confession was freely and voluntarily made, the burden is upon the defendant to show that it was in fact not a voluntary confession." That had not been the rule in Illinois since the Supreme Court of Illinois' decision in *Rogers*, decided three years before *Fox*, in which the court held that the burden was on the prosecution to prove that a confession was voluntary. That principle had been reaffirmed by the Illinois Supreme Court repeatedly in the years after it decided *Rogers*, most recently in its decision in *Roach* in 1937.[35]

Needless to say, the state also rejected Clayton and Evins's reliance on *Brown*, asserting dismissively that the defense's citation of *Brown v. Mississippi* "gives some insight into the origins of defendant's story." Having suggested, once again, that Nixon had invented the claims of torture out of whole cloth, at the behest of his dishonest lawyers and his cronies in the jailhouse, the state argued that the facts of *Brown* were so significantly different that it had no application to Nixon's case. In *Brown*, according to the state, the crucial point was that the judge and the prosecutor both knew about the torture applied to the three defendants and the defendants in *Brown* bore obvious signs of mistreatment, while Nixon showed no signs of physical abuse.[36]

The state also used the reference to *Brown* as an opportunity to recite, once again, the various refutations of Nixon's claims offered during the trial. Those claims, the state noted, were each disputed by "from one to ten witnesses." Then the state went through all the main claims Nixon made: Nixon's claim that he was hung out the window of the eleventh floor at 11th and State was refuted by the building engineer, who testified that the windows on that floor did not open enough to allow anyone other than an infant to be hung outside. His claim that he was beaten by Thurston on the eleventh floor was denied by Thurston, who said he was never on that floor with Nixon. Nixon's claim that he was driven to 95th and Stony Island, and kept there for several hours by Storms, Fitzgerald, Paradowski, and McGuire was denied by all four men, who claimed they never drove Nixon there. His claim that he was hit by Crane at the Hyde Park station was denied by Crane, who pointed out that he was not at the station at the time Nixon said he was hit. His claim that Paradowski, McGuire, and Kush told him they would show him "the seven devils" in Storms's office was denied by all three men. Each also denied that Nixon was beaten in Storms's office. And, the state noted, several of the things that Nixon claimed happened could not have happened because the people whom Nixon accused were not present at the time that Nixon said the things happened.[37]

The state responded to the procedural objections made by Clayton and Evins with alternative interpretations of the case law, going through them one-by-one. But the state generally ignored the larger issue of fairness and its relation to the rule of law. Instead, its appeal was to a labored common sense. The defense, it noted at one point, argued that it was prejudiced by Muehlberger's testimony because it did not have time to sensitize its own rabbit to test the results of his test, but, the state pointed out, the defense did not put on any evidence to show that there were no chemists in Chicago with sensitized rabbit serum, so it was not clear they were as badly harmed as they claimed.[38]

In their reply brief, Clayton and Evins returned to each of the arguments set out in their original brief. Few of their points added anything to the arguments they had made initially, though they reframed several of their claims somewhat. In responding to the prosecution's claim that the order of proof in a hearing over the admission of a confession did not matter, Clayton and Evins pointedly noted that the long-standing common law rule was that the party that had the burden of proof had to proceed first. The two lawyers also hammered at the state's claim that the various officers called to refute Nixon's claims of torture effectively demonstrated that none of the things that Nixon complained of had happened. Once again, they pointed out that the testimony of those officers at trial had been very precise and that those officers "merely testified that the defendant was not beaten while in their presence," which did not, Clayton and Evins added, prove that Nixon was not beaten outside their presence by other officers, whose identities were unknown to Nixon because he was blindfolded. They also suggested that Nixon's account of the events of May 27 through 31 was more consistent with the strange pattern of his alleged confessions: There was no reason, they argued, for Nixon not to have signed his first statement unless he was taken away and beaten after making it, as he claimed.[39]

They also dismissed the state's claim that Nixon's participation in the "so-called re-enactment" proved that the confessions were accurate. They noted that Nixon went through the reenactments "while still under the influence and domination of those who had already tortured" him. That meant, they asserted, that he was motivated to cooperate and do what he was told out of fear, and in order to avoid more torture. And they added that all these problems were particularly severe in Nixon's case, given his youth and the fact that he had been found to have a mental age of just eleven and a half. [40]

Illinois Supreme Court

In its decision dated April 19, 1939, the Illinois Supreme Court made quick work of these arguments, ignoring most of the issues raised by the defendant and only briefly addressing those that it did engage.[41]

The court easily dismissed the defense claim that the lower court erred in refusing to grant the motion for a change of venue, noting that when the defense filed the second of the two motions for a change of venue it failed to list Judge Lewe on the motion. The court also pointed out that the defense never pressed for a ruling on that motion and instead proceeded to trial before Judge Lewe without objection. With respect to the defense claim that the testimony of Muehlberger should have been barred because his name was left off the witness list, the court held that it was within the discretion of the trial court to allow testimony by witnesses whose names were not provided to the defendant before trial. The court admitted that there was an exception to the rule that that decision could not be reviewed on appeal, but concluded that exception only arose when the defendant was taken by surprise. In this case, the Supreme Court held, there was no evidence of surprise; on the contrary, the state had indicated that Muehlberger would be called during voir dire of the jury and again in its opening statement, without any objection by the defense. Although that would have seemed to resolve the issue, the Supreme Court went further, noting that the defense made no effort to determine whether there was another sensitized rabbit available that could be used to attempt to confirm Muehlberger's conclusions. Nor, the court pointed out, did the defense seek to have the court order the state to help it locate such a rabbit. As the argument about the rabbit suggests, the court in its opinion often adopted the state's argument as its own.[42]

The court spent slightly more time dismissing the argument that the joint statement by Nixon and Hicks should not have been admitted into evidence because Hicks did not take the stand, though in the end the court concluded that there was no problem admitting the joint confession. Resting its assessment on three Illinois Supreme Court cases, the court held that the rule was well settled that when "a Statement is made in the presence of the accused and he makes reply admitting the truth of the Statement either wholly or in materially incriminating parts, both the Statement and his reply are competent evidence."[43]

The court also rejected the defense arguments that the confessions that Nixon and Hicks made jointly and severally should not have been admitted because they were coerced through torture. The court treated this as two separate claims: first, a question about whether the trial court improperly put the burden of proof on the defense to prove that he had been tortured; and second, a question about whether the State had successfully refuted Nixon's claims of torture. In analyzing both questions, the Illinois Supreme Court once again borrowed heavily from the state's brief. With respect to the first point, the court held that it was true that the burden was on the state to prove that the confessions were not coerced by torture or other mistreatment. But, the court went on, *Costello* and *Fox* established that the state did not have to "produce all [its] evidence before any evidence is produced on behalf of the defendant". All that mattered was that there be a full hearing on the claim. Here, there was a full hearing, so that requirement had been met.[44]

The Illinois Supreme Court's treatment of the second issue was also influenced by the state's argument. As had the state, the court noted that twenty-three police officers, "shown to be all of the officers in charge of defendant from the time of his arrest until after the Statements and reenactment were made," had taken the witness stand. All of these witnesses, the court added, testified that they did not harm Nixon and they did not see anyone else do so. The court, like the state, also noted that Nixon made no complaint that he had been tortured while he was in custody, and that several witnesses, including the state's attorney, saw no signs that he had been injured.[45]

The court's reading of the record was mistaken. Indeed, the fact that the court referred to the testimony of twenty-three police officers, which was the erroneous number offered by the state, suggests once again that the court just copied much of the state's argument. It also suggests the court did not read the record on appeal. In addition, contrary to the court's finding, the evidence did show, as Nixon's lawyers claimed on appeal, that some of the police officers whom Nixon claimed participated in the beatings and abuse were not called to testify at his trial. The defense attorneys were also correct that the testimony of the officers did contain gaping holes: periods of time when one of them, or another officer, could have been subjecting Nixon to some sort of abuse. In this respect, the police denials were too precise; they may have established that Nixon was not beaten at the times that he claimed (though Nixon consistently testified that his guesses about the timing of various incidents were approximations because he had no watch). The evidence of the officers who testified that they did nothing to harm Nixon did not conclusively establish that Nixon was not abused at some point, even reading the police officers' testimony in the most forgiving light. Nor, of course, was the fact that no one who testified for the state saw bruises on Nixon particularly significant, since to a man those witnesses had agreed that they had done very little to examine Nixon for signs of mistreatment.

Robert H. Jackson, an associate justice on the United States Supreme Court from 1941 to 1954, once said of that court that "We are not final because we are infallible, we are infallible because we are final." One could say the same of the Illinois Supreme Court opinion in Nixon's case. There was no money for attempts to appeal the case to the United States Supreme Court. Once again, ministers in Chicago's African American community rallied behind Nixon and petitioned the governor for leniency. But this time, it did no good. On June 15, 1939, Illinois put Robert Nixon to death for the murder of Florence Johnson; he was not yet twenty years old. His codefendant, Earl Hicks, fared considerably better. Four months earlier, in February 1939, Judge Lewe sentenced Earl Hicks to fourteen years in prison for his part in Florence Johnson's murder.[46]

CHAPTER FIVE

NIXON'S CASE WAS NOT an anomaly. Other claims of police torture were made contemporaneous to his trial; still other claims followed it. In many respects, those claims resembled those that had come before. One change in the years following Nixon's trial was that torture claims became increasingly hidden from the public (and historical) eye. Newspapers reported them less than they had before; the rise of plea bargains meant fewer suspects had a chance to go to court to make a public claim that torture happened.[1]

Techniques of Invisibility

Of course, torture's invisibility had been a problem in Chicago even before Nixon went to trial. News accounts and court reports that described a sweating or the third degree often offered little detail about what that meant in any given case. Did it mean, as the police often claimed, that there had simply been a relentless but civil and nonviolent interrogation? Or did those words disguise a beating, the water cure, or something worse? Police denials, sometimes in the face of bruises and other evidence to the contrary, often made under oath, helped push the practice even further out of sight. Concealing torture was hardly unique to Chicago. In his study of torture in democratic countries, Darius Rejali notes that they often adopted "clean" forms of torture that are easier to conceal because they leave fewer marks. That was partly because governments in those countries had to answer to voters who were ambivalent about the practice, and partly because those governments were more interested in intimidating or coercing individual prisoners than they were concerned with leaving visible scars that might deter others. As significant, as Rejali and others have shown, is the fact that popular ambivalence was sometimes muted approval. As the *Tribune* and the Wickersham Commission both noted, many Chicagoans seemed willing to tolerate police torture because they thought it helped stop crime.

But during the 1920s, those Chicagoans became more like the stereotypical buyer of sausage: they liked the results but did not want to know about how it was made.[2]

In the mid-1920s, the police desire to keep torture hidden, particularly from judges who increasingly challenged their authority to use violence against suspects they were sure were guilty, apparently helped prompt the use of the rubber hose, the punch to the gut, the kick to the shin, and the slap to the head. Those techniques were painful, but rarely left permanent marks or scars. That same desire may also help to explain the rise of a specific practice that apparently came into use in the late 1920s. That was the practice of suspending a suspect by the wrists, sometimes accompanied with punches and slaps. The technique was called the "standing handcuff"; a variation of it, sometimes known as "picqueting," was a British military punishment used in India and on slaves in the Caribbean. Later, it was used, particularly on African Americans, in the Jim Crow South.[3]

Claims that the practice was employed in Chicago first appeared in the late 1920s. In 1928, Edward Grady said that he had been strung up by his ankles at the Gresham station by the chief of detectives. In the spring of 1936, seventeen-year-old Michael Livingston, a suspect in a murder case, claimed that John Sullivan and several detectives at 11th and State hung him from a door by his wrists. His codefendant, nineteen-year-old Emil Reck, said that he suffered the same treatment from officers interrogating him at the North Avenue station. In November 1936, lawyers for Rufo Swain charged that he confessed to killing Mary Louise Trammell after he was strung up by his wrists at 11th and State. A year later, Arthur LaFrana, suspected in a robbery-murder, claimed he was hung by his wrists on two separate occasions while being interrogated by Captain Goldberg. That same year, Thomas McCall claimed that he confessed to raping Virginia Austin only after he was beaten by police officers who also strung him up by his wrists, and Robert Conroy asserted that he falsely confessed to raping Anna Brasy after the police officers interrogating him hung him from a door by his wrists and beat him.[4]

Cases from the 1940s rested on claims of torture very similar to those made by Robert Nixon. In 1941, David Goldblatt was arrested and charged with murdering Anton Gorczak, a driver for a cleaning company. The murder itself was part gangland slaying and part economic terrorism: the police claimed that Goldblatt and Thomas Russo were hired by Samuel Ginsberg, the owner of another cleaning company, to beat Gorczak up because Gorczak was stealing customers from Ginsberg's firm. Ginsberg's partner in the cleaning firm was the wife of a "Capone gang chieftain." Russo,

Goldblatt, and a third, unidentified man, were accused of beating Gorczak with a rubber gear shift handle at a tailor shop in Chicago. Gorczak died from the assault.[5]

Goldblatt was arrested in September 1941, promptly confessed to the murder for hire, and implicated Russo and Ginsberg. A day later, he repudiated his confession and signed a statement claiming that he confessed under torture. In a petition his attorney filed that same day with the acting chief judge of the Cook County Criminal Court, he claimed that police officers working for the state's attorney's office hung him from a door by his wrists and beat him until he confessed. Judge Haas ordered that Goldblatt be examined by four doctors, two representing the state and two representing Goldblatt. Goldblatt's case went to trial in December 1941, at which time he repeated his claim that the confessions the state wanted to admit against him had been forced out of him by torture. The prosecution called Daniel Gilbert, still chief investigator for the state's attorney's office, and Wilbert Crowley, still first assistant state's attorney, to the stand to refute Goldblatt's claims. Gilbert said that when they accused Goldblatt of the murder, he responded: "I've thrown many sevens and elevens, but now it looks like I've thrown craps." Thereupon, Gilbert continued, Goldblatt freely and voluntarily confessed. Gilbert's version of the confession was echoed by Crowley, another witness from the state's attorney's office, William Crawford, and Chicago police detective Nicholas Disteldorf.[6]

There were, however, several reasons to doubt Goldblatt committed the murder: two eyewitnesses, Abraham Rubin who owned the tailor shop at which the attack occurred and his presser, Phillip Cloutier, both claimed they were unable to identify Goldblatt as one of the men involved in the attack. At best, they said, he seemed to be roughly the right size. In addition, Rubin recalled that the first time the police tried to have Goldblatt reenact the crime, he failed miserably to get the details right. It was only during a second reenactment that he seemed to know what had happened. There also were reasons to credit Goldblatt's claim of police torture. The four doctors who examined him after his arrest, including the two who worked for the state, all testified that Goldblatt was bruised when they examined him. Other witnesses testified that Goldblatt was with them at the time that he was supposed to be helping to beat Gorczak. And Goldblatt took the stand to repeat his claim that the police hung him from a door and beat him until he finally said "I killed anybody you say I did."[7]

In the end, that evidence did not matter. The jury convicted Goldblatt and he was sentenced to death. A few months later, the Chicago dry cleaners association announced that several staff members in the state's attorney's office would split the $2500 reward for information leading to the arrest and conviction of Gorczak's murderer. Two years later, however, the Illinois Supreme Court reversed that verdict. Not long after, the state decided not to retry him; without the confession, prosecutors conceded, they could not convict Goldblatt.[8]

The standing handcuff reappeared in the middle of the 1940s. In 1943, Edward Damiani was arrested and charged with killing a woman in the course of robbing a currency exchange. Damiani was arrested by the detectives in the robbery bureau at 11th and State and subjected to what they admitted was a grueling interrogation. Damiani was more specific: he claimed that they cuffed him and hung him from a door. Three years later, Suzanne Degnan, a six-year-old girl, disappeared from her bedroom on Chicago's North Side. A ransom note left in her room suggested that she was the victim of a kidnapping, but several days later parts of her dismembered body were found in a nearby sewer. The case was a sensation, which meant there was enormous pressure on the police to make arrests. They quickly did so, taking two janitors from the neighborhood, Desere Smet and Hector Verburgh, into custody. Both were held for several days and then released. Several months later, William Heirens, a seventeen-year-old student at the University of Chicago, was arrested during a burglary in the Degnan neighborhood. In the course of investigating that burglary, the police determined that Heirens had murdered Suzanne Degnan and two women, Josephine Ross and Frances Brown, who had been killed in separate incidents in 1945. Heirens subsequently pled guilty at a lengthy plea-bargaining session.[9]

Smet, Verburgh, and Heirens each claimed that he had been tortured by the police. Smet said that he was beaten during his several days in police custody. Verburgh went into greater detail, claiming that while he was held at the detective bureau at 11th and State he was kept incommunicado, denied food for extended periods, and hung by his cuffed wrists until his toes barely touched the floor. Heirens claimed he was beaten during arrest, held incommunicado for six days, given truth serum, burned with ether and deprived of food, and mistreated at the hospital (where he was taken after his arrest). Smet and Verburgh both sued the police department after they were released. Smet sought $50,000 in damages in his suit; Verburgh $100,000 on his own behalf and $25,000 for his wife, who was also arrested.[10]

There was considerable public outrage about the treatment of Smet and Verburgh. The ACLU called a meeting to denounce their treatment at the hands of the police. Four hundred people attended and passed a resolution calling on the police department to give officers more training about civil rights and to fire officers who used the third degree. The police department never admitted that any officers mistreated either Smet or Verburgh, and denied any wrongdoing to Heirens until his death in 2012. But the City of Chicago did pay Smet and the Verburghs to settle any claims they might have against the police department.[11]

That settlement does not seem to have stopped the practice. In 1947, Nicholas LoCoco said that he was strung up by his arms and beaten by detectives on the eleventh floor of police headquarters. A year later, John Wagoner said that he was cuffed with his hands against the wall during his interrogation at 11th and State. Others suggested that the practice continued into the 1950s and increasingly targeted African Americans. In 1952, an African American named Oscar Walden said that officers threatened to hang him by his wrists and beat him if he did not confess. Another African American, Paul Crump, arrested for murder a year later, claimed that police hung him by his wrists and beat him until he confessed. That claim was graphically recreated in a television documentary about Crump's arrest prepared in 1962 by the young filmmaker William Friedkin. Although the film won an award at the San Francisco International Film Festival, it was not aired in Chicago because the torture scenes were considered too controversial. In 1959, the ACLU of Illinois published a booklet, *Secret Detention by the Chicago Police*, which called attention to this practice and noted that so long as the victim's wrists were bandaged, it left no marks. The report noted that claims of that sort had been made "with alarming frequency" over the past twenty years but added that although the press occasionally covered such claims, "when the complainants are not involved in sensational murder investigations or are persons of no wealth and little community standing, they receive little attention."[12]

It may have been a coincidence, but the standing handcuff seems to have fallen out of favor around the time of the ACLU report's publication. About that same time, several claims of police torture suggested that the police were experimenting with new techniques. Robert Jackson, arrested in 1956 on suspicion of murder and robbery, said that a police officer and an assistant state's attorney took him to the basement of the Fillmore Street station, where they put some sort of bag over his head. Then they struck him behind the ear and hit him in the stomach as they interrogated him. That practice, known as bagging, figured prominently in some of the complaints made about the Chicago Police Department in the 1980s, but appeared only occasionally in complaints of police torture in the 1950s and 1960s. In 1962, Lyvon Draper, a black man, claimed that he was taken to the basement of a station, where detectives put a bag over his head and then put his head underwater, twice as they tried to get him to confess to murder. Draper's description was apparently believable. He was acquitted at trial, although one of his codefendants was convicted. Other black men arrested in the 1960s also said that the police held their heads under water to try to get them to confess. In 1962, Alex Gordon said that the officers interrogating him about a kidnapping case held his head in a pan of water for "long periods" of time, tied his arms behind him, and pointed a gun at him. Four years later, in 1966, Fred Alexander said that the officers who arrested him for robbery cuffed him to a chair for three hours, then took him to the basement of the station, where he was hit with a nightstick and with fists. He added that the officers held his head under water during part of his interrogation. Although the officers denied that Alexander had suffered any abuse, he presented evidence (including from doctors who had treated him) that he had a lacerated head and a swollen eye and nose.[13]

More of the Same

In 1940 the United States Supreme Court declared, once again, that torture intended to obtain a confession violated the due process clause of the Fourteenth Amendment to the Constitution. In that decision, *Chambers v. Florida*, the defendants claimed that they had been subject to physical violence during their interrogation, but the court did not focus on that aspect of their case. Instead, the court concluded that holding suspects incommunicado, in that case for more than a week, was coercive enough to make the process unconstitutional. The court also, and significantly, rejected the argument made by Florida on appeal that it had to defer to the judgment of the judge and jury about whether the confessions were voluntary. On the contrary, Justice Black wrote for the court, "we must determine independently whether petitioners' confessions" were obtained in a manner that violated the Constitution, "by review of the facts upon which that issue necessarily turns." Four years later, that court decided yet another police torture case, *Tennessee v. Ashcraft*. Once again, the defendants claimed that they were subject to physical torture. Once again, the court refused to consider that claim, noting, "As to what happened in the fifth-floor jail room during this thirty-six hour secret examination, the testimony follows the usual pattern and is in hopeless conflict." Rather than resolve the conflict, the court focused on the fact that Ashcraft had been held incommunicado and questioned for thirty-six hours, without respite. That was enough to suggest his confession was unconstitutional.[14]

The *Chicago Tribune* featured a lengthy editorial on the court's decision in *Ashcraft*. Noting that the court held that extended interrogation lasting overnight was impermissible, the *Tribune* declared that a "man who is deprived of sleep and forced to answer questions for 36 hours on end is being tortured quite as certainly as if he were being beaten with a rubber hose." Either practice, or holding prisoners incommunicado, was a violation of rights and plainly wrong, and it was time, the *Tribune* concluded, for police officers to "change their methods accordingly." Yet the editorial concluded on a low note, reflecting that it "remains to be seen if the ordinary police force will be found equal to the role assigned to it by the court." It seemed not. In 1944, the Republican candidate for state's attorney told members of the Chicago Civil Liberties Committee that he opposed the third degree. Three years later, in 1947, Judge Elmer Schnackenberg told a meeting of police officers that no officer should use the third degree.[15]

Those hints that observers thought torture continued seemed to be confirmed by claims made throughout the 1940s. In February 1940, Carl Hubert Erickson, a young white man accused of killing a friend in a dispute over a job, took the stand at his murder trial to claim that he only confessed after the police gave him the third degree. According to Erickson, he was taken to the East Chicago station, where he was shackled to a chair by police officers who then shined a bright light in his face and began to yell at him, demanding that he confess. When he refused, he was hit in the face by one of the officers. The state rebutted his claims with testimony by physicians at Cook County Jail, who claimed that when they examined Erickson after he was taken to the jail the day after his confession, they found no bruises. The jury either did not believe Erickson or decided they did not care; Erickson was convicted. In 1941, the *Chicago Defender* reported that detectives at the Fifth District station interrogated Arnold Bell, an African American minister, all night until he confessed to killing his wife in a fit of jealousy.[16]

In 1941, Alfred Jankowski, a white man suspected of attempting to rape a young woman at the south end of Grant Park, claimed he confessed to the crime after being beaten and threatened with future beatings. In the middle of the decade, two other white men, John Machul and Rudolph Deskler, confessed to committing seventy-five burglaries in Chicago over a period of nine months in 1943. At trial, Machul testified that he did so after being beaten by officers at the Town Hall station. That same year, eighteen-year-old Walter Tranowski, arrested for kidnapping and robbery, said he was beaten into confessing and displayed bruises across his back to support his claim. In response to his claim, Judge Donald McKinlay moved Tranowski, who was white, to the county jail, where he was outside the control of the police, incurring the wrath of Wilbert Crowley in the process. As the 1940s came to an end, there was still more evidence of abusive interrogations. In the fall of

1948, officers at the Woodlawn Street station interrogated John Holiday, an African American bartender and union officer, nonstop for two days until he confessed to killing his wife. That same year, Lawrence Kelly, a white man arrested on suspicion of being part of a gang that burglarized a number of schools and businesses, claimed that he only confessed to the crime after he had been abused by the officers at the Englewood police station. The police denied any wrongdoing, Kelly was convicted, and the verdict was affirmed on appeal.[17]

Police Torture and Race

In 1953, the *Chicago Tribune*, always optimistic, reported that under Police Chief O'Connor, Chicago's Police Department had begun to place greater emphasis on the use of scientific investigation. As a result, the story continued, there was a marked decline in the use of the third degree, much to the chagrin of some of the officers on the force. As evidence of the effectiveness of the new regime, the *Tribune* pointed to the recent arrest of five men suspected in the murder of the chief of the private police department at Libby, McNeill & Libby. Unfortunately, the Libby, McNeill & Libby case was yet another one in which the defendants claimed that the police used torture to get confessions. In March 1953, several men stole $21,000 in payroll money from the Libby, McNeill, & Libby plant in Chicago. During the theft, the chief of Libby's security force was killed. In April 1953, Chicago papers reported that the last of the men suspected in the robbery had been captured, and that twenty-two-year-old Paul Crump had confessed to killing the guard. All the suspects were black. After one of the suspects, nineteen-year-old Hudson Tillman, also gave a statement that implicated four other men (including Crump) in the crime, the other men also confessed. Tillman's statement was crucial, since three of the men whom he named as participants had previously been arrested on suspicion but released because there was no evidence to tie them to the crime. In July 1953, all the defendants but Tillman, who served as the state's main witness against the other defendants and was ultimately never tried, were convicted. For the next two decades, Crump challenged his conviction in state and federal courts, winning retrials and stays of execution. In 1962, the governor of Illinois commuted Crump's death sentence to 199 years in prison without parole. That decision rested on the evidence that Crump, who had written a novel while on death row, had been completely rehabilitated. But while the courts and the governor engaged many of Crump's arguments in his long struggle with the legal system, none directly considered his claims that he had confessed after being subjected to extended torture that included being held incommunicado, kneed, struck in the face, and kicked while he was suspended by his arms.[18]

In 1955, two years after Crump was first arrested, the Chicago police located Richard Carpenter, who was wanted for killing one police officer and shooting another. Carpenter, who was white, was taken captive after taking a family hostage, and his arrest followed a manhunt that took several days and thirty squads of police officers. His capture, which was covered by local TV and radio stations, was unquestionably violent. The *Chicago Tribune* ran a photo of Carpenter after he was captured. In the photo, he was lying on the floor of the North Avenue police station, apparently unconscious. One of his arms is pinned down by a police officer's shoe, his hands are cuffed over his head, his eyes are swollen shut, and blood seems to be pouring from a wound on his head. A story in that paper recounting his arrest reported that Carpenter was "beaten before police found that he was unarmed." Not long after his arrest, Carpenter confessed to the murders. He then repudiated his confessions a few days later; commenting on his repudiation, his lawyer said that the cuts and bruises on his client made it "obvious" that Carpenter did not confess voluntarily. Carpenter was found guilty and was executed in December 1958. Roosevelt Scott, an African American arrested for murder in 1959, claimed that the officers at the Warren Street station questioned him for twenty-four hours, during which time they struck him with a black-jack and a baseball bat, hit him on the head with a phone book, and forced him to sit, naked, on a chair while officers struck his testicles.[19]

The sense that police torture increasingly had become a racial issue led the Chicago branch of the NAACP to discuss police abuse in a forum on civil rights issues it sponsored in 1958. Not all opponents of the practice saw the problem in racial terms. The next year, the ACLU of Illinois issued a report, *Secret Detention by the Chicago Police*. The report, which did not consider whether blacks were more likely to be subject to abuse than whites, condemned the police practice of holding suspects for extended periods of time and argued that the longer a person remained in custody without access to a judge or an attorney, the more likely it was that the suspect would be tortured by the police. In February 1960, Northwestern University hosted a two-day conference on criminal law administration. At the meeting, Bernard Weisberg, the general counsel for the Illinois branch of the American Civil Liberties Union, called for an end to secret interrogations and the third degree. Fred Inbau, professor at Northwestern and noted criminologist, argued, against Weisberg, that secret interrogations were sometimes the only way that crimes could be solved, and that they only way the third degree could be stopped was if a law was passed outlawing the use of confessions as evidence. While Weisberg suggested that suspects being interrogated should have access to counsel and other rights in order to protect them from police abuse, other participants, including Orlando Wilson, dean of the Department of Criminology at the University of California and the head of a task force that was to select the next commissioner of Chicago's police department, argued that the only way to reduce the crime rate was to reduce the number of restrictions on police rather than increase them.[20]

Interestingly, Wilson's committee picked him to be the next superintendent of police, and Inbau went on to publish articles arguing that police should be subject to fewer restrictions, particularly during interrogation, since often confessions were the only way to break a case. Inbau suggested that if police were properly trained, compensated, and freed of political pressure they would be able to interrogate without abusing suspects. The federal government was not so sure. In 1962, the Justice Department called on Congress to pass a civil rights law that would increase the penalties on law enforcement officers who beat or threatened suspects. That same year, the Chicago Police Department's youth division formally banned use of the third degree, though the *Chicago Tribune* reported that many of the "old-timers" in the unit objected to the ban.[21]

It's hard to say why those old-timers complained, since claims of police torture made in the 1960s often sounded as if they had been ripped from the pages of the *Chicago Tribune* in the 1920s and 1930s. In 1960, Roosevelt Freeman, an African American, said that he was beaten with fists and struck with a rubber hose by police officers during an interrogation. That same year, Lennette Brown, another African American man, said he was beaten by police officers who told him what to say at the coroner's inquest and in his confession. As the 1960s began, white suspects also complained they were subject to police torture. A year after Lennette Brown's arrest, Robert Earl asserted that he was punched, kicked, threatened with a beating, and deprived of food or drink until he agreed to confess, while his codefendant, seventeen-year-old Vernon Cocroft, said he had been punched; kicked; denied food, drink, and cigarettes; and prevented from calling his family while he was being interrogated. In 1962, Eugene Izzi claimed that he confessed to murder after being abused by members of the Cook County Sheriff's Police Department, and that same year, Robert Hartgraves said that he was held incommunicado and deprived of sleep by officers who questioned him all night and also beat him. A year later, James McCasle asserted that he was beaten and forced to play Russian roulette by police officers during his interrogation. In 1965, Otis McNeill claimed that the officers at 11th and State beat him and threatened that his ill father would remain in custody if he did not confess to robbery. Although the records are unclear, all six men were apparently white.[22]

Torture as Control

Most people who complained of torture at the hands of Chicago's police between 1930 and 1970 claimed that they were beaten or otherwise abused in an effort to get them to confess. Some, however, made another claim. At the start of the 1930s, the Wickersham Commission noted that the police in Chicago sometimes used beatings and other forms of violence to punish suspects rather than to induce confessions, and there was plenty of evidence of this form of summary justice. In August 1931, two African American men involved in a Communist Party–sponsored march to protest an eviction were shot by police officers who claimed the men posed a threat to public safety. A third man, also African American, was found shot to death shortly after the protest. The party charged that all three had been assassinated by the police and led rallies and protests to condemn police violence. In 1933, Joseph Merkel complained that police officer Anthony Bradtke beat him on the street after Merkel asked to see Bradtke's identification. That same year, William Marston said he was beaten by a police officer during a routine traffic stop. A year later, after James Troutman died following a police beating that broke several of his vertebrae, the Chicago branch of the NAACP began to investigate police abuse at the Wabash Avenue station on Chicago's West Side. Troutman, nineteen years old, had been arrested with several other African American suspects after the murder of a police officer, and there were claims he was beaten by several of the officers during his arrest. Three years later, on Memorial Day 1937, a police squad of over two hundred men met striking steelworkers on a field on Chicago's far South Side. By the end of the day, ten of the marchers were dead or dying of gunshot wounds, dozens more marchers had been shot, and sixty others had injuries as a result of beatings they received at the hands of the police during the Memorial Day Massacre. The officer in charge of the police response on Memorial Day was John Prendergast, one of the new breed of "humanitarian" leaders of the police department that the *Tribune* had celebrated in 1932.[23]

In 1938, the ILD magazine *Equal Justice* reported that John Robinson, an African American man who was arrested for intoxication, claimed that the officers at the Maxwell Street station beat and kicked him during his arrest and then dragged him down the stairs at the station. Tony Santucci, a white youth arrested for robbery, said he was beaten by officers two days before his arrest and then threatened with a second beating at the time of his arrest by the same officers. These practices apparently continued into the 1940s and beyond. Richard Heirens, arrested for murder in 1946, claimed he was beaten on the head during his arrest in addition to being burned with ether; deprived of food, drink, and sleep; and held incommunicado for six days. That same year, Leslie Wakat, arrested on suspicion of robbery, claimed he was struck in the face, beaten with a stick, and had his arm twisted behind his back while he was handcuffed at the scene of the crime. The results of that mistreatment were more dramatic than that list suggests. According to the ACLU, Wakat had "broken bones in his right hand, multiple bruises on his chest, arms, buttocks, shins and shoulders, and . . . injuries to his left leg and knee so serious as to require eight months of treatment." The ACLU report indicates that the police claimed Wakat suffered those injuries after grabbing an officer's gun and falling down a flight of stairs in the resulting tussle.[24]

The complaints just went on. In 1952, Casimir Koprowski, a white, disabled navy veteran, filed a federal lawsuit claiming that two Chicago police officers beat him after he was ticketed for parking illegally. At a hearing on his claim in 1954, Koprowski testified that two officers, Ben Oratowski and Tod Porterfield from the Summerdale station, pushed him into their squad car, where Porterfield kneed him in the groin, punched him, and hit him in the face with his hat. This continued once they got to the station, where Oratowski joined in beating Koprowski and calling him names. In 1953, police officers looking for a child molester on Chicago's West Side seized a white man who fit the description as he was walking a small dog in the park and pushed and knocked him down before they took him to the station. There, the officers learned to their chagrin that their supposed rapist was Judge John T. Dempsey, who was quickly released with apologies. In 1957, Louis Wright said he was beaten in the squad car by the officers who took him into custody on a rape claim. Four years later, in 1961, Joseph Nischt said he was beaten by officers who arrested him for murder, and two years after that Donald DeLong charged that one of the officers who arrested him for burglary kneed him in the groin while he was putting him into the squad car. In 1964, the *Chicago Defender* reported that police officers at the Fillmore station beat Eldridge Johnson as a form of summary punishment. The next year, Jeffroe Chandler, accused of theft, said he was struck at the scene by arresting officers.[25]

The Wickersham Commission described the tendency of the Chicago police to engage in "brutal arrests" but did not consider individual claims of brutal arrests as part of its study of the third degree. Today we draw a similar distinction, considering acts of police violence during arrest to be misconduct rather than police torture. But the arrests of Lesley Wakat, Richard Carpenter, and others suggest that it is often hard to draw a clear line between violence at the point of arrest and violence intended to coerce a confession. Indeed, the United Nations Declaration Against Torture draws no distinction between torture used to obtain confessions, and "any act by which severe pain or suffering, whether physical or mental, is intentionally inflicted on a person for such purposes as . . . punishing him for an act he or a third person has committed or is suspected of having committed, or intimidating or coercing him or a third person."[26]

Failure of the Courts

From the 1930s through the end of the 1960s, the reception of claims of police torture at trial was much as it had been in Nixon's case. Even defendants like Carl Erickson, who had neutral witnesses who testified to hearing complaints about abuse or seeing evidence of bruising, rarely were able to convince jurors to credit their claims of torture. Most could not even point to obvious bruises, since they had been hit in the stomach or over the kidneys, or other places where bruises did not show, and often the police kept suspects in custody at station houses, rather than taking them to court or county jail where any marks might be seen.[27]

The police continued to categorically deny that they used the third degree or beat suspects during interrogations. In 1941, when Alfred Jankowski testified that he confessed to attempted rape after being beaten, Sergeant Truska testified that Jankowski was assaulted by outraged bystanders during his arrest. At a pretrial hearing on Hector Verburgh's claim that he had been tortured by the police, Police Commissioner John Prendergast swore that he opposed use of the third degree when he was chief of police, and Frank Pape, an officer who helped arrest and examine Verburgh, denied that any of the officers involved in the investigation used the third degree.

In 1946, when Leslie Wakat was arrested for burglary, the police at the Town Hall station put him through torture so extreme that by the time he confessed he had broken bones in addition to the bruises on his legs and arms and an injury to his knee. At trial, the jury found him guilty after the police testified he suffered those injuries resisting arrest. In 1953, seven years after his conviction, the Illinois Supreme Court credited his claims of torture and ordered him released. Four years after that, a federal jury ruled in Wakat's favor in a civil rights claim against the arresting officers and awarded him $15,000 in damages. As the ACLU noted in its coverage of Wakat's case, his was a rare instance where a victim of police torture was able to win some sort of a verdict against the officers who assaulted him. In most of the rare occasions when police officers were prosecuted for abusing suspects, jurors failed to convict.[28]

In 1953, five police officers were charged with aggravated assault and attempted murder after Anthony DeDosa claimed that they beat him while they questioned him about a theft in November 1952. The officers were tried twice in 1953. At the first trial, the jury found them not guilty of assault with intent to murder but did find them guilty of aggravated assault. They were then tried a second time on the assault claims and acquitted. In 1950, nineteen-year-old Andrew Johnson collapsed and died from a lacerated kidney during an interrogation at the detective bureau. At the inquest hearing on his death, Andrew Aitken, chief of detectives, and John Golden, homicide lieutenant, both testified that the police did not beat prisoners. A police doctor testified that they found no bruises on his body, and the coroner's physician speculated that Johnson's kidney might have been injured when he fainted and fell off the chair he was sitting in during the interrogation.[29]

Failures of Appeal

In the 1940s and 1950s, most defendants still did not appeal their convictions. Most often, the problem was the cost of the appeal; the price of the trial transcript was a bar for most defendants. That changed in the late 1950s, when the Supreme Court of the United States held that criminal defendants were entitled to a free transcript on appeal. But before that, appeals were the exception, not the rule. Those defendants who did appeal had mixed results. Tony Santucci, convicted the same year as Robert Nixon, did win a new trial based on his claims that he was beaten by officers both before and after his arrest. David Goldblatt, the so-called goon killer, had his conviction for murder reversed on appeal because the Illinois Supreme Court credited his claims that his confession was coerced from him by physical abuse.[30]

In 1949, the Illinois General Assembly passed a postconviction hearing act, which allowed individuals to raise constitutional challenges to their convictions. Although the act was denounced, notably in a *Chicago Tribune* editorial, it was written to help those who had not been able to afford to appeal their convictions, particularly those whose convictions rested on confessions obtained through the third degree. Yet as the case of Emil Reck demonstrates, that law did not provide much help. Reck was convicted of the murder of Silber Peacock in 1936, and sentenced to 199 years in prison, notwithstanding the fact that Reck claimed that he confessed only after he had been tortured for several days by police at the North Avenue station. Reck's claims of torture were corroborated by witnesses at his hearing to exclude his confession, witnesses that included codefendants who testified that they also had suffered torture at the hands of the police, or saw or heard Reck being beaten or pleading for mercy; doctors who treated him at Cook County Hospital and heard his complaints that he had been "scuffling with police"; or those who saw him during the interrogation and agreed he looked unwell. Reck's family could not afford to pay for an appeal, so it was not until the 1940s that he was able to appeal his case. At his first, direct appeal in 1945, Reck could not afford to have his lawyer obtain a transcript, so he had to appeal on issues raised in the files with the clerk of the court. As a result, the torture claim, which only appeared in the trial and hearing testimony, was not a subject of an appeal. Reck lost. In the 1950s, he found another lawyer, who was able to file a postconviction petition on his behalf. That petition did raise the issue of torture, and Reck was given a hearing on that claim. But in the end, the judge who heard Reck's postconviction petition was unwilling to reconsider the decisions of the judge and jury at the original trial, and so Reck's conviction stood. That decision was affirmed, once again, by the Illinois Supreme Court. After that, Reck's attorneys filed a federal habeas corpus claim. The claim was considered by a federal district judge who wrote an elaborate opinion that concluded, in the end, that even while Reck's claims of torture were credible, it was improper to use collateral review so long after the fact of his conviction to release him from prison. The Seventh Federal Circuit Court of Appeals affirmed that decision, and Reck's lawyers appealed to the United States Supreme Court. That court reversed his conviction in 1961, but its ruling did not touch his claims that he had confessed after being subject to extended physical abuse. Instead, the court reversed his conviction on the ground that his extended detention, particularly in light of his low IQ, made it more likely than not that Reck's confession had been coerced.[31]

   In its decision in *Reck*, the United States Supreme Court refused to do what it declared in *Chambers v. Florida* was the thing that all courts should do in torture cases: to look closely into the trial court record. As the court's opinions on police torture claims in the 1950s made clear, the court was also influenced by a concern that it not involve itself too far in state court criminal matters. Theories of federalism, in this instance the idea that even the United States Supreme Court should leave it to the states to set the standards for their courts and monitor criminal justice in their own jurisdictions, first arose in dissenting opinions in police torture cases in the late 1940s and early 1950s. As is sometimes the case, those dissents gradually became the majority opinion. By the late 1950s, the United States Supreme Court had adopted a policy regarding torture claims that deferred to the rulings of the trial judge and the determinations of the judge or jury. This sort of deference was not unique to claims of police torture; scholars have argued that the United States Supreme Court has deferred to local perceptions and standards in cases involving the death penalty. But in police torture cases, as in other instances, it meant that constitutional principles of due process and other rights were subject to local norms.[32]

A few years after it ruled in Emil Reck's case, the United States Supreme Court tried to solve the problem of police torture indirectly. In *Miranda v. Arizona*, the court adopted the so-called Miranda rules in part to try to give suspects in police custody the opportunity to be advised by a lawyer. The court was quite explicit about its hope that this would, finally, bring the third degree to an end. After referring to cases and studies that had found that the third degree had not yet come to an end, and noting that the third degree created a serious danger of false confessions, the court concluded that the best way to bring police interrogations under control was to set a limit on custodial interrogations by the police. The answer, the court concluded, was to make it more likely that an individual would have a lawyer present whenever he or she was interrogated by the police. The Miranda rules were intended to serve that purpose.[33]

A New Era?

A year after *Miranda* was decided, the Chicago Police Department created the Gang Intelligence Unit (GIU) in 1967 to bring street gangs under control. Although the interracial unit, which worked out of police headquarters, was supposed to target all youth gangs, it quickly focused its attention on African American and Hispanic gangs on Chicago's South and West Sides. The unit, which began with ten officers, grew rapidly, first to thirty-eight officers, and then to two hundred in late 1968, and ultimately to more than two hundred in early 1969. Its decline was nearly as fast as its growth. In early 1971, Chicago declared victory over the gangs and reduced the unit from 185 to 52 officers.[34]

Perhaps coincidentally, the reduction of the GIU came in the midst of a criminal trial that raised serious questions about the unit's tactics. On August

13, 1970, detective James Alfano of GIU was shot in the back as he sat in an unmarked police car behind the Southmoor Hotel in Chicago's Woodlawn neighborhood. Three days later, Alfano died. In the days that followed the shooting, other members of GIU, joined by Chicago detectives, police officers, and Cook County sheriff's deputies, swarmed over the Woodlawn and South Shore neighborhoods around the Southmoor, hunting for members of the Black P. Stone Rangers, an African American gang whose leaders purportedly had ordered a sniper attack on Alfano and other officers. By October, nearly twenty men believed to be members of the gang, several as young as fifteen years old, were in custody as part of the investigation into the murder. In mid-December, the trial of seven of the suspects began at the criminal courts at Twenty-sixth and California Avenue. A month later, all seven defendants were found not guilty.[35]

There were a number of problems with the prosecution's case: its chief witness admitted he lied repeatedly during the course of the investigation. Four witnesses for the state, including three police officers, claimed to be able to see various defendants and other evidence at the scene of the murder by way of a street light that the prosecution's own photographs demonstrated did not exist. In addition, the defense team of James Montgomery Jr., Sam Adam, and R. Eugene Pincham made repeated efforts to show that their clients were tortured by the Chicago police. Cross-examining Caesarei Marsh, a gang member turned state's witness, Montgomery asked Marsh if it was not true that he was at police headquarters when a black police officer threw one member of the Rangers into an interrogation room. Montgomery also asked Marsh if that same man did not come out of the interrogation room thirty minutes later bleeding, gasping for air, and nearly unable to walk. The trial judge sustained the prosecution's objection to the question, so Marsh did not answer. At another point, however, Montgomery and his cocounsel were able to put a statement Marsh made into evidence. In that statement, which he gave to Montgomery during an interview in September 1970, Marsh claimed that after he was arrested on August 14, he was threatened, beaten, and tortured by officers associated with GIU until he implicated the seven defendants on trial.[36]

The defense team had put on considerably more evidence about the torture meted out to their clients and other suspects at the pretrial hearing to suppress the confession of Dennis Griffin, one of the defendants. Altogether, the defense offered nearly a week's worth of testimony that elaborated that claim. At the hearing, fifteen-year-old James Ownes testified that after he was arrested, he was taken to police headquarters, where he was interrogated for nearly fourteen hours between his arrest at noon until 2:00

the next morning. During the interrogation he claimed he was beaten in the chest, and hit in the stomach by Ronald Smith, an African American officer working for GIU. Another witness, seventeen-year-old Ronald Florence, testified that he saw Dennis Griffin at 11th and State the morning after his arrest and that Griffin had a swollen right eye and was wearing a bloody shirt. Toward the end of the hearing, Griffin himself testified that he signed his confession only after suffering through several rounds of torture. At first, he was beaten by two detectives from GIU, who hit him on the legs and stomach with "a hard object" after covering his head with a typewriter cover. On a second occasion, when he refused to cooperate during the investigation, the same officers put another plastic cover over his head and then "pulled down my pants, made my penis hard, and then I felt an electric shock. I passed out." Griffin testified that when he came to, he was hanging out of a window head first, with a rope tied around his ankles. One of the officers told him that if he did not sign the statement, the police would kill Griffin and his mother. Another defendant, Ronald Florence, also testified that he was beaten and hung out of a window on the eighth floor of police headquarters. Both Griffin and Florence claimed that an assistant state's attorney, James Meltreger, was present during most of their interrogations and knew what was being done, although he was out of the room when the officers tortured them. In the end, Griffin's confession was barred, but not because of the claims of torture. Instead, Judge Louis Garippo excluded the confession because the police violated Griffin's rights by not allowing him to have his lawyer present while he was interrogated. Even earlier in the case, at a bond hearing on August 18, 1970, Montgomery asked the judge conducting the hearing to take notice of the fact that one of the men in custody, Lee Jackson, had "a swollen upper lip and several teeth missing."[37]

After the verdict, there was outrage over the state's failure to obtain a conviction in the case, but it tended to focus on the weakness of the state's evidence rather than the claims about police practice. There was little attention paid to the claims of police torture or the charge, made by the defense attorneys at trial, that the state's attorneys trying the case attempted to put into evidence materials that had been prepared after the trial began, rather than during the investigation into the crime. The ruling by Judge Garippo seems to prove that the *Miranda* rules could be a significant check on police misconduct, since it was the failure of the police to let Griffin consult his lawyer, rather than what Griffin claimed the police did to him during the interrogation, that led to his confession being excluded from evidence. But if any of the claims by any of the defense witnesses that they were tortured by the police at 11th and State were true, then Judge Garippo's ruling was a sign that *Miranda* failed to stop police torture.[38]

Writing about the use of torture in Brazil, Paul Chevigny concluded that the people who were tortured were those who were "marginal." These were people who were only quasi-citizens, as Darius Rejali put it in his study of torture, the people who solid citizens did not feel were entitled to the full protections of the law. The logic in Chicago was similar; as the city's police captains and state's attorneys put it in the 1920s, it was okay to torture the guilty. The claims of police torture made in the 1940s, 1950s, 1960s, and early 1970s suggest that logic continued to influence criminal justice in Chicago even after the Supreme Court decided *Brown v. Mississippi* in 1936. Across that same period, the people who claimed they were subject to police torture were almost invariably male and increasingly were African American. That shift is not unexpected, in that period, crime, as Khalil Gibran Muhammad has argued, became equated with race, and blacks became presumptively criminals.[39]

CONCLUSION

THE BURDEN OF PROOF

VICTIMS, LAWYERS, AND HISTORIANS all find it hard to prove that police torture happened. There are few records that document actual instances of torture; individual claims of torture are easily dismissed as overwrought exaggerations or outright lies, particularly when they are made by individuals accused of crimes and are denied by scores of police officers and state's attorneys. Those problems of proof are made more complicated when the individual claiming torture is unable to point to any obvious marks or bruises. But it is also hard to prove torture when we do not want to believe it has happened or are willing to look the other way because torture gets results or provides just one more layer of punishment to the criminals who terrorize our neighborhoods. Those difficulties are compounded when courts of appeal are so willing to defer to the decisions of jurors that they ignore uncontroverted evidence of bruises, uncontradicted testimony about being interrogated through the night, or the simple fact that a suspect was held incommunicado for several days to facilitate the process.

The history of police torture in Chicago between 1871 and 1971 demonstrates that individual claims of torture are, unfortunately, as easy to dismiss as they are hard to substantiate. Robert Nixon's case may raise questions about whether he was tortured. Certainly the confused and contradictory evidence at his trial, and the many inconsistencies and inaccuracies in the confessions offered in his case, raise serious and reasonable doubts about his guilt. Reasonable doubt is supposed to be enough to keep a person from being found guilty in our criminal justice system. In this case, those doubts should have been enough to keep Nixon from being convicted or executed for Florence Johnson's murder. They do not, in and of themselves, prove his claim that he was tortured.

Yet the claims of police torture in Chicago between 1871 and 1971 reveal patterns that lend credence to the general claim that some officers in that city used torture to get confessions and other evidence from suspects and witnesses throughout that period. Those patterns of practice, in turn, help us assess the likelihood of individual claims, like those made by Robert Nixon. We may never know beyond any doubt that Robert Nixon was tortured, but by tracing patterns and practices and examining his case in light of them we may be able to decide if his story was more likely true than not. The long history of police torture claims in Chicago suggests, initially, that the patterns of torture changed over time. An initial wave, from just after 1870 to roughly 1910, chiefly relied on nonviolent methods of coercion. This was the era of the sweatbox and isolation, where suspects were put into the uncomfortable cells or rooms until they agreed to talk, were held incommunicado for extended periods of time, or were questioned through the night or kept awake. A second, more violent wave began shortly after 1910 and lasted through the 1920s. In this period, officers complemented the older tools, especially holding suspects incommunicado, with fists, shoes, blackjacks, rubber hoses, phone books, and any object that came to hand as they beat, kicked, and struck suspects until they confessed. Especially in the early part of this period, there was nothing secret about these techniques. Torture left marks and suspects were able to show their bruises to lawyers, judges, even the Chicago City Council. That caused a popular and judicial backlash, particularly when the people bearing the marks of police violence appeared to be respectable and middle-class. While the backlash did not end police torture, it drove it into hiding. And so, in the third wave, which began after the Supreme Court's decision in *Brown v. Mississippi*, police torture was increasingly concealed. Violence was focused on the stomach and other areas that bruised less easily or obviously, and suspects were, like Nixon, often kept from court and their lawyers for extended periods of time, to allow their bruises to fade.

The torture claims suggest other patterns, as well. Familiar names and places appear in claims of torture: In the last decades of the nineteenth century, Inspectors Schaak and Bonfield were tied to claims of police abuse, most notably in the Haymarket case. By the early decades of the twentieth century, Captains Wheeler and Schuettler and Inspector Hunt appear in several claims of torture, and their stations (Harrison, Hyde Park, Maxwell Street) were named in others. In the 1910s, State's Attorney Hoyne and his assistants figured in a series of complaints. Beginning in the 1920s, members of the detective bureau, particularly the robbery squad, which prided itself on its aggressive policing, were mentioned in several complaints of torture.

The claims tie certain names and places to the practice of torture, but they suggest another pattern, like a family tree, as well. Schuettler worked with Schaak and Bonfield in the nineteenth century. John Sullivan worked as an investigator at the state's attorney's office before he became chief of detectives, while Daniel Gilbert, the chief investigator at the state's attorney's office who played such a shadowy role in Nixon's case, began in the detective bureau in the 1920s. Frank Pape, whose name was linked to torture and abuse claims in the 1950s and 1960s, got his start in the detective bureau in the 1930s.[1]

Seeing patterns is a step, but to truly understand the patterns, to truly know how to evaluate all those claims of torture, we need more. We need to see the records that show us how long suspects were held, we need the reports that show who participated in their interrogations, we need to read through the trial transcripts and confessions, and, perhaps most of all, we need the documents that will help us piece together professional genealogies. All this evidence of patterns and practices helps historians trying to make sense of a partially concealed and obstructed past; it is also a way for the legal system to assess claims of police torture.

Notes

Notes to Introduction

1. Fran Spielman, "City Council Approves $5.5 Million in Reparations for Burge Torture Victims," *Chicago Sun-Times*, May 6, 2015; Ordinance: "Call for Reparations for Victims and Family Members Affected by Law Enforcement Torture and Abuse," Chicago City Council, Record no. 02014-7069.

2. Michael Milner, "Hot Type," *Chicago Reader*, July 8, 2010, available at http://www.chicagoreader.com/chicago/john-conroy-jon-burge-police-torture/Content?oid=2074209; Michael Milner, "The Sentencing of Jon Burge," *Chicago Reader*, January 24, 2011, http://www.chicagoreader.com/Bleader/archives/2011/01/24/the-sentencing-of-jon-burge.

3. Alfred McCoy, *Policing America's Empire: The United States, The Philippines, and the Rise of the Surveillance State* (Madison: University of Wisconsin Press, 2009), 12. For a discussion of the sources I have used for this study, see the bibliography.

4. Darius Rejali, *Torture and Democracy* (Princeton, NJ: Princeton University Press, 2007), 6. "Three Slayers Scheduled to Go to Chair Tonight," *Chicago Tribune*, June 15, 1939; "Murderer Dies in Chair," *Chicago Tribune*, June 16, 1939 (Nixon's execution).

5. Richard Wright, *Native Son and How "Bigger" Was Born* (New York: Perennial Classics, 1940, 1999), 273, 309. See also "How Bigger Was Born," reprinted in ibid., 453.

6. Stanley Cohen, *States of Denial: Knowing about Atrocities and Suffering* (Cambridge, UK: Polity Press, 2001); Richard A. Leo, *Police Interrogation and American Justice* (Cambridge, MA: Harvard University Press, 2008); Jinee Lokaneeta, *Transnational Torture: Law, Violence, and State Power in the United States and India* (New York: New York University Press, 2011).

7. Kim D. Chanbonpin, "Truth Stories: Credibility Determinations at the Illinois Torture Inquiry and Relief Commission," *Loyola University Chicago Law Journal* 4 (2014): 1085; M. Spencer Green and Don Babwin, "Another Man Freed in Chicago Police Torture Saga," *USA Today*, Dec. 11, 2013, accessed May 9, 2014, http://www.usatoday.com/story/news/nation/2013/12/11/chicago-police-torture-stanley-wrice/3991469/. See generally, John Conroy, *Unspeakable Acts, Ordinary People: The Dynamics of Torture, an Examination of the Practice of Torture in Three Democracies* (Berkeley: University of California Press, 2000).

Notes to Chapter One

1. United States, Wickersham Commission, *Report on Lawlessness in Law Enforcement* (Washington, DC: United States Government Printing Office, 1931; reprint, Montclair, NJ: Patterson Smith, 1968), 19. On the commission, see Marilynn Johnson, *Street Justice: A History of Police Violence in New York City* (Boston: Beacon, 2003), 122.

2. *Stallings v. Owens*, 51 Ill. 92 (1869) (the jury entered a verdict for Stallings and that verdict was affirmed on appeal); *Miller v. Illinois*, 39 Ill. 457, 462 (1866).

3. *Illinois Statutes*, ch. 38, paras. 370, 374 (1874).

4. In his exhaustive study of torture, Darius Rejali cites sources that establish the use of sweatboxes during the Civil War. Rejali, *Torture and Democracy*, 69. The WPA slave narratives suggest

that some slave owners used them on enslaved people before that war. See, e.g., "Interview with Janie Scott on July 14, 1937," in Works Projects Administration, *Slave Narratives: A Folk History of Slavery in the United States*, Vol. 1: Alabama Narratives (Washington, DC, 1941), Project Gutenberg, http://www.gutenberg.org/files/36020/36020-h/36020-h.html.

5. "A Canadian Dude," *Chicago Tribune*, May 27, 1885; "The Iron Mountain Express Robbery," *Chicago Tribune*, October 12, 1887; "'True Bill' Voted Against Him," *Chicago Tribune*, November 30, 1895; "Gallagher's Case," *Chicago Tribune*, December 26, 1884.

6. "Namuth Nabbed," *Chicago Tribune*, January 24, 1878; "The Match-Bonds," *Chicago Tribune*, July 4, 1879; "Uncle Sam's Trap," *Chicago Tribune*, April 18, 1895; "Indicted for Arson," *Chicago Tribune*, September 29, 1893.

7. Sam Mitrani, *The Rise of the Chicago Police Department: Class and Conflict, 1850–1894* (Urbana: University of Illinois Press, 2013), ch. 6.

8. "Filed Out," *Chicago Tribune*, December 16, 1884; Elizabeth Dale, *The Chicago Trunk Mystery* (DeKalb: Northern Illinois University Press, 2011); "Chapek Had a Hard Time," *Chicago Tribune*, July, 25, 1888; "The People in Charge of the Sweat-box in Chicago," *Milwaukee Journal*, December 22, 1893.

9. Paul Avrich, *The Haymarket Tragedy* (Princeton, NJ: Princeton University Press, 1986), 221–232; "The Chicago Anarchists," *Chicago Tribune*, July 21, 1886 (referring to unnamed suspect in the Haymarket case who had been sweated); "M. J. Schaak Dies," *Chicago Tribune*, May 19, 1898 (noting his use of the sweatbox and his work on the Haymarket case).

10. Gillian O'Brien, *Blood Runs Green: The Murder that Transfixed Gilded Age America* (Chicago: University of Chicago Press, 2015); "Wing Speaks for the Defense," *Chicago Tribune*, February 25, 1894. On the petition for habeas corpus in 1889, see "Kennedy Is Surprised," *Chicago Tribune*, August 8, 1889.

11. Erik Larson, *The Devil in the White City: Murder, Magic and Madness at the Fair That Changed America* (New York: Vintage, 2003); "Bad Slip of Holmes," *Chicago Tribune*, July 25, 1895; "Find a New Victim," *Chicago Tribune*, July 26, 1895; "Two Women in the Sweat Box," *Chicago Tribune*, July 26, 1895; "New Victim Is Emily Van Tassel," *Chicago Tribune*, July 28, 1895; "Castle Is a Tomb," *Chicago Tribune*, July 28, 1895; "Recover a Portion of a Skeleton," *Chicago Tribune*, July 30, 1895.

12. See discussion in Rejali, *Torture and Democracy*, 66.

13. "Killing Emma Werner," *Chicago Tribune*, May 27, 1893; "Bandits Well Born," *Chicago Tribune*, August 27, 1894; "Man Believed to Be Dead Returns," *Chicago Tribune*, December 12, 1895; "Nine Boys Are Placed Under Arrest," *Chicago Tribune*, May 26, 1895; "Lover Is Made a Target," *Chicago Tribune*, August 15, 1896; "Rounding up the Thugs," *Chicago Tribune*, July 14, 1896; "Emil Sohlern Is Slain," *Chicago Tribune*, April 29, 1897; "Man and Wife Shot," *Chicago Tribune*, August 28, 1897; "Ryan May Tell All," *Chicago Tribune*, November 27, 1897; "Raid on Thieves' Booty," *Chicago Tribune*, June 2, 1897; "To Go to Coroner," *Chicago Tribune*, November 16, 1897; "Stories Do Not Fit," *Chicago Tribune*, December 28, 1897; "Confesses to Brutal Murder," *Chicago Tribune*, December 23, 1898; "Takes Hickey Case from Hayes," *Chicago Tribune*, September 27, 1898; "Police Hold Meier's Neighbor," *Chicago Tribune*, June 14, 1899; "Sweatbox Methods Fail," *Chicago Tribune*, March 4, 1899; "Own to Meier Murder," *Chicago Tribune*, July 8, 1899; "Becker Owns Murder," *Chicago Tribune*, March 2, 1899; "Light on Becker's Life," *Chicago Tribune*, February 27, 1899.

14. "Her Papers Stolen," *Chicago Tribune*, January 28, 1893; "Confessed to Robbing the Safe," *Chicago Tribune*, April 11, 1893; "Suspected of Robbing Mr. Forsyth," *Chicago Tribune*, February 27, 1894; "Seeley or His Twin," *Chicago Tribune*, December 11, 1894; "Nab Five Bad Men," *Chicago Tribune*, July 18, 1895; "Five in the Sweat-box," *Chicago Tribune*, March 26, 1896; "Stealing from the Mails," *Chicago Tribune*, September 21, 1888; "Thugs in the Toils," *Chicago Tribune*, June 27, 1896; "After the Lane Drug Store Looters," *Chicago Tribune*, July 4, 1896; "Short One Gives Up," *Chicago Tribune*, July 13, 1896; "Rounding up the Thugs," *Chicago Tribune*, July 14, 1896; "Plan to Kill the Chief," *Chicago Tribune*, July 14, 1896; "Spot Two of the Thugs," *Chicago Tribune*, July 15, 1896; "Holds Thugs at Bay," *Chicago Tribune*, July 26, 1896; "Schultz Quickly Identifies Cronin," *Chicago Tribune*, April 4, 1897; "Raids on Thieves' Booty," *Chicago Tribune*, June 2, 1897; "Nye Acts on Tip," *Chicago Tribune*, September 28, 1897.

15. "To Probe a Mystery," *Chicago Tribune*, December 28, 1892; "Fields Owns He Is Murderer," *Chicago Tribune*, February 22, 1896; "Three Bandits in Irons," *Chicago Tribune*, July 16, 1896; "Maud Cooper Is the Bad Burglar," *Chicago Tribune*, October 31, 1895; "Nine Boys Placed under Arrest," *Chicago Tribune*, May 26, 1895; "Ends in Mysteries," *Chicago Tribune*, January 2, 1898; "Five in the Sweat-Box," *Chicago Tribune*, March 26, 1896; "Recover a Portion of a Skeleton," *Chicago Tribune*, July

30, 1895; "Held for a Girl's Death," *Chicago Tribune*, September 26, 1896; "Thugs in the Toils," *Chicago Tribune*, June 27, 1897; "Two Women in Sweatbox," *Chicago Tribune*, July 26, 1895.

16. "Filed Out," *Chicago Tribune*, December 16, 1884; "Progress of Murder Trial," *Chicago Tribune*, October 19, 1897; "Wife's Body Found," *Chicago Tribune*, November 28, 1897.

17. "Editorial," *Chicago Tribune*, March 25, 1888; "To Do Away with the 'Sweat-Box,'" *Chicago Tribune*, February 1, 1889; "'Sweat-Box' Methods Denounced," *Chicago Tribune*, January 25, 1889; "The Cause of Personal Liberty," *Chicago Tribune*, January 30, 1889; "Of Private Detective Agencies," *Chicago Tribune*, January 5, 1896.

18. "Patrolman Dodd Makes a Capture," *Chicago Tribune*, June 25, 1896.

19. "Police Quiet about Hill," *Chicago Tribune*, August 30, 1898; "Peril of the Cells," *Chicago Tribune*, December 6, 1896.

20. "Freed of Holdup Charge: Lawyer Carl Lindenman Puts Police on Defensive," *Chicago Tribune*, August 24, 1901; "Complains to O'Neill of Sweatbox Treatment," *Chicago Tribune*, August 23, 1902.

21. "Couple Edwards with Batholin," *Chicago Tribune*, August 15, 1902; "Torturing a Prisoner," *Chicago Tribune*, August 15, 1902; "Sweatbox Held to Be Barbaric," *Chicago Tribune*, August 16, 1902; "Thompson Held to Grand Jury," *Chicago Tribune*, August 17, 1902; "Citizens Denounce Sweatbox," *Chicago Tribune*, August 17, 1902; Charles McCormick, "Letter to the Editor: Quotes Law on Civil Rights," *Chicago Tribune*, August 18, 1902; J. K. McMahon, "Letter to the Editor: Time to Close the Sweatbox," *Chicago Tribune*, August 18, 1902; Margaret Irving Hamilton, "Letter to the Editor: Unlawful, Inhumane Custom," *Chicago Tribune*, August 19, 1902; John W. Talbot, "Letter to the Editor: Says Mayor Is Responsible," *Chicago Tribune*, August 19, 1902; W. J. Reed, "Letter to the Editor: Law Should Stop Sweating," *Chicago Tribune*, August 19, 1902; "'Sweatbox' an Outrage," *Chicago Tribune*, August 19, 1902; "Just Praise and Unjust Blame," *Chicago Tribune*, August 20, 1902; "Our 'Sweat Boxes' Cozy!" *Chicago Tribune*, October 12, 1902.

22. "Admits Helping to Kill Duffy," *Chicago Tribune*, May 10, 1902; "Boy of 15 Is Held for Robbing a Strong Box," *Chicago Tribune*, July 8, 1902; "Say They Were Abused by Two City Detectives," *Chicago Tribune*, October 24, 1902; "Kills Detective; Scores Arrested," *Chicago Tribune*, May 2, 1902; "Dragnet Is Used in Bribery Case," *Chicago Tribune*, April 30, 1902; "Two Youths in Trial for Life," *Chicago Tribune*, July 18, 1902; "Sweatbox Held to Be Barbaric," *Chicago Tribune*, August 16, 1902.

23. "Wing Speaks for the Defense," *Chicago Tribune*, February 25, 1894; "Dragnet Is Used in Bribery Case," *Chicago Tribune*, April 30, 1902; "Sweatbox Held to Be Barbaric," *Chicago Tribune*, August 16, 1902.

24. "Leopold Sets Up 'Alibi,'" *Chicago Tribune*, November 6, 1906; "Nicholas Helps Leopold's Alibi," *Chicago Tribune*, April 2, 1907; *Chicago Tribune*, October 24, 1906; *Chicago Tribune*, September 28, 1907; *Chicago Tribune*, September 22, 1907; "Hat Leads to Evidence," *Chicago Tribune*, May 1, 1900; "Wife Gives Clew to Robber Band," *Chicago Tribune*, June 2, 1904; "Reject Alibi of Suspect," *Chicago Tribune*, November 28, 1905; "Sees Doom for Kendall," *Chicago Tribune*, December 4, 1905; "Alderman Heads Flying Squadron," *Chicago Tribune*, September 9, 1904; "Boy of 15 Is Held for Robbing a Strong Box," *Chicago Tribune*, July 8, 1902; "Prisoner Who Escaped May Know of Murder," *Chicago Tribune*, September 10, 1902; "Think 'Tailor Shop' Gang Caught," *Chicago Tribune*, January 18, 1902.

25. "Hat Leads to Evidence," *Chicago Tribune*, May 1, 1900; "Robber's 'Pal' Tells All," *Chicago Tribune*, December 20, 1900; "Hunt for Water Fraud," *Chicago Tribune*, May 15, 1900; "Find Fire Plot; Make Arrests," *Chicago Tribune*, June 19, 1901; "Seek the Train Robbers," *Chicago Tribune*, August 2, 1901, 3; "Freed of Holdup Charge: Lawyer Carl Lindenman Puts Police on Defensive," *Chicago Tribune*, August 24, 1901, 1.

26. "Accuses Police of Torture," *Chicago Tribune*, August 24, 1903.

27. "Seeks Death after 'Sweat,'" *Chicago Tribune*, August 10, 1907; "Holdup Men Kill One More Victim," *Chicago Tribune*, January 6, 1908.

28. John F. Geeting, "Innocent Men Forced to Admit Guilt," *Chicago Tribune*, January 13, 1907; "Police Sweating Given Hot Roast," *Chicago Tribune*, February 27, 1907; "House Solid for 'Sweatbox' Cure," *Chicago Tribune*, March 22, 1907; Andrew J. Birschi, "Editorials by the Laity: Laws that Allow Criminals to Escape," *Chicago Tribune*, November 17, 1907; "Confessions as Evidence," *Chicago Tribune*, June 30, 1909. On the water cure, see Rejali, *Torture and Democracy*, 68, 273.

29. "The 'Third Degree,'" *Chicago Tribune*, May 5, 1910.

30. "Torture in Cells Is Proven Myth," *Chicago Tribune*, May 26, 1910.

31. "Italian Kills Unknown Man," *Chicago Tribune*, November 22, 1910; "Fiance Held in Drowning of Phone Girl," *Chicago Tribune*, July 6, 1914; "Finger Prints Move Slayer to Confess," *Chicago Tribune*, May 18, 1915; "Mrs. Barnes Shot Husband After He Fell," *Chicago Tribune*, September 7, 1916; "Fitch Is Called 'Soft' by Prosecutor," *Chicago Tribune*, August 1, 1917; "Trap Reynolds Burglars: Arthur Quinn Held as Suspect; Gems Found," *Chicago Tribune*, January 20, 1917; "Spooks Stalk in Courtroom to Accuse Mable Jackman," *Chicago Tribune*, October 28, 1919.

32. "Alderman Fights Police Torturers," *Chicago Tribune*, February 2, 1913; "Haas Puts Police in Perilous Pose," *Chicago Tribune*, February 3, 1913.

33. "Admits Weakness in Alibi," *Chicago Tribune*, April 13, 1910, 5; "Tortured by Police, He Says," *Chicago Tribune*, June 13, 1913; "Charges Police Beat Him Until He Confessed Crimes," *Chicago Tribune*, March 26, 1914; "Fiancé Held in Drowning of Phone Girl," *Chicago Tribune*, July 6, 1914; "'Glass Pistol' Thief Confesses to 19 Robberies," *Chicago Tribune*, December 20, 1915; "Brentano Acts to End Police 'Third Degree,'" *Chicago Tribune*, November 23, 1918; "Trio on Joy Ride with Slain Girl Face Hard Grill," *Chicago Tribune*, April 9, 1917; *Illinois v. Colvin*, 294 Ill. 196 (1920).

34. "Fleming Denies Third Degree to Grand Jury," *Chicago Tribune*, December 3, 1918; "Alderman Says He Helped Free Crime Suspect," *Chicago Tribune*, December 19, 1919.

35. Burton Rascoe, "Chicago's Seventeen Unsolved Murders in 1915," *Chicago Tribune*, January 9, 1916; "The Third Degree," *Chicago Tribune*, May 5, 1910; "Admits Weakness in Alibi," *Chicago Tribune*, April 13, 1910; "'Glass Pistol' Thief Confesses to 19 Robberies," *Chicago Tribune*, December 20, 1915; "Trio on Joy Ride with Slain Girl Face Hard Grill," *Chicago Tribune*, April 9, 1917, 13; "'Third Degree' Yarn Fizzles," *Chicago Tribune*, September 3, 1916.

36. "Report Condemns Legal Kidnapping," *Chicago Tribune*, August 5, 1911; "Illegal Methods of Law," *Chicago Tribune*, August 7, 1911; "Accuses Police of 'Third Degree,'" *Chicago Tribune*, January 30, 1913; "Only Occasionally?," *Chicago Tribune*, January 31, 1913; "Alderman Fights Police Tortures," *Chicago Tribune*, February 2, 1913; "Haas Puts Police in Perilous Pose," *Chicago Tribune*, February 3, 1913; "On Trial for Life, She Eats Peanuts," *Chicago Tribune*, March 4, 1913; "Police Put Crime on Innocent Man," *Chicago Tribune*, April 25, 1913; "Hoyne et al. Sued by Arrest Victim," *Chicago Tribune*, July 31, 1913; "Sweated 4 Days; Sues Hoyne," *Chicago Tribune*, August 2, 1913; "U.S. Bar Committee Decries 'Third Degree,'" *Chicago Tribune*, August 16, 1913 (of course, as the story made clear, the report did not do any such thing); "The 'Third Degree,'" *Chicago Tribune*, May 5, 1910; "Asks Law to End Third Degree," *Chicago Tribune*, November 10, 1912; "On Trial for Life, She Eats Peanuts," *Chicago Tribune*, March 4, 1913.

37. "Fitch Is Called 'Soft' by the Prosecutor," *Chicago Tribune*, August 1, 1917; "Fleming Denies Third Degreeing to Grand Jury," *Chicago Tribune*, December 3, 1918; "Brentano Acts to End Police 'Third Degrees,'" *Chicago Tribune*, November 23, 1918.

38. "No Felony for Police to Beat a Man," *Chicago Tribune*, November 24, 1918; "The Leslie Verdict," *Chicago Tribune*, April 11, 1907; "Judge Asks for Third Degree Investigation," *Chicago Tribune*, November 28, 1918; "'Third Degree' Charges Bring Official Denial," *Chicago Tribune*, April 13, 1919; "'Third Degree in My Office? Bring on the Quiz': Hoyne," *Chicago Tribune*, April 19, 1919; "'Third Degree' Charges Bring Official Denial," *Chicago Tribune*, April 13, 1919. Subsequently the Cook County Grand Jury found no evidence that Assistant State's Attorney John Owen used the third degree against Radakowitz and instead praised his conduct of the investigation. "Judge Hazen Acts to Refute Jury's Attack," *Chicago Tribune*, May 3, 1919; Maclay Hoyne, "Letter to the Editor," *Chicago Tribune*, April 13, 1919. See also "Gang Confesses to 31 Crimes, Hoyne Says," *Chicago Tribune*, April 20, 1919 (claiming that all the gang members confessed voluntarily, without being subjected to the third degree).

39. "Thief at 16, Irving Schlig, Rum Fly, Murdered at 21," *Chicago Tribune*, August 29, 1925; "Judges Testify in 'Third Degree' Inquiry by Jury," *Chicago Tribune*, October 26, 1922.

40. "Picks Out Cop As Flogger in Third Degree," *Chicago Tribune*, January 31, 1923; "Story of Police Third Degree Methods Told Alderman Nearly Causes Riot in City Council Chamber," *Chicago Tribune*, January 31, 1923; "Chicago 'Clean-Ups,'" *Chicago Defender*, May 23, 1925; "Court Rebukes Schoemaker for 'Third Degree,'" *Chicago Tribune*, August 29, 1920; "Warrants for Four Cops on 'Third Degree' Charge," *Chicago Tribune*, April 21, 1921; "Judges Testify in 'Third Degree' Inquiry by Jury," *Chicago Tribune*, October 26, 1922; "Foster May Slip Police Grip," *Chicago Tribune*, December 16, 1922; "Seize $200,000 Gem Bandit," *Chicago Tribune*, January 30, 1925.

41. *Illinois v. Colvin*, 294 Ill. 196, 198 (1920); *Illinois v. Rogers*, 303 Ill. 578 (1922); *Illinois v. Frugoli*, 334 Ill. 324 (1929).

42. "Fail to Accuse Police," *Chicago Tribune*, June 20, 1924, 1; *Illinois v. Rogers*, 303 Ill. at 588; *Lawless Law Enforcement*, 136.

43. "How We Protect Our Murderers," *Chicago Tribune*, June 20, 1921; "Lyle Clawing at Cops to Aid Self, Fitzmorris Says," *Chicago Tribune*, February 23, 1923; Philip Kinsley, "'Third Degree' Bill Talked into Senate Discard," *Chicago Tribune*, March 14, 1923.

44. "Rubber Judges Blamed as Aids of Gun Toters," *Chicago Tribune*, November 15, 1924; "Chief Says Cops Shouldn't Beat Up Innocent Men," *Chicago Tribune*, July 3, 1927.

45. "Chief Says Cops Shouldn't Beat Up Innocent Men," *Chicago Tribune*, July 3, 1927.

46. "Killer Stabs Killer in County Jail," *Chicago Tribune*, June 21, 1925; "Foster May Slip 'Police Grip'," *Chicago Tribune*, December 16, 1922; "Jury Finds Beulah Annan Is 'Not Guilty'," *Chicago Tribune*, May 25, 1924; "Rum Juror and Woman Held: Questioned in Inquiry into Smale Verdict," *Chicago Tribune*, January 12, 1924; "Boy Killers Get 25 Years," *Chicago Tribune*, May 1, 1928.

47. *Illinois v. Chrfrikas*, 295 Ill. 222 (1920); *Illinois v. Rogers*, 303 Ill. 578 (1922); "Boy in $10,000 Theft Declares Cops Beat Him," *Chicago Tribune*, April 19, 1921; "Perry the Innocent," *Chicago Tribune*, December 24, 1925.

48. *Illinois v. Holick*, 337 Ill. 333 (1930); *Illinois v. Coffey*, 342 Ill. 56 (1930); "Police Slayer Guilty," *Chicago Tribune*, August 11, 1929.

49. "Immunity Claimed by Eller," *Chicago Tribune*, August 6, 1928; "Indict Two Eller Gang Witnesses," *Chicago Tribune*, November 17, 1928; "Loesch Orders Hughes before Jury," *Chicago Tribune*, June 26, 1928; "Chief Hughes Pledges Aid to Terrorist Jury," *Chicago Tribune*, June 27, 1928.

50. "The Prosecutor (in Chicago) in Felony Cases," Illinois Association for Criminal Justice in Chicago and Chicago Crime Commission, *The Illinois Crime Survey (Chicago: Blakely, 1929)*, 289, 289–291.

51. "Judge Hazen Acts to Refute Jury's Attack," *Chicago Tribune*, May 3, 1919, 1, 4; *Illinois v. Vinci*, 295 Ill. 419 (1920); *Lawless Law Enforcement*, 126.

52. "The Third Degree," *Chicago Tribune*, August 18, 1931; "Orders Quiz as Prisoner Shows Beating Marks," *Chicago Tribune*, September 18, 1931; "Policeman Today Expert in His Field," *Chicago Tribune*, May 1, 1932 (quoting a longtime observer who claimed that over the past three years the third degree was dying out).

53. *Brown v. Mississippi*, 297 U.S. 278 (1936).

54. "Trio Is Saved from Legal Lynching," *Chicago Tribune*, March 15, 1936; "A Tale of Horror," *Chicago Tribune*, March 15, 1936; "The Supreme Court and the Negro," *Chicago Tribune*, March 23, 1936; "Mississippi Torture Case in U.S. High Court," *Chicago Defender*, January 11, 1936; "Press Favors Judgment in Cropper Case," *Chicago Defender*, February 29, 1936; "Full Text of Mississippi Torture Case," *Chicago Defender*, February 29, 1936; "Supreme Court Reverses Mississippi Mock Trial," *Chicago Defender*, February 29, 1936. Richard A. Leo, *Police Interrogation and American Justice* (Cambridge, MA: Harvard University Press, 2008).

55. "Chicago Police Head Denies Use of the Third Degree," *Chicago Tribune*, August 21, 1931.

Notes to Chapter Two

1. "Lightning Perils Four; More Rains Expected Today," *Chicago Tribune*, May 27, 1938; "The Weather," *Chicago Tribune*, May 27, 1938; "Sift Mass of Clews for Killer," *Chicago Tribune*, May 28, 1938; "Brick Slayer's Prints Checked with Suspects," *Chicago Daily News*, May 28, 1938; "Woman Beaten to Death in Bed; Suspect Grilled," *Chicago Daily News*, May 27, 1938; *People v. Robert Nixon*, Trial Transcript [hereafter Tr.] at 94.

2. Tr. 284. Illinois Central Railroad, *Electric Suburban Schedules between Randolph St., Matteson, South Chicago, and Blue Island*. No. 366.

3. Michael Dennis, *The Memorial Day Massacre and the Movement for Industrial Democracy* (New York: Palgrave Macmillan, 2010).

4. "Hunt Four Fast Talkers in Gem Fraud, Robbery," *Chicago Tribune*, May 27, 1938; "Moron Rescued by Police from Angry Women," *Chicago Tribune*, May 27, 1938; "Woman Victim Snares Parolee; Solve 7 Holdups," *Chicago Tribune*, May 27, 1938; "Corner N.Y. Parolee in Hotel After Gun Chase; Held as Bandit," *Chicago Tribune*, May 27, 1938.

5. Dawn Rae Flood, *Rape in Chicago: Race, Myth, and the Courts* (Urbana: University of Illinois Press, 2012), 33–35.

6. Drake and Cayton, *Black Metropolis*, 63 and Fig. 6; Chicago Commission on Race Relations, *The Negro in Chicago: A Study of Race Relations and a Race Riot* (Chicago: University of Chicago Press, 1922); William M. Tuttle Jr., *Race Riot: Chicago and the Red Summer of 1919* (Urbana: University of Illinois Press, 1970).

7. Drake and Cayton, *Black Metropolis*, 63 and Fig. 6; *The Negro in Chicago*; Tuttle, *Race Riot*; Mary Pattillo, *Black on the Block: The Politics of Race and Class in the City* (Chicago: University of Chicago Press, 2007).

8. "Chicago Police Detain 14 in Brick Killing," *Washington Post*, May 28, 1938; "Mother Murdered by Brick Wielder as She Lies in Bed," *Atlanta Constitution*, May 27, 1938.

9. Tr. 98; "Chicago Police Detain 14 in Brick Killing," *Washington Post*, May 28, 1938, X3; "Mother Murdered by Brick Wielder as She Lies in Bed," *Atlanta Constitution*, May 27, 1938, 10. Sunrooms were a characteristic piece of Chicago's turn of the century architecture. For a discussion, see Justin Manley, "A Sunroom of One's Own," *Grey City Journal* 18 (Spring 2014): 3.

10. Tr. 179–180.

11. Tr. 84-93, 172–184, 230, 241.

12. Tr. 85, 89, 93, 154, 175, 202-203, 206.

13. Tr. 172, 184, 191–193. J. Walfred Lewis, "Newly Made Police Captains," *Chicago Daily News*, June 1, 1937; "Shifts 1 Captain, 5 Lieutenants, 102 Other Police," *Chicago Tribune*, April 16, 1937.

14. Tr. 172, 184, 191–193, 238. "Brick Slayer's Prints Checked with Suspect," *Chicago Daily News*, May 28, 1938. Unfortunately, I have been unable to find copies of these photos in any of the case files.

15. J. Walfred Lewis, "Who They Are—The Officers Newly Made Police Captains," *Chicago Daily News*, June 1, 1937; Tr. 219, 225. See also Otto Erlanson, "The Scene of a Sex Offense as Related to the Residence of the Offender," *Journal of Criminal Law and Criminology* 31 (1940): 339–342; "Woman Beaten to Death in Bed," *Chicago Daily News*, May 27, 1938.

16. "Brick Slayer's Prints Checked with Suspect," *Chicago Daily News*, May 28, 1938.

17. Tr. 280–292.

18. Tr. 280–306. "Brick Moron Tells of Killing 2 Women," *Chicago Tribune*, May 29, 1938; "Science Traps Negro Moron in Five Murders," *Chicago Tribune*, June 3, 1938.

19. Tr. 208–209, 211, 226–227, 230–232, 252–255, 256-257, 297–298. Carothers was Julius Carothers, born in 1910. In 1940 he lived with his parents and several siblings at 221 East 50th Street. *1940 Federal Census*; Census Place: Chicago, Cook County, Illinois; Roll: T627_926; Page: 10A; Enumeration District: 103–152.

20. Tr. 300–301. "Brick Slayer's Prints Checked with Suspects," *Chicago Daily News*, May 28, 1938.

21. "New Police Building Ready," *Chicago Tribune*, September 9, 1928; "City Detectives at Home in New Edifice," *Chicago Tribune*, September 16, 1928; "Science Traps Moron in Five Murders," *Chicago Tribune*, June 3, 1938; Ken Alder, *The Lie Detectors: The History of an American Obsession* (New York: Free Press, 2007), 115–116; Simon Cole, *Suspect Identities: A History of Fingerprinting and Criminal Identification* (Cambridge, MA: Harvard University Press, 2001); Calvin Goddard, "Scientific Crime Detection Laboratories in Europe, Part I," *American Journal of Police Science* 1 (1930): 13.

22. "Brick Slayer's Prints Checked with Suspects," *Chicago Daily News*, May 28, 1938; "Brick Moron Tells of Killing 2 Women," *Chicago Tribune*, May 29, 1938.

23. "Sift Mass of Clews for Killer," *Chicago Tribune*, May 28, 1938; Tr. 86–87.

24. "Brick Slayer's Prints Checked with Suspects," *Chicago Daily News*, May 28, 1938.

25. "Woman Beaten to Death in Bed; Suspect Grilled," *Chicago Daily News*, May 27, 1938; "Brick Slayer's Prints Checked with Suspect's," *Chicago Daily News*, May 28, 1938; "Brick Moron Tells of Killing 2 Women," *Chicago Tribune*, May 29, 1938 (the *Tribune* characterized Nixon as slow-witted); "Link Chicago Youth to 4 Brick Slayings," *New York Times*, May 30, 1938.

26. Tr. 311–314, 317–319. The court reporter took down their statements; the transcriptions of their statements were read to the jury and survive in the court records.

27. Tr. 314–315, 397-398, 783-819.

28. Tr. 783-819. "2 Accuse Each Other in Brick Killing," *Chicago Tribune*, May 30, 1938; "Brick Slayer Is Likened to Jungle Beast," *Chicago Tribune*, June 5, 1938: "Wire Report: Husband of White Woman Murdered in Chicago Apartment Starts Fight with Accused Negro at Inquest," *American Negro Press*, June 17, 1938.

29. Tr. 783-819. "2 Accuse Each Other in Brick Killing," *Chicago Tribune*, May 30, 1938.

30. Tr. 783-819, 960-961, 995-997. "2 Accuse Each Other in Brick Killing," *Chicago Tribune,* May 30, 1938.

31. "2 Accuse Each Other in Brick Killing," *Chicago Tribune,* May 30, 1938.

32. "Brick Moron Tells of Killing 2 Women," *Chicago Tribune,* May 29, 1938; "Brick Slayer Quizzed Over Nurse's Death," *Chicago Daily News,* May 31, 1938.

33. "Fasten Double Murder in West on Brick Killer," *Chicago Tribune,* May 31, 1938; "At Funeral," *Chicago Tribune,* June 1, 1938; Tr. 315.

34. "Science Traps Moron in Five Murders," *Chicago Tribune,* June 3, 1938; Charles Leavelle, "Brick Slayer Is Likened to a Jungle Beast," *Chicago Tribune,* June 5, 1938; "Confessed Brick Slayer Re-Enacts Three Killings," *Chicago Tribune,* June 3, 1938.

35. "Science Traps Moron in Five Murders," *Chicago Tribune,* June 3, 1938. See also Tr. 263–279.

36. "Confesses to Crime Proved on Another," *New York Times,* June 7, 1938; "Negro Admits Killing Seven Women Here," *Los Angeles Times,* May 29, 1938.

37. People's Exhibit 12, Tr. 725-745; People's Exhibit 13, Tr. 746-782; People's Exhibit 14, Tr. 783-819.

38. Tr. 731, 733, 761, 767, 768, 769, 752–753, 763, 770, 771, 774, 811, 813.

39. Tr. 732, 761, 767, 798, 799-800, 804-805.

40. Tr. 729, 754–755, 786, 787–788.

41. Tr. 728, 757, 791, 793.

42. Tr. 737, 759, 805.

43. Tr. 759, 801–802.

44. Tr. 760, 761, 763, 796.

45. Tr. 733, 770-771.

46. Tr. 771, 816–818.

47. Richard A. Leo and Richard Ofshe, "The Consequences of False Confessions: Deprivations of Liberty and Miscarriages of Justice in the Age of Psychological Interrogations," *Journal of Criminal Law and Criminology* 88 (1998): 429.

48. On *Native Son* and the Nixon case, see "How Bigger Was Born," in Wright, *Native Son and How "Bigger" Was Born,* 453. On Wright's assumptions on black alienation and crime, see Naomi Murakawa, *The First Civil Right: How Liberals Built Prison America* (New York: Oxford University Press, 2014).

49. "2 Accuse Each Other in Brick Killing," *Chicago Tribune,* May 30, 1938; Charles Leavelle, "Brick Slayer Is Likened to a Jungle Beast," *Chicago Tribune,* June 5, 1938. See also "Victims Listed in 2 Year Wave of Sex Crimes," *Chicago Tribune,* May 28, 1938; "Brick Slayer's Prints Checked with Suspects," *Chicago Daily News,* May 28, 1938; "Confesses to Crime Proved on Another," *New York Times,* June 7, 1938.

50. "Confesses to Crime Proved on Another," *New York Times,* June 7, 1938; "Negro Admits Killing Seven Women Here," *Los Angeles Times,* May 29, 1938.

51. "Blame Press for Attack on Shackled Boy," *Chicago Defender,* June 18, 1938; "Ask for Change of Venue," *Plain Dealer,* June 28, 1938; Chicago Upset Over Sex Case 'Confessions,'" *New York Amsterdam News,* June 18, 1938.

52. "Chicago Upset over Sex Case 'Confessions,'" *New York Amsterdam News,* June 18, 1938; "Ask Change of Venue for Alleged Slayers," ANP Wire Service, June 24, 1938; "Chicago Youth Kicked, Hung by Ankles to Get Rape Confession," CNA Wire Service, June 1938.

53. Harry R. Hoffman, M.D., and Harry A. Pankind, M.D., "Psychiatric Examination: Robert Nixon," dated July 6, 1938; Harry R. Hoffman, M.D., and Harry A. Pankind, M.D., "Psychiatric Examination: Earl Hicks," dated July 6, 1938, in Record on Appeal.

54. Tr. 402-403, 970, 1040–1044. Hoffman and Pankind, "Psychiatric Examination: Robert Nixon."

55. "Robert Nixon" entry, 1930; Census Place: New Orleans, Orleans, Louisiana; Roll: 808; Page: 70B; Enumeration District: 0174; "Thomas Crosby" entry, 1930; Census Place: Morehead Parish, Louisiana; Roll: 799; Page: 15A; Enumeration District: 0019; "Andrew J. Servier" entry, 1930; Census Place: Tallulah, Madison, Louisiana; Roll: 795; Page: 20A; Enumeration District: 0005; "Andrew J. Servier" entry, 1940; Census Place: Tallulah, Madison, Louisiana; Roll: T627_1412; Page: 62B; Enumeration District: 33–8; Frederick Pretzie Jr. Report on Case No 38–1077, Division of Pardons and Paroles, dated October 24, 1938. In Pardon File, Robert Nixon. "Fasten Double Murder on Brick Killer," *Chicago Tribune,* May 31, 1938.

56. "Earle Hicks" entry, 1930; Census Place: Greenville, Washington, Mississippi; Roll: 1171; Page: 15A; Enumeration District: 0009; "Fasten Double Murder on Brick Killer," *Chicago Tribune*, May 31, 1938.

57. "Florence Whitton" entry, 1910; Census Place: Manhattan Ward 12, New York, New York; Roll: T624_1013; Page: 4A; Enumeration District: 0293; "Florence Whitton" entry, 1920; Census Place: Chicago Ward 5, Cook (Chicago), Illinois; Roll: T625_308; Page: 4A; Enumeration District: 259; Image: 240.

58. "Elmer Johnson" entry, 930; Census Place: Chicago, Cook, Illinois; Roll: 425; Page: 29A; Enumeration District: 0284.

59. "Beats Slayer of Wife," *Chicago Tribune*, June 8, 1938; "Husband Beats Confessed Slayer of Wife at Inquest," *Washington Post*, June 8, 1938; "Blame Press for Attack on Shackled Boy," *Chicago Defender*, June 18, 1938. Indictment 38–1077 (Florence Johnson murder); Indictment 38–1078 (Anna Kuchta murder); Indictment 38–1079 (Florence Thompson Castle murder); Indictment 38–1091 (Betty Bryant rape), Felony Criminal File Copies, Case No. 38 CR 1077, 1078, 1079, and 1091, Archives Department, Clerk of the Circuit Court of Cook County; Memorandum of Orders, Case no. 38–1077 in Record on Appeal, People v. Nixon. See also "Grand Jury Acts to Speed Trial of Rapist Nixon," *Chicago Tribune*, June 9, 1938; "Rapist Indicted for Slaying of Three Women," *Chicago Tribune*, June 11, 1938.

60. "Chicago Cops Third Degree Threatens New Victims," *Equal Justice* (June 1938): 4; "Rapist Slayer of Three Women to Be Arraigned," *Chicago Tribune*, June 12, 1938; "Confessed Brick Murderers Deny Crimes in Court," *Chicago Tribune*, June 15, 1938.

61. Randi Storch, *Red Chicago: American Communism at its Grassroots, 1928–1935* (Urbana: University of Illinois Press, 2009); Richard C. Cortner, *A "Scottsboro" Case in Mississippi: The Supreme Court and* Brown v. Mississippi (Jackson: University Press of Mississippi, 1986), 33–39; Dan Carter, *Scottsboro: A Tragedy of the American South* (rev. edition, Baton Rouge: Louisiana State University Press, 2007).

62. "600 Pay Final Tribune to Atty. Joseph E. Clayton Jr.," *Chicago Defender*, September 18, 1956.

63. Oral History Interview, EPISODES: William Sylvester White, September 5, 2000, *The History Makers*, http://www.idvl.org/thehistorymakers/Bio40.html.

64. "W. Crowley, Judge for 29 Years, Dies," *Chicago Tribune*, October 3, 1976; "J. S. Boyle, Helped Consolidation of the Courts," *Chicago Tribune*, November 29, 1983.

65. "Husband of White Woman Murdered in Chicago Apartment Starts Fight with Accused Negro at Inquest," *ANP Newswire*, June 17, 1938; "Memorandum of Orders," Case no. 38–1077, in Record on Appeal.

66. "Petition on behalf of Robert Nixon," dated June 28, 1938; "Petition on behalf of Earl Hicks," dated June 28, 1938; "Order" dated June 28, 1938; Hoffman and Pankind, "Psychiatric Examination: Robert Nixon;" Harry R. Hoffman, M.D., and Harry A. Pankind, M.D., "Psychiatric Examination: Earl Hicks," dated July 6, 1938, in Record on Appeal.

67. "Chicago Youth Kicked, Hung by Ankles to Get Rape Confession," CNA Wire Service, June 1938; "Police Beat Us, Charge Accused Pair: Hicks and Nixon Say They Confessed After Third Degree Tactics," *Chicago Defender*, June 25, 1938; "Chicago Upset over Sex Case 'Confessions,'" *New Amsterdam News*, June 18, 1938; "Youth, 18, Says Officers Tortured Him to Gain Assault-Murder Convictions," *Atlanta Daily World*, June 18, 1938.

Notes to Chapter Three

1. "Chicago Youth Kicked, Hung by Ankles to Get Rape 'Confession,'" *Capitol Plaindealer*, June 24, 1938; Memorandum of Orders, Case No. 38–1077.

2. Memorandum of Orders, Case No. 38–1077; "Chicago Youth Coerced to Plea of Guilty," *CNA Wire Service*, August 1938; Youth Held Sane at Trial Admits Part in Killing," *Chicago Daily News*, July 25, 1938. The jury at the sanity hearing was composed of Thomas Martin Doran, John Wickawski, Joseph Novak, Bernart Zinder, Carl Flersheim, Earl Petterin, Lawrence Samuelson, Alex Esones, Otto Krahm, Peter Jensen, John Shaller, and William Rodenbostel. Record on Appeal, People v. Nixon, 37–41.

3. The jury that sat to hear the trial was composed of Harold Guy Brent, Frank Cepak, William W. Hadnott, W. E. McClure, Jerry Sulan, Lawrence D. Chouinard, Frank J. Finger, Leonard Heih,

August E. Sandberg, Ezra S. Stevens, and Charles J. Weir; Record on Appeal, People v. Nixon, 42–43; "State Excuses Race Juror as Swain Trial Opens," *Chicago Defender*, November 28, 1936.

4. Tr. 71–79, 80.

5. Tr. 80–83.

6. Tr. 84-87, 88-93.

7. Tr. 90, 91.

8. Tr. 94, 96, 107, 108.

9. Tr. 96–97, 132-136. "Victim's Sister Again Identifies 'Brick-Slayer,'" *Chicago Daily News*, July 28, 1938.

10. Tr. 96–97, 109, 112–114, 117–119, 123, 132–136.

11. Tr. 126–129, 148, 150, 168-170.

12. Tr. 137, 142-146, 167, 169.

13. Tr. 176–178, 248, 251.

14. Tr. 212-216, 219-222, 246-247, 259-262, 263–279; Fred Inbau, "Clarence W. Muehlberger, 1896–1966," *Journal of Criminal Law and Criminology* 57 (1967): 517.

15. Tr. 274.

16. Tr. 263–265. "Sift Mass of Clews for Sex Killer," *Chicago Tribune*, May 28, 1938. Karl Landsteiner standardized blood types in 1901. By 1932, Dr. Leon Lattes in Italy had developed two ways to test bloodstains on fabric to determine type.

17. Tr. 280–306; 1940 Federal Census, Chicago, Cook County, Illinois, Tract 584-A, Pages 130–197.

18. Allan H. Spear, *Black Chicago: The Making of a Negro Ghetto, 1890–1920* (Chicago: University of Chicago Press, 1967); Drake and Cayton, *Black Metropolis*; Arnold R. Hirsch, *Making the Second Ghetto: Race and Housing in Chicago, 1940–1960* (Chicago: University of Chicago Press, 1998), 4–5. For examples, see *1940 Federal Census; Census Place: Chicago, Cook, Illinois*; Roll: *T627_926*; Page: *10A*; Enumeration District: 130–201; 1940 Census, 130–184A; 1940 Census, 130–197.

19. Tr. 284, 296, 305-306.

20. Tr. 307–311, 311-327. For the moments when Harvey testified that he did not see any promises or threats made, or see either suspect abused, see Tr. 321, 323–324.

21. Tr. 313, 313, 318, 320, 330. The confessions were People's Exhibits 12, 13, 14, 15, 16, 16A, and 16B.

22. Tr. 331-332. "Fight in Court over Confessions in Sex Slaying," *Chicago Daily News*, July 29, 1938.

23. Tr. 328, 331, 339, 369, 371. "Police Beat Us, Charge Accused Pair: Hicks and Nixon Say They Confessed after Third Degree Tactics," *Chicago Defender*, June 25, 1938; "Chicago Upset over Sex Case 'Confessions,'" *New Amsterdam News*, June 18, 1938; "Youth, 18, Says Officers Tortured Him to Gain Assault-Murder Convictions," *Atlanta Daily World*, June 18, 1938; "Chicago Youth Kicked, Hung by Ankles to Get Rape Confession," *Capital Plaindealer*, June 24, 1938. That motion is a bit of a mystery: it was filed with the court, and the proof of service on the petition indicated that it was received by the state's attorney's office by J. J. Hussey. But while the motion itself indicated it would be presented on July 21, there is no mention of the motion in the Memorandum of Orders for the case. Instead, that docket sheet shows that a second motion for a severance, this one filed by Keys on behalf of Hicks, was heard and denied on July 22. Hicks's petition in support of his motion for a severance does not make any claim of torture. Notice of Motion and Petition for Severance, filed on behalf of Robert Nixon, Case No. 38-1077; Notice of Motion and Petition for Severance, filed on Behalf of Earl Hicks, Case No. 38-1077. Both are in the Record on Appeal. "Brick Slayer's Confession Up for Trial Today," *Chicago Tribune*, July 29, 1938; "Fight in Court Over Confessions in Sex Slaying," *Chicago Daily News*, July 29, 1938; "Charge and Deny 3d Degree Used on Brick Slayer," *Chicago Tribune*, July 30, 1938.

24. Tr. 371–450.

25. Tr. 373-374.

26. Tr. 375-376, 377-378, 380-381, 382.

27. Tr. 381-384, 430.

28. Tr. 384-385, 386-387, 388.

29. Tr. 387-388, 389–390.

30. Tr. 391–392.

31. Tr. 399-400, 401, 402, 412.

32. Tr. 546–550.

33. Their evidence may be found in the Trial Transcript 450–710. For Erwin's evidence, see Tr. 545–551.

34. Tr. 474, 476, 483, 485, 488, 490, 506, 555-556, 564, 569, 571, 574-575, 577.

35. Tr. 483, 490-491, 509, 511-512, 525, 529, 536, 555, 578-579, 590-591, 600, 604-605, 687-688, 692, 697.

36. Tr. 459, 536, 537, 542-543, 648, 651, 688, 689, 697, 701-702, 704, 707.

37. Tr. 459-463, 464, 514-515, 650, 655-657, 708-709.

38. Hussey, in fact, was "positive" Nixon was not taken out of the lockup between 8:00 a.m. and 4:00 p.m. on Friday, May 27, Saturday, May 28, Sunday, May 29, or Monday, May 30. Tr. 555. Since Hussey did not work Monday, May 30, he probably meant May 31. Tr. 553. There was considerable evidence, not just from Nixon, that Nixon was taken from the lockup several times on each of those days during that period. On cross examination, Hussey modified his testimony somewhat, to say that he was not sure if Nixon was taken out of the lockup while he was on duty. Tr. 558–559. On the trip to the reenactment, see Tr. 517, 526-527, 538, 689, 699.

39. Tr. 653. Wilson, in contrast, said he did specifically ask Nixon if anyone had beaten, misused, or mistreated him and that Nixon said no. Tr. 463.

40. Tr. 536–704. See also transcript 627 (no records of prisoners being taken out of lockup, no way to know when prisoners were removed or by whom).

41. Tr. 725–819. "Brick Slaying Confessions Put before the Jurors," *Chicago Tribune*, August 2, 1938.

42. Tr. 884–928.

43. Tr. 930, 94-943, 944, 947, 950-951, 954.

44. Tr. 957, 958, 960, 961-962.

45. Tr. 968, 969-985, 970 (Memphis), 984-985 (map), 995-997 (apple), 1094 (map).

46. Tr. 1027, 1034–1039, 1300–1304. Robert Mearns Yerkes, *Psychological Examination in the United States Army* (Washington, DC: General Printing Office, 1921).

47. Tr. 1039, 1045–1049.

48. Tr. 1060–1061, 1064, 1086, 1114–1115.

49. Tr. 1062, 1092, 1125, 1127.

50. Tr. 1134–1140, 1141–1145, 1155, 1166–1167, 1177–1184, 1207–1208.

51. Tr. 1125–1127; Drake and Cayton, *Black Metropolis*, ch. 21.

52. Tr. 1224–1229, 1231, 1234–1239, 1241; "Brick Moron Tells of Killing 2 Women," *Chicago Tribune*, My 29, 1938.

53. Tr. 1242–1249.

54. Tr. 1250–1254, 1254–1261.

55. Tr. 1261–1266.

56. Tr. 1267–1271, 1271–1272, 1272–1274, 1275–1277, 1281–1289.

57. Tr. 1290–1299.

58. Tr. 1307–1319.

59. Tr. 1321, 1325-13-26, 1334, 1341, 1495–1497.

60. Tr. 1329–1331.

61. Tr. 1351, 1352, 1353-55, 1357, 1361-1362, 1363–1366, 1368-1370, 1371.

62. Tr. 1372, 1376-1377, 1378–1387.

63. Tr. 1394–1397, 1399-1406.

64. Tr. 1406, 1408, 1412, 1415-1416, 1422-1424, 1425, 1426, 1432-1436, 1436-1438, 1443-1449.

65. Tr. 1468, 1473, 1489.

66. Tr. 1484, 1487.

67. Tr. 1468–1469, 1493, 1496.

68. Jury Instructions, Case No. 38–1077 in Record on Appeal.

69. Memorandum of Orders, Case No. 38–1077 in Record on Appeal; "Rapist-Slayer Wins 7th Stay of Execution," *Chicago Tribune*, December 15, 1938.

Notes to Chapter Four

1. Tr. 1521, 1528–1529, 1536, 1538. "Order, dated August 12, 1938," Record on Appeal, unnumbered pages between 49B and 50.

2. "Rapist-Slayer Wins 7th Stay of Execution," *Chicago Tribune*, December 15, 1938.

3. Telegram dated October 18, 1938; Telegram dated October 25, 1938; Telegram dated October 26, 1938; Petition stamped received November 4, 1938; Letter from Rev. W. L. Sledge to B. K. Phillips, Clerk of the Parole Board, dated November 3, 1938; Letter from Henry Mason, President, International Literary Society, to Henry Horner, dated December 12, 1938; Letter from Harry L. Broom, President, Ethiopian World Federation Incorporated, dated December 12, 1938; see also "Citizens Ask Horner's Aid in Nixon Case," *Chicago Defender*, November 12, 1938; "Baptist Ministers Seek Justice for Nixon," *Chicago Tribune*, November 5, 1938; "Drafting Plea for Nixon (photo)," *Chicago Defender*, November 5, 1938; "Fight to Save Nixon from Chair," *Chicago Defender*, November 5, 1938.

4. "Rapist-Slayer Wins 7th Stay of Execution," *Chicago Tribune*, December 15, 1938; Anon., Letter to Governor Horner, dated December 5, 1938. Clemency Case File.

5. Stenographic Verbatim Transcript, Hearing Before the Illinois Parole Board, October 27, 1938; Letter from Thomas J. Courtney, State's Attorney, to Robert B. Phillips, Chief Clerk of Parole Board, dated October 25, 1938. Both documents are part of the Record on Appeal, People v. Robert Nixon.

6. Stenographic Verbatim Transcript, Hearing Before the Illinois Parole Board, October 27, 1938 in the Record on Appeal, Case No. 53032, People of the State of Illinois v. Robert Nixon.

7. *Moore v. Dempsey*, 261 U.S. 86 (1923); *Powell v. Alabama*, 287 U.S. 45 (1932). On the Scottsboro case, see Carter, *Scottsboro: A Tragedy of the American South*.

8. *Brown v. Mississippi*, 297 U.S. 278, 285–286 (1936). On the Brown case, see Cortner, *A "Scottsboro" Case in Mississippi*; *Mississippi v. Brown*, 173 Miss. 542, 553–554, 566–567 (1935).

9. 297 U.S. at 281–283.

10. 297 U.S. at 285–286.

11. *Illinois v. Frugoli*, 334 Ill. 324, 333 (1929), citing sections 161, 165 of the Illinois Criminal Code; *Illinois v. Colvin*, 294. Ill. 196, 198–199 (1920).

12. John Henry Wigmore, *A Treatise on Anglo-American Systems of Evidence at Trials of Common Law* (2nd edition, 1923), 2: 216–219; *Illinois v. Butler*, 343 Ill. 146 (1931); *Illinois v. Roach*, 369 Ill. 95, 96–97 (1938); Elizabeth Dale, *Criminal Justice in the United States, 1789-1939* (New York: Cambridge University Press, 2011), 60, 71.

13. *Illinois v. Roach*, 369 Ill. at 96–97. A year after Nixon's appeal was denied, the Supreme Court of the United States decided another police torture case, *Chambers v. Florida*, 309 U.S. 227 (1940). In *Chambers*, the court held that because the use of improperly obtained confessions could constitute a denial of due process, "we must determine independently whether petitioners' confessions were so obtained, by review of the facts upon which that issue necessarily turns." 309 U.S. at 229. That was, of course, too late for Robert Nixon.

14. *Lawless Law Enforcement*, 130.

15. *Illinois v. Vinci*, 295 Ill. 419, 423–424 (1920).

16. "Fail to Accuse Police," *Chicago Tribune*, June 20, 1924. See also *Illinois v. Sweeney*, 304 Ill. 502, 511 (1922) (also claims he was told he was being taken to see the gold fish, which was a beating); "Aldermen Gasp as Youth Bares Wounds," *Chicago Tribune*, January 30, 1923; "Picks out Cop as Flogger in Third Degree," *Chicago Tribune*, January 31, 1923.

17. 345 Ill. 278, 285 (1928).

18. Susan Bandes, "Pattern of Injustice: Police Brutality in the Courts," *University of Buffalo Law Review* 47 (1999): 1275.

19. *Illinois v. Vinci*, 295 Ill. at 427; *Brown v. Mississippi*, 297 U.S. at 287; *Illinois v. Rogers*, 303 Ill. at 589–590; *Illinois v. Frugoli*, 334 Ill. at 333.

20. *Illinois v. Albers*, 360 Ill. 73, 81 (1935); *Illinois v. Frugoli*, 334 Ill. at 331; *Illinois v. Holick*, 337 Ill. 333, 336–339 (1929). See also Wigmore, *A Treatise on Anglo-American Systems*, 2:216.

21. 356 Ill. 171, 174 (1934).

22. 355 Ill. 451, 455 (1934).

23. 345 Ill. 278 (1931).

24. *Illinois v. Arendarczyk*, 367 Ill. 534, 537 (1937); *Illinois v. Cope*, 349 Il. 278 (1932); *Illinois v. Basile*, 356 Ill. 171 (1934); *Illinois v. Rogers*, 303 Ill. 578 (1922); *Illinois v. Sweeney*, 304 Ill. 502 (1922); *Illinois v. Holick*, 337 Ill. 333 (1929).

25. Brief and Argument for Plaintiff in Error, filed January 27, 1939, People of the State of Illinois v. Robert Nixon, Case No. 53032, Record on Appeal [hereinafter Nixon's Br.].

26. Nixon's Br. 112–114, citing *Illinois v. Holick*, 337 Ill. 333 (1929); *Illinois v. Cope*, 345 Ill. 278 (1931), *Illinois v. Basile*, 356 Il. 171 (1934), *Illinois v. Campbell*, 359 Ill. 286 (1935), *Illinois v. Arendarczyk*, 367 Ill. 534 (1937), and *Illinois v. Roach*, 369 Ill. 93 (1937).

27. Nixon's Br. 114–115, 120-123, 123-129. *Illinois v. Fox*, 319 Ill. 606 (1925).

28. Nixon's Br. 128–129.

29. Nixon's Br. 99–105, 110-111,129–131, 132-133, 135-139, 139-146, 146-152.

30. Nixon's Br. 153–159.

31. Brief and Argument of the Defendant in Error, filed February 16, 1939, People of the Stte of Illinois v. Robert Nixon, Case No. 53032, Record on Appeal [hereinafter State Br.] 62–63, quoting *Illinois v. Costello*, 320 Ill. 79 (1926) without citation. The quoted language is from pages 103–104 in *Costello*; the state collapsed several separate sentences together, added words that are not in the opinion, and, bizarrely, omitted the crucial quote about the order of proof in the process. In its entirety, the part of the opinion the state quoted reads:

An admission or confession of a defendant to which no objection is made is properly admitted in evidence without the introduction of any preliminary proof. If objection is made, it is the duty of the court to hear, out of the presence of the jury, such evidence as either side may present as to the circumstances under which the confession was made, with a view to determining whether it was voluntarily made or was procured by the pressure of hope of fear applied for the purpose of producing it. The motive of the defendant does not affect the competency of his confession if it was made voluntarily, but the means used to obtain it will be examined to determine whether it was voluntary. There is no rigid rule as to the order of proof. This preliminary question must be decided by the court upon the evidence heard, and its decision will not be reversed unless manifestly against the weight of the evidence.

32. Reply Brief of the Plaintiff in Error, filed February 25, 1939, People of the State of Illinois v. Robert Nixon, Case No. 53032, Record on Appeal [hereinafter Nixon's Reply Br.], 9, citing *Illinois v. Frugoli*, 334 Ill. 324 (1929) for this point.

33. State Br. 62-63, *Illinois v. Holick*, 337 Ill. 333 (1929).

34. *Illinois v. Rogers*, 303 Ill. 578, 589–590 (1922); *Illinois v. Frugoli*, 334 Ill. 324, 333–334 (1929).

35. *Sims v. Florida*, 59 Fla. 38, 43 (1910). Compare *Illinois v. Rogers*, 303 Ill. 578, *Illinois v. Roach*, 369 Ill. 93.

36. State Br., 64.

37. State Br., 64-66.

38. State Br., 54-58 (change of venue), 58-60 (exclusion of Muehlberger), 66-76 (Hicks's statements), 78-79 (closing argument), 81-83 (Whitton identification of Nixon).

39. Nixon's Reply Br., 13–14.

40. Nixon's Reply Br., 32–33.

41. *Illinois v. Nixon*, 371 Ill. 318 (1939). The court refused to address several of the arguments, asserting that because there had been no objection made at the time of trial there was no need to consider the objection on appeal. 371 Ill. at 332 (admission of testimony by Sullivan and Storms regarding Hicks's statement that Nixon hit Johnson with the brick), ibid. (argument by state's attorney that referred to Nixon as a "brick killer" during closing argument).

42. 371 Ill. at 326, 326–328.

43. 371 Ill. at 331-332.

44. 371 Ill. at 328–330.

45. 371 Ill. at 324–325, 329-330.

46. *Brown v. Allen*, 344 U.S. 443, 540 (1953); Letter from Rev. J. L Logan and the Ethiopian World Federation to State Patrol Board, dated June 5, 1939; Letter from Rev. J. J. Dockery and the Ethiopian World Federation to Henry Horner, dated June 5, 1939; Telegram dated June 14, 1939. All letters and telegrams are in Robert Nixon Clemency File. "Second Suspect Convicted in Chicago Slaying," *Atlanta Daily World*, February 7, 1939.

Notes to Chapter Five

1. On the rise of plea bargains, see *Illinois Crime Survey*, 48.

2. Rejali, *Torture and Democracy*, 34, 329–330, 339. Rejali notes that citizens can have a hard time "seeing" torture in their neighborhoods, and points to Chicago between 1970 and 1990 as an

example. Rejali, *Torture and Democracy*, 251. See also Silvan Niedermeier, "Violence, Visibility, and the Investigation of Police Torture in the American South, 1940–1955," in *Violence and Visibility in Modern History*, ed. Jürgen Martschukat and Silvan Niedermeier (New York: Palgrave Macmillian, 2013), 91; ACLU of Illinois, *Secret Detention by the Chicago Police* (Glencoe, IL: Free Press, 1959), 12–13.

3. James Epstein, *Scandal of Colonial Rule: Power and Supversion in the British Atlantic during the Age of Revolution* (New York: Cambridge University Press, 2012), 20–21; Rejali, *Torture and Democracy*, 343–344; Niedermeier, "Violence, Visibility, and the Investigation of Police Torture."

4. *Illinois v. LaFrana*, 4 Ill. 2d 261 (1954); "Police Beating Charged by Reck in Peacock Case," *Chicago Tribune*, May 8, 1936; "Peacock Killer Loses Nerve as Mother Faints," *Chicago Tribune*, May 9, 1936; "Cook County Bar Launches Swain Quiz," *Chicago Defender*, September 12, 1936; "Found Guilty, Gets 5 Years in Hotel Rape," *Chicago Tribune*, December 14, 1937; *United States ex rel. Conroy v. Pate*, 240 F. Supp. 237 (1965).

5. "Hunt Two Named in Confession of Cleaning Killer," *Chicago Tribune*, September 12, 1941.

6. "Confessed Goon Examined after Beating Charge," *Chicago Tribune*, September 14, 1941; "Fight Admission of Confessions in Bat Slaying," *Chicago Tribune*, December 9, 1941; "Deny Goon Death Confession Was the Result of Force," *Chicago Tribune*, December 18, 1941.

7. "Tell of Bruises on Defendant in Goon Death Case," *Chicago Tribune*, December 11, 1941; "Fail to Identify Goldblatt as Gorczak Killer," *Chicago Tribune*, December 13, 1941; "Repudiates His Confession in Bat Slaying," *Chicago Tribune*, December 17, 1941.

8. "Courtney Aids Will Get Goon Killing Reward," *Chicago Tribune*, February 7, 1942; "Free Suspect Once Doomed as Goon Murderer," *Chicago Tribune*, June 10, 1943.

9. Adamson, *The Toughest Cop in America* (Indianapolis: First Books Library, 2001), 20–21, 23; "Confesses Gas Holdup Killing," *Chicago Tribune*, September 20, 1943; "'I Loosed Gas on Woman,' Killer Admits," *Chicago Tribune*, February 9, 1944; "How Officials Build Case in Kidnap-Killing," *Chicago Tribune*, July 13, 1946.

10. "Verburghs Sue for $125,000 in Degnan Jailing," *Chicago Tribune*, February 2, 1946; Amended Petition for Executive Clemency, filed on behalf of William Heirens (Illinois, 2002 Docket), 15, 20–21, 35–37.

11. "400 Voice Protest on Police Handling of Degnan Inquiry," *Chicago Tribune*, January 25, 1946; "Witness," *Chicago Tribune*, September 9, 1947; M. V. L. "Letter to the Editor," *Chicago Tribune*, February 26, 1948; Richard French, "Letter to the Editor," *Chicago Tribune*, March 4, 1948.

12. "Confession Admitted to Record in Trial of 'Tunnel Burglars,'" *Chicago Tribune*, July 13, 1948; *Illinois v. Wagoner*, 8 Ill. 2d 188 (1956); *Illinois v. Walden*, 19 Ill. 2d 602 (1960); "The People vs. Paul Crump" (1962); David Weiner, "The Forgotten Case of Paul Crump," *Chicago Tribune*, June 20, 2010; ACLU of Illinois, *Secret Detention*, 14.

13. *Illinois v. Jackson*, 41 Ill. 2d 102 (1968); *Chicago Defender*, February 7, 1962; *Chicago Defender*, April 19, 1962; *Illinois v. Alexander*, 96 Ill. App. 2d 113 (1st Dist. 1968). On bagging in general and in Chicago, see Rejali, *Torture and Democracy*, 236, 335.

14. *Chambers v. Florida*, 309 U.S. 227, 228–229 (1940); *Ashcraft v. Tennessee*, 322 U.S. 143, 149–150, 153–154 (1944). Ashcraft, who was white, was charged with asking John Ware, a black man, to kill Ashcraft's wife. Ware's conviction rested on Ashcraft's confession, so the Supreme Court reversed on both convictions. It did not consider Ware's separate claims of torture at the hands of the police.

15. "Torture Forbidden," *Chicago Tribune*, May 4, 1944; "Dempsey Tells His Opposition to the Third Degree," *Chicago Tribune*, October 3, 1944; "Dempsey Vows He Won't Shirk Job for Votes," *Chicago Tribune*, October 28, 1948; "Judge Decries Use of Force on Crime Suspects," *Chicago Tribune*, March 26, 1947.

16. "Accused Killer of Friend Calls Confession Fake," *Chicago Tribune*, February 17, 1940; "Churchman Slays Wife," *Chicago Defender*, June 14, 1941.

17. "Returns to Scene of His Crime and Is Arrested," *Chicago Tribune*, November 17, 1941 (the *Tribune* erroneously calls him John Jankowski); *Illinois v. Jankowski*, 391 Ill. 298 (1945); "Judge M'Kinlay Stays Aloof on Crowley Blast," *Chicago Tribune*, February 16, 1943; "Two Confess to 75 Store Burglaries," *Chicago Tribune*, April 2, 1943; *Illinois v. Machul*, 387 Ill. 556 (1944); "Arrest Ex-Convict, Stepson in Robbery and Burglary Cases," *Chicago Tribune*, June 8, 1948; "Seek Secret Motive in Slaying of Glamour Girl," *Chicago Defender*, October 2, 1948; "2 Get Prison Terms in $300 Holdup of Real Estate Office," *Chicago Tribune*, December 1, 1948; *Illinois v. Kelly*, 404 Ill. 281 (1949).

18. "Police Prove Effective in Major Crime," *Chicago Tribune,* April 17, 1953; "Nab 5 for $21,000 Robbery," *Chicago Defender,* April 4, 1953; "Crump Wins Fight for Life," *Chicago Defender,* August 2, 1962; *Illinois v. Crump,* 5 Ill. 2d 251 (1955); *Illinois v. Crump,* 12 Ill. 2d 402 (1957).

19. "The Man Who Killed a Policeman," *Chicago Tribune,* August 19, 1955; "Slayer of Cop Captured," *Chicago Tribune,* August 19, 1955; "W-G-N, WGN-TV Air Stories of Killer Capture," *Chicago Tribune,* August 19, 1955; "Attorney Says Carpenter to Plead Innocent," *Chicago Tribune,* August 21, 1955; "Police Killer Executed," *Chicago Tribune,* December 19, 1958; *Illinois v. Scott,* 29 Ill. 2d 97 (1963).

20. "Plan Lectures on Problems Facing Negro," *Chicago Tribune,* April 27, 1958; ACLU, *Secret Detention;* "Finds Crime Outstrips Birth Rate," *Chicago Tribune,* February 20, 1960.

21. "Courts Often Hinder Police, Inbau Claims," *Chicago Tribune,* January 15, 1961; Clay Gowran, "Inbau Blames Crime on Rise of 2 Soft Ideas," *Chicago Tribune,* December 1, 1964; "Inbau Backs Interrogation by Policemen," *Chicago Tribune,* March 14, 1965; "Asks Tighter Laws to Curb Third Degree," *Chicago Tribune,* March 21, 1962; David Halvorsen, "Youth Division Police Ban the 'Third Degree,'" *Chicago Tribune,* December 23, 1962.

22. *Illinois v. Freeman,* 25 Ill. 2d 88 (1962); *Illinois v. Brown,* 30 Ill. 2d 297 (1964); *Illinois v. Earl,* 34 Ill. 2d 11 (1966); 37 Ill. 2d 19 (1967); "Denies 'Ride' Killing; Tells Police 'Abuse,'" *Chicago Tribune,* December 25, 1962; *Illinois v. Hartgraves,* 31 Ill. 2d 375 (1964); *Illinois v. McCasle,* 35 Ill. 2d 552 (1966); *Illinois v. McNeil,* 99 Ill. App. 2d 273 (1st Dist. 1968).

23. *Lawless Law Enforcement,* 128; Storch, *Red Chicago,* 99–100; "Police Captain Opens Quiz in Brutality Case," *Chicago Tribune,* June 25, 1933; "Seek Indictment of Police Blamed for Prisoner's Death," *Chicago Defender,* August 4, 1934; "Lockup Visitor for 20 Hours," *Chicago Tribune,* July 1, 1933; Dennis, *Memorial Day Massacre.*

24. *Equal Justice,* May 1938, 5; *Illinois v. Santucci,* 374 Ill. 395 (1940); Heirens petition, 15, 20–21; 35–37; *Illinois v. Wakat,* 415 Ill. 610 (1953); *Wakat v. Harlib,* 253 F.2d 59 (7th Cir. 1958); ACLU, *Secret Detention,* 16–17.

25. "Cripple Tells of Beating by Two Traffic Cops," *Chicago Tribune,* April 13, 1954; ACLU *Secret Detention,* 5; *Illinois v. Nischt,* 23 Ill. 2d 284 (1961); *Illinois v. Dulong,* 33 Ill. 2d 140 (1965); M. Wilson Lewis, "Charge Westside Police Brutality," *Chicago Defender,* March 5, 1964; *Illinois v. Chandler,* 84 Ill. App. 2d 231 (1st Dist. 1967).

26. Rejali, *Torture and Democracy,* 56.

27. "Accused Killer of Friend Calls Confession Fake," *Chicago Tribune,* February 17, 1940.

28. *Illinois v. Wakat,* 415 Ill. 610 (1953); *Wakat v. Harlib,* 253 F.2d 59 (7th Cir. 1958).

29. "Returns to Scene of His Crime and Is Arrested," *Chicago Tribune,* November 17, 1941 (the Tribune erroneously calls him John Jankowski); *Illinois v. Jankowski,* 391 Ill. 298 (1945); "Witness," *Chicago Tribune,* September 9, 1947; *Wakat v. Harlib,* 253 F. 2d 59 (7th Cir. 1958); ACLU, *Secret Detention,* 16; "5 Policemen Acquitted in Second Trial," *Chicago Tribune,* November 21, 1953; "Deny at Death Quiz That Cops Beat Subjects," *Chicago Tribune,* February 9, 1951.

30. "Charges Police Brutality and Wins New Trial," *Chicago Tribune,* October 12, 1940; "Court Reverses 1941 Conviction in Goon Slaying," *Chicago Tribune,* May 21, 1943; "Free Suspect Once Doomed as Goon Murderer," *Chicago Tribune,* June 10, 1943.

31. Stanley Levin, "Post Conviction Remedies in Illinois," *Journal of Criminal Law and Criminology* 40 (1950): 606 (1949–1950); John Paul Stevens, "Letter to the Editor: Bar Association Defends Post Conviction Act," *Chicago Tribune,* October 18, 1952; *Illinois v. Reck,* 392 Ill. 311(1945); *Reck v. Illinois,* 7 Ill. 2d 261 (1955); *United States ex rel. Reck v. Ragen,* 172 F. Supp. 734 (N.D. Ill. 1959); *United States ex rel. Reck v. Ragen,* 274 F.2d 250 (7th Cir 1960); *Reck v. Pate,* 367 U.S. 433 (1961).

32. On the evolution of the court's treatment of deference, consider the dissenting opinion of Justice Burton in Haley v. Ohio, 332 U.S. 596, 607 (1948), and the majority opinion by Justice Jackson and the dissenting opinion of Justice Frankfurter in Stein v. New York, 346 U.S. 156, 181, 199–200 (1953). For other examples of deference by the United States Supreme Court, see Jonathan Simon, *Governing through Crime: How the War on Crime Transformed American Democracy and Created a Culture of Fear* (New York: Oxford University Press, 2007); David Garland, *Punishment and Modern Society: A Study in Social Theory* (Chicago: University of Chicago Press, 2012).

33. *Miranda v. Arizona,* 384 U.S. 436 (1966). This had been the solution urged by groups like the ACLU of Illinois. ACLU, *Secret Detention.*

34. "Police Start Unit to Fight Youth Gangs," *Chicago Tribune,* March 22, 1967; Rashaad Shabaz, "'Sores in the City': A Genealogy of the Black P. Stone Nation," in Karen M. Morin and Dominque

Moran, eds., *Historical Geographies of Prisons: Unlocking the Usable Carceral Past* (New York: Rutledge, 2015), 51, 58; "Conlisk Tells Plans to Enlarge Gang Unit," *Chicago Tribune*, November 8, 1968; "93 Policemen Are Shifted to Help Curb Teen-Age Gangs," *Chicago Tribune*, March 5, 1969; "Police Cut Gang Unit by 133 Men," *Chicago Tribune*, January 7, 1971.

35. "State Seeking Death Penalty in Alfano Case," *Chicago Tribune*, October 21, 1970; "Alfano List Grows," *Chicago Tribune*, October 24, 1970; "Judge Swears In Jury for Alfano Murder Trial," *Chicago Tribune*, December 19, 1970; Philip Caputo, "7 in Alfano Murder Trial Found Innocent," *Chicago Tribune*, January 18, 1971.

36. Philip Caputo, "Credibility Is Issue in Alfano Trial," *Chicago Tribune*, December 30, 1970; Philip Caputo, "7 in Alfano Murder Trial Found Innocent," *Chicago Tribune*, January 18, 1971; Philip Caputo, "Evidence in Alfano Case Hit," *Chicago Tribune*, January 19, 1971; Toni Anthony, "Alfano Witness Says Cops Used 'Threats,'" *Chicago Defender*, December 31, 1970.

37. Bonne J. Nesbitt, "Claim Cops Beat Suspects Jailed for Alfano Murder," *Chicago Defender*, November 19, 1970; "Charges GIU in 'Torture,'" *Chicago Defender*, November 21, 1970; "Continue Fight to Kill Confessions by Stones," *Chicago Defender*, November 23, 1970; Bonne Nesbitt, "Nix Confession in Alfano Case," *Chicago Defender*, November 25, 1970; "Court Told Gang Plot to Kill Cop," *Chicago Tribune*, August 18, 1970.

38. Philip Caputo, "7 in Alfano Murder Trial Found Innocent," *Chicago Tribune*, January 18, 1971; Philip Caputo, "Evidence in Alfano Case Hit," *Chicago Tribune*, January 19, 1970; "Another Botched Prosecution," *Chicago Tribune*, January 20, 1971; Mark Ogan, "Letter to the Editor: Weak Prosecution," *Chicago Tribune*, January 29, 1971; Philip Caputo, "State Files Impounded in Alfano Murder Trial," *Chicago Tribune*, January 8, 1971.

39. Paul Chevigny, "Changing Control of Police Violence in Rio de Janeiro and Sao Paulo, Brazil," in *Policing Change, Changing Police: International Perspectives*, ed. Otwin Marenin (New York: Garland, 1996), 30; Rejali, *Torture and Democracy*, 56; Khalil Gibran Muhammad, *The Condemnation of Blackness: Race, Crime, and the Making of Modern Urban America* (Cambridge, MA: Harvard University Press, 2010). The available records do not always identify the race of the individuals claiming they were tortured. It appears, however, that although white men continued to make the claim in the 1950s and 1960s, in that same period African American men claimed they were tortured out of proportion to their numbers in the population. For a similar argument about an earlier period, see Marilyn S. Johnson, *Street Justice: A History of Police Violence in New York City* (Boston: Beacon Press, 2003), 136.

Notes to Conclusion

1. Richard C. Lindberg, *To Serve and Collect: Chicago Politics and Police Corruption from the Lager Beer Riot to the Summerdale Scandal, 1855–1960* (Carbondale: Southern Illinois University Press, 1991), 68, 244; "Trappers," *Chicago Tribune*, June 2, 1920; "Sullivan Named Chief of Detectives," *Chicago Tribune*, August 4, 1934; Adamson, *Toughest Cop in America.*

Selected Bibliography

The data on claims of police torture come from three main sources: The *Chicago Tribune*, the *Chicago Defender*, and the Illinois Supreme Court and Illinois Appellate Court reports. Those sources have been supplemented by the others cited below.

Court and Government Records

Chicago Police Department, *Annual Report*. Chicago, 1938.

Clemency Case File, People v. Robert Nixon, Illinois State Archives, Springfield, Illinois.

Felony Court Records, People v. Robert Nixon, Case No. 38-1077, 38-1078, 38-1079, 38-1091, Circuit Court of Cook County Archives, Daley Center, Chicago.

People of the State of Illinois v. Robert Nixon, Case No. 25032, Record on Appeal, Illinois Supreme Court, Illinois Archives, Springfield, Illinois.

Ashcraft v. Tennessee, 322 U.S. 143 (1944).

Brown v. Allen, 344 U.S. 443 (1953).

Brown v. Mississippi, 297 U.S. 278 (1936).

Chambers v. Florida, 309 U.S. 227 (1940).

Haley v. Ohio, 332 U.S. 596 (1948).

Illinois v. Alexander, 96 Ill. App. 2d 113 (1st Dist. 1968).

Illinois v. Albers, 360 Ill. 73 (1935).

Illinois v. Ardelean, 368 Ill. 274 (1938).

Illinois v. Arendarczyk, 367 Ill. 534 (1937).

Illinois v. Armstrong, 51 Ill. 2d 471 (1972).

Illinois v. Basile, 356 Ill. 171 (1934).

Illinois v. Berardi, 321 Ill. 47 (1926).

Illinois v. Bowman, 40 Ill. 2d 116 (1968).

Illinois v. Butler, 343 Ill. 146 (1931).

Illinois v. Campbell, 359 Ill. 286 (1935).

Illinois v. Chandler, 84 Ill. App. 2d 231 (1st Dist. 1967).

Illinois v. Chrfrikas, 295 Ill. 222 (1920).

Illinois v. Coffey, 342 Ill. 56 (1930).

Illinois v. Colvin, 294 Ill. 196 (1920).

Illinois v. Cope, 345 Ill. 278 (1931).

Illinois v. Costello, 320 Ill. 79 (1926).

Illinois v. Crump, 12 Ill. 2d 402 (1957).

Illinois v. Cunningham, 30 Ill. 2d 433 (1964).

Illinois v. Dale, 20 Ill. 2d 532 (1960).

Illinois v. Davis, 399 Ill. 265 (1948).

Illinois v. Davis, 35 Ill. 2d 202 (1966).

Illinois v. Dulong, 33 Ill. 2d 140 (1965).

Illinois v. Dwyer, 397 Ill. 599 (1947).

Illinois v. Evans, 25 Ill. 2d 194 (1962).

Illinois v. Evenow, 355 Ill. 451 (1934).
Illinois v. Fisher, 21 Ill. 2d 142 (1961).
Illinois v. Fisher, 340 Ill. 216 (1930).
Illinois v. Fox, 319 Ill. 606 (1925).
Illinois v. Frugoli, 334 Ill. 324 (1929).
Illinois v. Goldblatt, 383 Ill. 176 (1943).
Illinois v. Golson, 32 Ill. 2d 398 (1965).
Illinois v. Guido, 321 Ill. 397 (1926).
Illinois v. Hayes, 38 Ill. 2d 329 (1967).
Illinois v. Heide, 302 Ill. 624 (1922).
Illinois v. Hester, 39 Ill. 2d 489 (1968).
Illinois v. Holick, 337 Ill. 333 (1929).
Illinois v. Ickes, 370 Ill. 486 (1939).
Illinois v. Jackson, 23 Ill. 2d 263 (1961).
Illinois v. Jackson, 41 Ill. 2d 102 (1968).
Illinois v. Jankowski, 391 Ill. 298 (1945).
Illinois v. Jennings, 11 Ill. 2d 610 (1957).
Illinois v. Kees, 32 Ill. 2d 299 (1965).
Illinois v. Kelly, 404 Ill. 281 (1949).
Illinois v. Kozlowski, 368 Ill. 124 (1938).
Illinois v. La Coco, 406 Ill. 303 (1950).
Illinois v. LaFrana, 4 Ill. 2d 261 (1954).
Illinois v. Lego, 32 Ill. 2d 76 (1965).
Illinois v. Maggio, 324 Ill. 516 (1927).
Illinois v. McCasle, 35 Ill. 2d 552 (1966).
Illinois v. Meaderds, 21 Ill. 2d 145 (1961).
Illinois v. Miller, 13 Ill. 2d 84 (1958).
Illinois v. Miller, 33 Ill. 2d 439 (1965).
Illinois v. Nemke, 23 Ill. 2d 591 (1962).
Illinois v. Nemke, 46 Ill. 2d 49 (1970).
Illinois v. Nischt, 23 Ill. 2d 284 (1961).
Illinois v. Nixon, 371 Ill. 318 (1939)
Illinois v. Reck, 392 Ill. 311 (1945).
Illinois v. Roach, 369 Ill. 95 (1938).
Illinois v. Rogers, 303 Ill. 578 (1922).
Illinois v. Rogers, 413 Ill. 554 (1953).
Illinois v. Royals, 356 Ill. 628 (1934).
Illinois v. Sammons, 17 Ill. 2d 316 (1959).
Illinois v. Santucci, 374 Ill. 395 (1940).
Illinois v. Sims, 21 Ill. 2d 425 (1961).
Illinois v. Sinclair, 27 Ill. 2d 505 (1963).
Illinois v. Sloss, 412 Ill. 61 (1952).
Illinois v. Smith, 42 Ill. 2d 547 (1969).
Illinois v. Spranger, 314 Ill. 602 (1924).
Illinois v. Sprinkle, 27 Ill. 2d 398 (1963).
Illinois v. Sweeney, 304 Ill. 502 (1922).
Illinois v. Terry, 12 Ill. 2d 56 (1957).
Illinois v. Thomlison, 400 Ill. 555 (1948).
Illinois v. Topolski, 360 Ill. 586 (1935).
Illinois v. Vinci, 295 Ill. 419 (1920).
Illinois v. Wagner, 81 Ill. 2d 188 (1956).
Illinois v. Wakat, 415 Ill. 610 (1953).
Illinois v. Walden, 19 Ill. 2d 602 (1960).
Illinois v. Wallace, 35 Ill. 2d 251 (1966).
Illinois v. Wilson, 29 Ill. 2d 82 (1963).
Illinois v. Witherspoon, 27 Ill. 2d 483 (1963).
Illinois v. Ziderowski, 325 Ill. 232 (1927).

Illinois v. Zielinski, 10 Ill. 2d 473 (1957).
Miranda v. Arizona, 384 U.S. 436 (1966).
Moore v. Dempsey, 261 U.S. 86 (1923).
Needham v. Illinois, 98 Ill. 275 (1881).
Powell v. Alabama, 287 U.S. 45 (1932).
Reck v. Illinois, 7 Ill. 261 (1955)
Reck v. Pate, 367 U.S. 433 (1961).
Reck v. Ragen, 274 F.2d 250 (7th Cir. 1960).
Stein v. New York, 346 U.S. 156 (1953).
United States ex rel. Conroy v. Pate, 240 F. Supp. 237 (N.D. Ill. 1965).
United States ex rel. Reck v. Ragen, 172 F. Supp. 734 (N.D. Ill. 1959).
Wakat v. Harlib, 253 F. Supp. 2d 59 (1958).

Films

The Chair (1962). VHS. Directed by Gregory Shuker, Richard Leacock, and D. A. Pennebaker. Santa Monica, CA: Direct Cinema, Ltd.
People v. Paul Crump (1962). DVD. Directed by William Friedkin. Chicago: Facets, Inc.

Newspapers

Atlanta Constitution
Capital Plaindealer
Chicago Daily News
Chicago Defender
Chicago Times
Chicago Tribune
Christian Science Monitor
Equal Justice
Los Angeles Times
New Amsterdam News
New York Times
Plain Dealer
Washington Post

Books and Articles

ACLU, Illinois Division. *Secret Detention by the Chicago Police*. Glencoe, IL: Free Press, 1959.
Adamson, Charles F. *The Toughest Cop in America*. Indianapolis: First Books Library, 2001.
Adler, Jeffrey. *First in Violence, Deepest in Dirt: Homicide in Chicago, 1875–1920*. Cambridge, MA: Harvard University Press, 2006.
Alder, Ken. *The Lie Detectors: A History of an American Obsession*. New York: Free Press, 2007.
Avrich, Paul. *The Haymarket Tragedy*. Princeton, NJ: Princeton University Press, 1986.
Baldwin, Davarian. *Chicago's New Negroes: Modernity, the Great Migration, and Black Urban Life*. Chapel Hill: University of North Carolina Press, 2007.
Balko, Radley. *Rise of the Warrior Cop: The Militarization of America's Police Forces*. New York: Public Affairs, 2013.
Bandes, Susan. "Patterns of Injustice: Police Brutality in the Courts." *Buffalo Law Review* 47 (1999): 1275.
Bates, Beth Tompkins. "A New Crowd Challenges the Agenda of the Old Guard in the NAACP." *American Historical Review* 102 (1997): 340.
Black, Joel. "A Theory of African American Citizenship: Richard Westbrooks, the Great Migration, and the Chicago Defender's 'Legal Helps' Column." *Journal of Social History* 46 (2013): 896.
Carter, Dan. *Scottsboro: A Tragedy of the American South*. Revised edition. Baton Rouge: Louisiana State University Press, 2007.

Chevigny, Paul. "Changing Control of Police Violence in Rio de Janeiro and Sao Paulo, Brazil." In Otwin Marenin, ed., *Policing Change, Changing Police: International Perspectives*. New York: Garland, 1996.

Chicago Commission on Race Relations. *The Negro in Chicago: A Study of Race Relations and a Race Riot*. Chicago: University of Chicago Press, 1922

Cohen, Stanley. *States of Denial: Knowing about Atrocity and Suffering*. Cambridge, UK: Polity Press, 2001.

Cole, Simon A. *Suspect Identities: A History of Fingerprinting and Criminal Identification*. Cambridge, MA: Harvard University Press, 2001.

Conroy, John. *Unspeakable Acts, Ordinary People: The Dynamics of Torture*. Berkeley: University of California Press, 2000).

Cortner, Richard C. *A "Scottsboro" Case in Mississippi: The Supreme Court and Brown v. Mississippi*. Jackson: University Press of Mississippi, 1986.

Dale, Elizabeth. *The Chicago Trunk Mystery: Law and Justice at the Turn of the Century*. DeKalb: Northern Illinois University Press, 2011.

———. *Criminal Justice in the United States, 1789–1939*. New York: Cambridge University Press, 2011.

Dennis, Michael. *The Memorial Day Massacre and the Movement for Industrial Democracy*. New York: Palgrave Macmillan, 2010.

Drake, St. Clair, and Horace R. Cayton. *Black Metropolis: A Study of Negro Life in a Northern City*. New York: Harcourt, Brace, 1945.

Epstein, James. *Scandal of Colonial Rule: Power and Subversion in the British Atlantic during the Age of Revolution*. New York: Cambridge University Press, 2012.

Erlanson, Otto. "The Scene of the Sex Offense as Related to the Residence of the Offender." *Journal of Criminal Law and Criminology* 31 (1940): 339.

Fish, John Hall. *Black Power/White Control: The Struggle of the Woodlawn Organization in Chicago*. Princeton, NJ: Princeton University Press, 1973.

Flood, Dawn Rae. *Rape in Chicago: Race, Myth, and the Courts*. Urbana: University of Illinois Press, 2012.

Friedman, Lawrence M. *Crime and Punishment in American History*. New York: Basic Books, 1994.

Futterman, Craig, H. Mellissa Mather, and Melanie Miles, "The Use of Statistical Evidence to Address Police Supervisory and Disciplinary Practices: The Chicago Police Department's Broken System." In *Civil Rights Litigation and Attorney Fees Annual Handbook*. Steven Saltzman ed. Eagen, MN: Thomson Reuters, 2007.

Garland, David. *Punishment and Modern Society: A Study in Social Theory*. Chicago: University of Chicago Press, 2012.

Gellman, Erik. *Death Blow to Jim Crow: The National Negro Congress and the Rise of Militant Civil Rights*. Chapel Hill: University of North Carolina Press, 2012.

Gilmore, Glenda. *Defying Dixie: The Radical Roots of Civil Rights, 1919–1950*. W.W. Norton, 2013.

Goddard, Calvin. "Scientific Crime Detection Laboratories in Europe, Part I." *American Journal of Police Science* 1 (1930): 13.

Green, Adam. *Selling the Race: Culture, Community and Black Chicago, 1940–1955*. University of Chicago Press, 2009.

Grossman, James. *Land of Hope: Chicago, Black Southerners and the Great Migration*. Chicago: University of Chicago Press, 1991.

Hirsch, Arnold R. *Making the Second Ghetto: Race and Housing in Chicago, 1940–1960*. Chicago: University of Chicago Press, 1998.

Hogan, John F. *The 1937 Chicago Steel Strike: Blood on the Prairie*. Charleston, SC: History Press, 2014.

Huggins, Martha K., Mika Haritos-Fatouros, and Philip G Zimbardo. *Violence Workers: Police Torturers and Murders Reconstruct Brazilian Atrocities*. Berkeley: University of California Press, 2002.

Illinois Association for Criminal Justice in Chicago and Chicago Crime Commission. *The Illinois Crime Survey*. Chicago: Blakely, 1929.

Inbau, Fred. "Clarence W. Muehlberger, 1896-1966." *Journal of Criminal Law and Criminology* 57 (1967): 517.

Johnson, Marilynn S. *Street Justice: A History of Police Violence in New York City*. Boston: Beacon, 2003.

Langbein, John H. *Torture and the Law of Proof: Europe in the Ancien Régime*. Chicago: University of Chicago Press, 1976, 2006.

Larson, Erik. *The Devil in the White City: Murder, Magic and Madness at the Fair That Changed America*. New York: Vintage, 2003.

Lemann, Nicholas. *The Promised Land: The Great Black Migration and How It Changed America*. New York: A.A. Knopf, 1991.

Leo, Richard A. *Police Interrogation and American Justice*. Cambridge, MA: Harvard University Press, 2008.

Leo, Richard A., and Richard Ofshe, "The Consequences of False Confessions: Deprivations of Liberty and Miscarriages of Justice in the Age of Psychological Interrogations." *Journal of Criminal Law and Criminology* 88 (1998): 429.

Lesly, Michael. *Murder City: The Bloody History of Chicago in the Twenties*. New York: W.W. Norton, 2007.

Levin, Stanley. "Post Conviction Remedies in Illinois." *Journal of Criminal Law and Criminology* 40 (1950): 606.

Lindberg, Richard C. *To Serve and Collect: Chicago Politics and Police Corruption from the Lager Beer Riot to the Summerdale Scandal, 1855-1960*. Carbondale: Southern Illinois University Press, 1998.

Lokaneeta, Jinee. *Transnational Torture: Law, Violence, and State Power in the United States and India*. New York: New York University Press, 2011.

McCoy, Alfred W. *Policing America's Empire: The United States, The Philippines, and the Rise of the Surveillance State*. Madison: University of Wisconsin Press, 2009.

Mack, Kenneth. *Representing the Race: The Creation of the Civil Rights Lawyer*. Cambridge, MA: Harvard University Press, 2012.

Martschukat, Jürgen, and Silvan Niedermeier, eds. *Violence and Visibility in Modern History*. New York: Palgrave MacMillan, 2013.

Mitrani, Sam. *The Rise of the Chicago Police Department: Class and Conflict, 1850-1894*. Urbana: University of Illinois Press, 2013.

Monkkonen, Eric. *Police in Urban America, 1860-1920*. New York: Cambridge University Press, 2004.

Morin, Karen M., and Dominique Moran, eds. *Historical Geographies of Prisons: Unlocking the Usable Carceral Past*. New York: Routledge, 2015.

Muhammad, Khalil Gibran. *The Condemnation of Blackness: Race, Crime, and the Making of Modern Urban America*. Cambridge: Harvard University Press, 2010.

O'Brien, Gillian. *Blood Runs Green: The Murder that Transfixed Gilded Age America*. Chicago: University of Chicago Press, 2015.

Parry, John. *Understanding Torture: Law, Violence, and Political Identity*. Ann Arbor: University of Michigan Press, 2010.

Pattillo, Mary. *Black on the Block: The Politics of Race and Class in the City*. Chicago: University of Chicago Press, 2007.

Peters, Edward. *Torture*. Philadelphia: University of Pennsylvania Press, 1999.

Philpott, Thomas Lee. *The Slum and the Ghetto: Neighborhood Deterioration and Middle-Class Reform, Chicago 1880-1930*. New York: Oxford University Press, 1978.

Reed, Christopher Robert. *The Depression Comes to the South Side of Chicago: Protest and Politics in the Black Metropolis, 1930-1933*. Bloomington: Indiana University Press, 2011.

Rejali, Darius. *Torture and Democracy*. Princeton, NJ: Princeton University Press, 2007.

Schulz, William, ed. *The Phenomenon of Torture: Readings and Commentary*. Philadelphia: University of Pennsylvania Press, 2007.

Shabazz, Rashid. "Sores in the City: A Genealogy of the Black P. Stone Nation." In Morin, Karen M., and Dominique Moran, eds. *Historical Geographies of Prisons: Unlocking the Usable Carceral Past*. New York: Routledge, 2015, 51.

———. *Spatializing Blackness: Architectures of Confinement and Black Masculinity in Chicago*. Urbana: University of Illinois Press, 2015.

Simon, Jonathan. *Governing Through Crime: How the War on Crime Transformed American Democracy and Created a Culture of Fear*. New York: Oxford University Press, 2007.

Skolnick, Jerome, and James J. Fyfe. *Above the Law: Police and the Excessive Use of Force*. New York: Free Press, 1993.

Smith, Clay. *Emancipation: The Making of the Black Lawyer, 1844-1944*. Philadelphia: University of Pennsylvania Press, 1999.

Spear, Allan H. *Black Chicago: The Making of a Negro Ghetto, 1890-1920.* Chicago: University of Chicago Press, 1967.

Storch, Randi. *Red Chicago: American Communism and Its Grassroots, 1928–1935.* Urbana: University of Illinois Press, 2007.

Strange, Carolyn. "The 'Shock' of Torture: A Historiographical Challenge." *History Workshop Journal* 61 (2006): 135.

Stuntz, William. *The Collapse of American Criminal Justice.* Cambridge, MA: Belknap Press of Harvard University Press, 2011.

Sullivan, Patricia. *Lift Every Voice: The NAACP and the Making of the Civil Rights Movement.* New York: New Press, 2010.

"Symposium: Wickersham Commission." *Marquette Law Review* 96 (2013): 993–1219.

Thomas, George C., and Richard A. Leo. *Confessions of Guilt: From Torture to Miranda and Beyond.* New York: Oxford University Press, 2012.

Tuttle, William M. *Race Riot: Chicago and the Red Summer of 1919.* Urbana: University of Illinois Press, 1970.

Uhlmann, Jennifer Ruthanne. "The Communist Civil Rights Movement." PhD diss., UCLA, 2007.

United States, Wickersham Commission. *Report on Lawlessness in Law Enforcement.* Washington, DC: Government Printing Office, 1931.

Wigmore, John Henry. *A Treatise on Anglo-American Systems of Evidence at Trials of Common Law.* 2d ed., 1923.

Wilkerson, Isabel. *The Warmth of Other Suns: The Epic Story of America's Great Migration.* New York: Random House, 2009.

Wright, Richard. "How 'Bigger' Was Born." Reprinted in Richard Wright, *Native Son and How 'Bigger' Was Born.* New York: Harper Perennial, 1993.

———. *Native Son and How 'Bigger' Was Born.* New York: Perennial Classics, 1993.

Yerkes, Robert Mearns. Psychological Examination in the United States Army. Washington, DC: Government Printing Office, 1921.

Index

Acknowledgments

Thanks to Molly Kennedy of Springfield and David Joens and Stacey Skeeters from the Illinois Archive, Springfield. For comments, criticisms, and corrections, many thanks also to Kenneth Mack, Jeffrey Adler, Clifford Zimmerman, Locke Bowman, Michael Meranze, and Joseph Spillane.